PLANTS AND LANDSCAPES FOR SUMMER-DRY CLIMATES

PLANTS AND LANDSCAPES FOR SUMMER-DRY CLIMATES

of the San Francisco Bay Region

EAST BAY MUNICIPAL UTILITY DISTRICT

Published by East Bay Municipal Utility District
375 Eleventh Street, Oakland, California 94607
www.ebmud.com

Principal author and editor: Nora Harlow
Cover and text design and photography layout: Beth Hansen-Winter
Photographs: Saxon Holt
Illustrations: Richard Pembroke
Indexing: Nora Harlow

Mediterranean climate areas map (p. 2) adapted from Dallman, P.R., *Plant Life in the World's Mediterranean Climates*, 1998, with permission from the University of California Press and the California Native Plant Society, adapted from diCastri, F. *et al.*, *Ecosystems of the World II, Mediterranean-type shrublands*, 1981. Bay Region weather map (p. 4) adapted from Gilliam, Harold, "Weather as Varied as the People," *San Francisco Chronicle*, 1998, with permission from the author, adapted for Gilliam, Harold, *Weather of the San Francisco Bay Region*, 2002. Climate map (p. 38) adapted from *Sunset Western Garden Book*, 2001, with permission from Sunset Publishing Corp.

Typeset in Cochin and Trajan

Printed and bound in the United States of America
Printing by Graphic Press in Los Angeles, California
Binding by Roswell Bookbinding in Phoenix, Arizona
Printed on recycled paper

Hardcover edition: ISBN 0-9753231-0-5   Softcover edition: ISBN 0-9753231-1-3

COVER PHOTO: *Miscanthus sinensis*, LAVENDER, LAVATERA AND *Calamagrostis* X *ACUTIFLORA* 'KARL FOERSTER'
PHOTOS, PAGE i: *Leucospermum cordifolium*   PAGES ii-iii: *Calamagrostis* X *ACUTIFLORA* 'KARL FOERSTER'
PAGE v: *Rosa* 'MUTABILIS' NEXT TO GARDEN BENCH   PAGES vi AND viii-ix: *Muhlenbergia dubia*

Photographs by SAXON HOLT

Prepared by Water Conservation staff
NORA HARLOW, *editor*

Design by BETH HANSEN-WINTER

Illustrations by RICHARD PEMBROKE

CONTENTS

ACKNOWLEDGMENTS

A book of this scope benefits greatly from the expertise and viewpoints of many people. EBMUD wishes to acknowledge the input and assistance of members of the project's Advisory Committee, including Judy Adler, Bethallyn Black, Peter Boffey, Katy Foulkes, Anthony Garza, Kristin Hathaway, Annie Hayes, Glenn Keator, Aerin Moore, Sean O'Hara, Michael Thilgen, Susan Vogel, and Stewart Winchester. EBMUD's long-standing Landscape Advisory Committee also provided early input to decisions about the general direction of the project.

In addition to the project Advisory Committee, more than fifty people were invited to participate in developing a list of plants for inclusion in the book. The process of review and comment on the emerging plant list continued through several iterations over many months. Participants represented a wide range of professional interests in plants and landscapes in the Bay Region, including landscape designers, nursery owners, horticulturists, botanists, educators, native plant experts, environmentalists, and grounds maintenance personnel. The goal was to include a wide variety of local people with hands-on experience in growing and propagating plants in the Bay Region.

There were, not unexpectedly, a wide range of opinions about and experience with particular plants, as well as philosophies about ornamental landscapes. Some participants urged us to include only plants native and indigenous to the Bay Region; others advised a more cosmopolitan approach. Although decisions ultimately fell to EBMUD staff, these experts added immeasurably to the ongoing dialogue and to the value of the book. Our thanks to Judy Adler, Suzanne Arca, Liz Bade, Nancy Bauer, Russell Beatty, Bethallyn Black, Peter Boffey, Noah Booker, Chris Carmichael, Betsy Clebsch, Charli Danielsen, Analice Decker, John Dotter, Paul Doty, Kathy Echols, Steve Edwards, Bobbi Feyerabend, Daniel Gallagher, Anthony Garza, Shirley Harmon, Kristin Jakob, Glenn Keator, Kathy Kramer, Barry Lehrman, Ron Lutsko, Jane Miller, Aerin Moore, Bird Morningstar, Stephanie Morris, Chari Ogogo, Sean O'Hara, Wayne Roderick, Jeff Rosendale, Christine Schneider, Tamara Shulman, Nevin Smith, Tamara Smith, Michael Thilgen, Tomas Torres, and Jinx Tyler. Jill Singleton and Kris Sandoe assisted with plant research.

Special thanks to Phyllis Faber, who offered wise counsel throughout the project; to Christine Finch and Susan Handjian, whose knowledge of plants and concern for the environment helped set the tone for this book; to Michael Thilgen for ongoing inspiration and support and for technical review of several chapters; and to Dick Dunmire, Bobbi Feyerabend, and Kara Stephens-Flemming, who read proofs and commented on the plant descriptions. Katherine Grace Endicott, Katherine Greenberg, Phyllis Faber, and Richard G Turner, Jr, reviewed the final draft and made many useful comments.

We extend our appreciation to those who guided our photographer to gardens in which featured plants were grown, including Michael Barry, David Feix, Michael

Nassella tenuissima SPILLING DOWN SLOPE

Frappier, David Fross, Bill Grant, Katherine Greenberg, Chris Jacobson, Phil Johnson, Ron Lutsko, Don Mahoney, Jo O'Connell, Gary Ratway, Warren Roberts, Jeff Rosendale, Marlene Slutsky, Michael Thilgen, Judy Thomas, Dick Turner, Stewart Winchester, and Phil Van Solen.

We also thank those who welcomed our photographer into their public and private gardens, including Suzanne Arca, Blake Garden, California Flora Nursery, Julie Chen, Rich and Claire Clancy, Claire Dungan, Kathy Echols, Emerisa Nursery, Jeff Eichenfield and Jay Stowsky, Filoli Gardens, Paul and Kay Fireman, Gamble Garden, Gail Giffen, Katherine Greenberg, Sara Hammond, P.J. Herring, Kern and Arlene Hildenbrand, Anni Jensen and Carol Manahan, Peter Latourette, Leaning Pine Arboretum, Los Angeles County Arboretum, Judith Lowry, Luther Burbank Garden, Merritt College, Native Sons Nursery, Suzanne Porter, Sarah Puyans, Roger Raiche, Rancho Santa Ana Botanic Garden, Regional Parks Botanic Garden, Mary and Lou Reid, Wayne Roderick, Ruth Bancroft Garden, San Francisco Garden for the Environment, San Luis Obispo Botanic Garden, Santa Barbara Botanic Garden, Jack Schiefflelin, Mary Te Selle, Robin Sherrill, Sierra Azul Nursery, Nathan Smith, Katherine Spann, Susan Springer, Strybing Arboretum, Suncrest Nursery, Sunset Publishing, Susan's Succulent Nursery, John Taft, David Turner, University of California Botanical Garden, University of California, Davis, Arboretum, University of California, Santa Cruz, Arboretum, David and Kathy Welch, Western Hills Nursery, and Kristin Yanker-Hansen.

We thank Sunset Publishing Corporation for permission to use the zone designations and map from *Sunset Western Garden Book*. We also thank Suzanne Arca, Harold Gilliam, Don Mahoney, Deborah Rogers, Glen Schneider, Michael Thilgen, and Roger Waters for contributions in their areas of expertise.

We are grateful to all who contributed to the production of this book. Errors and omissions are the responsibility of the editor.

LAVENDER, AGAVE, PHORMIUM, AND *STIPA GIGANTEA*

PREFACE

The East Bay Municipal Utility District published the first edition of *Water-Conserving Plants and Landscapes for the Bay Area* in 1986. The book was enormously popular, widely distributed, and reprinted several times. By the late 1990s, with requests for the book exceeding supply, staff was faced with a decision: to continue reprinting or to prepare a new book that reflects the increased availability of native and mediterranean-climate plants and the growing public awareness of water supply reliability and of environmental issues of which water conservation is a part.

It is possible to create and maintain ornamental landscapes in ways that conserve water and energy, protect air and water quality, minimize impacts on landfills, provide habitat for wildlife, reduce fire hazard, and help to preserve natural wildlands. The idea of gardening with nature is hardly new, but it couldn't be more timely. California's population is projected to grow from 35 million in 2000 to over 50 million in 2025, and an additional 15 to 20 million acres of land will be needed to provide these new residents with homes, jobs, services, and transportation. The least any of us can do is to be mindful of our individual and collective impacts on natural resources — clean air, clean water, energy, open space, and biotic diversity — and to accept personal responsibility for our actions.

This book was written for the nine counties of the San Francisco Bay Region, though its principles apply to other parts of the world with similar climates. The counties of the Bay Region obtain their potable water from various sources, but their residents hike the same trails, travel the same freeways, marvel at the same natural wonders, and depend for their livelihoods on the health of the regional economy. The bay, delta, oceanside beaches, rivers and creeks, mountains, forests, and oak-studded grasslands are shared resources the benefits of which cross all county lines. It is in our own interest to learn about their importance to our quality of life, and their fragility, and to take steps, large or small, to protect and preserve them.

The plants described and depicted in this book are by no means the only plants suitable for dry-summer, wet-winter climates common to the San Francisco Bay Region. This volume is intended only to suggest possibilities for regionally appropriate ornamental landscapes and to inspire gardeners and landscape designers to explore and expand on them. Some will choose to plant only species native to the region or to the immediate locale. Others will want to grow a wider variety of water-conserving plants, native and nonnative, suited to local soils and microclimates. Each will contribute, to different degrees and in different ways, to a reduction in impacts of ornamental landscapes on natural resources and the environment. We encourage and applaud them all.

Pittosporum tobira 'Variegata' with *Erysimum* 'Bowles Mauve',
Geranium incanum, and *Erigeron karvinskianus*

Chapter One

GARDENING WHERE YOU ARE

Some call it natural gardening. Others describe it as sustainable, ecological, regional, or bioregional. Whatever it's called, the approach to landscaping outlined here is attuned to local climate, microclimate, topography, and soils and responsive to the reality of limited resources. The natural approach to landscape design and maintenance conserves water and energy, protects wildlands, limits green waste, and provides habitat for wildlife. At the same time, it requires less upkeep than traditional landscapes, and it connects the gardener— and those who live, work, or play in the garden—to the rhythms of life: the seasons, the weather, the daily miracles of the natural world.

When we consider what's missing from so many contemporary landscapes, especially in the West, the top of the list has to be what landscape designers and garden writers call the "sense of place"—that elusive quality of landscape design that subtly but unmistakably tells us where we are.

This is the San Francisco Bay Region. It may be Oakland, Palo Alto, or Santa Rosa, Alameda, Walnut Creek, or San Jose. Each of these parts of the larger region has its own soils, topography, and weather patterns, and within each subregion are a multitude of street-by-street or even lot-by-lot variations on the theme.

But it's not Milwaukee, it's not Atlanta, and it's not New York. Like most of California, and much of the West, summers in the Bay Region are warm and dry, and, if we're lucky, winters are wet. Soils may be sandy, rocky, or mostly clay, but, as is true of most low-rainfall regions, they tend to be low in organic matter—they rarely resemble the loamy soils of Midwestern prairies or English garden books.

The region around San Francisco Bay also has a unique physical and cultural geography—a geologic, biologic, and social history that has shaped what we see today. To ignore local history, including our own personal history, is to miss the opportunity to experience and express the authentic character of the place we live. When our gardens and landscapes are informed by our physical, cultural, and personal heritage, they become more than interior decoration taken outside. They feel "right," and they satisfy a basic human need for meaning.

Many plants are well suited to the Bay Region's climate and soils, and many garden styles can be adapted to express a regional landscape ethic. The English border or cottage garden can be reinterpreted using drought-tolerant native or mediterranean plants and gravel paths. A formal Italian- or French-inspired design might substitute

ARTEMISIA 'POWIS CASTLE', *LAVANDULA* X *INTERMEDIA* 'GROSSO', AND *L. STOECHAS* 'MADRID PINK' CREATE A LUSH LOOK WITH MINIMAL WATER

OPPOSITE: NATURALIZED PLANTINGS, STONEWORK, AND NATIVE TREES AND SHRUBS SOFTEN THE BOUNDARIES OF CULTIVATION AND WILDLANDS BEYOND

lavender or germander for boxwood edging. A Japanese garden effect could be achieved using local rock and native grasses to lend regional character. A genuinely California landscape can be created using plants indigenous to the San Francisco Bay Region.

The best part is you can start where you are. You don't have to tear up the lawn and plant a garden of native plants, although you could, and perhaps one day you will. Leave the grass clippings on the lawn. Skip a watering day or two. Let the insects nibble the leaves of your roses. Stash the leaf blower in the back of the garage.

The next time the opportunity presents itself, consider creating a new landscape, or revamping an old one, with plants that thrive in your microclimate without special care, provide food and shelter for wildlife, and conserve water and other natural resources. The benefits go beyond environmental to include nourishment of the soul.

CLIMATES OF THE BAY REGION

The San Francisco Bay Region, and most of California west of the Sierra Nevada, enjoys what is called a mediterranean climate. This distinctive climate pattern is found in only two percent of the world's land mass and in only four other areas of the world: the region surrounding the Mediterranean Sea, southern and western parts of Australia, central Chile, and the western Cape Province of South Africa.

Two of these regions are in the northern hemisphere and three are in the southern hemisphere, but all are on the west coasts of continental land masses, adjacent to the sea, and a little less than halfway between the equator and either the north or the south pole. All are influenced by subtropical high-pressure systems that inhibit summer rainfall.

MEDITERRANEAN CLIMATE AREAS

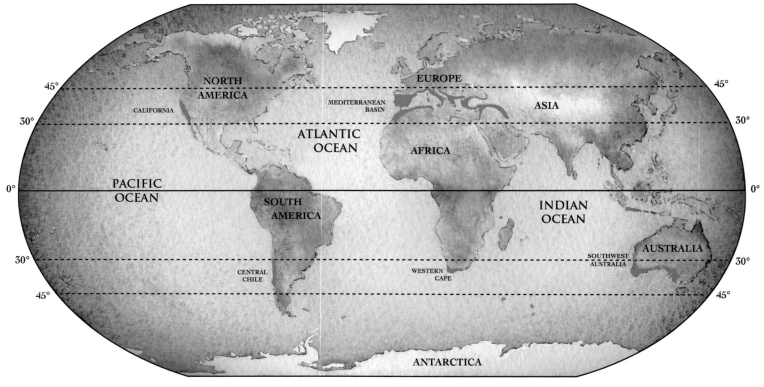

Mediterranean climates typically are characterized by short, mild, rainy winters and long, warm to hot, dry summers. But these regions can experience floods or hard freezes in winter and multiple years of drought when little or no rain falls. Rainfall varies widely from year to year—the seemingly abnormal droughts and floods are normal for mediterranean climates.

The five mediterranean climate regions differ in the specifics of their weather patterns. There is wide variation in the timing and length of the summer dry period in different parts of the Mediterranean Basin. In mediterranean regions of Australia, there are no high mountains and winters are mild, snow is rare, and stream flows are highest in rainy winter months. In Chile and California, snowmelt in the mountains concentrates runoff in spring and early summer. South Australia experiences occasional thunderstorms in summer.

COASTAL FOG MODERATES CLIMATE IN THE BAY REGION

Many plants from other mediterranean regions adapt to our summer-dry climate and blend well with plants native to the San Francisco Bay Region. However, in selecting plants for the regionally appropriate garden, gardeners should compare the native habitats of the plants they want to grow with the soils and seasonal characteristics of their own microclimates.

Just as not all plants native to California are suited to all California microclimates, not all mediterranean plants grow well or easily in all parts of the San Francisco Bay Region.

Influences on Climate in California

Variations within California's mediterranean climate are affected by several factors: latitude, coastal influence, elevation, and topography or orientation to the sun.

The wettest parts of California's mediterranean climate are to the north and the driest are to the south, with the San Francisco Bay Region approximately in the middle and characterized by moderate amounts of winter rainfall. Summer dry periods also tend to be longer as one moves further south.

California's north-south-trending mountain ranges mediate the effects of coastal fog and ocean breezes. The ocean plays an important role in moderating temperatures, both hot and cold. Temperature differentials cause short-term pressure gradients that create land-sea breezes—onshore during the day and offshore in the evening. Longer-term pressure gradients occur seasonally: a regional high-pressure system generally precludes summer storms.

Both temperature and rainfall vary with elevation. As onshore breezes from the ocean reach the mountain ranges, air rises and cools and moisture condenses. As air heats up on descent on the inland side of the mountains, moisture is drawn from the soil and vegetation. In general, mountains and hilly areas have higher rainfall on the western, coastal side and drier "rain shadows" on the eastern slopes.

Topography and orientation to the sun also affect climate or microclimate, with south- or west-facing slopes usually warmer and drier than north- or east-facing slopes. Vegetation naturally reflects these differences.

WEATHER AS VARIED AS THE PEOPLE

"If you don't like the weather," they say in New England, "wait a few minutes." In the San Francisco Bay Area, that advice might be revised: "If you don't like the weather, walk a few miles."

The Bay Area's cultural diversity is matched by its climatic diversity: a dazzling variety of microclimates, each with its special qualities of sunlight, fog, wind, rain, heat and cold, varying day to day, summer and winter, spring and fall.

The greater the distances, the more intense the weather extremes. In late spring, when cool coastal communities register in the 50s, eastern Contra Costa County may be sweltering at 100 degrees. There are times when the microclimates are overwhelmed by large-scale weather phenomena and the differences are eliminated. But normally, especially when the summer fog penetration reaches its maximum during July and August, microclimates predominate.

The reasons for this extraordinary variety of weather lie deep in the geologic past—in the clash of tectonic plates. The Pacific plate of the earth's crust, moving eastward over the eons, smashed into the edge of the North American continental plate, prying it up into monumental chains of mountains, including the Sierra Nevada, and, much later, California's coast ranges.

It is this rumpled landscape, this hill-and-valley topography, this heterogeneous diversity of land forms that give the Bay Area its multiple climates, microclimates, and submicroclimates. Eastward from the Pacific, each successive valley has less of a damp seacoast climate and more of a dry continental climate—hotter in summer and colder in winter. Diversity within

COOL MARINE AIR FLOWS INLAND THROUGH GAPS IN THE COASTAL RANGES AS HOT AIR RISES IN THE CENTRAL VALLEY (ADAPTED FROM GILLIAM, 2002)

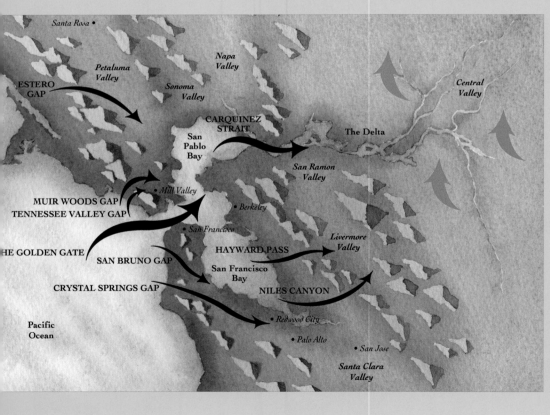

Microclimates of the Bay Region

Within the San Francisco Bay Region, the various microclimates often are so close together that one can drive a few miles from bright sun to overcast skies and feel a temperature change of thirty degrees. Summer temperatures are dramatically higher

diversity is provided within each range by subranges and within each valley by subvalleys.

The Golden Gate is the only sea-level break in the mountains along the coast, permitting the Pacific's marine weather to flow directly inland. But there are land gaps throughout the Bay Area, "little Golden Gates," where the oceanic influence penetrates the interior. Marine air flowing in through these gaps may drop the temperature only slightly, but a few degrees can make a big difference in comfort.

On the Peninsula, the biggest break in the Santa Cruz Mountains is the gap south of San Bruno Mountain, second only to the Golden Gate in its influence on Bay Area climate. Farther south on the Peninsula, the San Andreas Fault cuts through the range, producing the Crystal Springs gap. The breeze through this gap causes Redwood City to be a bit less warm in summer, and the cooling effect sometimes extends as far south as San Jose.

North of the Golden Gate, Mill Valley in summer is cooled several degrees not only by the strait itself but by two lesser gaps, a narrow opening through Tennessee Valley and a higher pass above Muir Woods. Cutting through the Marin Hills farther north is the Estero Gap, bringing to the Petaluma Valley a salt breeze that sometimes extends as far north as Santa Rosa, which is also cooled by ocean air moving through the canyon of the Russian River. Cooling, of course, is relative, and it might be more accurate to say that the gaps cause interior areas to be less hot than they would be otherwise.

San Francisco Bay generates its own breezes, which cool the communities around its shores. Some of that bay-cooled air flows through three gaps in the East Bay hills. Two of them, Niles Canyon and Hayward Pass, channel that air, warmed by its passage over land areas, to the Livermore Valley and beyond to Altamont Pass. The Carquinez Strait is a sea-level break in the hills that funnels ocean and bay air toward the Sacramento-San Joaquin River Delta and the Central Valley.

In most cities of the world, people commuting in from different points of the compass can assume that everyone is having the same weather experience: "Some weather we're having lately, isn't it?" But in the Bay Area, the opening gambit is more likely to be: "What's your weather like today?" No one is surprised if Berkeley is fogged in while Alameda basks in the sun, or if Mill Valley has rain while Palo Alto is dry.

Some historians believe that the climate of the region shapes the character of its people. If so, there may be a connection between this region's microclimates and its diversity of human temperaments and viewpoints, creating a distinctive Bay Area climate of the mind.

Harold Gilliam, author
Weather of the San Francisco Bay Region, 2002

inland than along the coast. Gardeners in the same town but on slopes that face different directions may experience difficulty growing the same plants, or the same plants may bloom a month apart.

The major variations in Bay Region microclimates result from the amount of coastal influence. Summer fog is an important source of moisture in coastal zones, which experience a more moderate, maritime version of the mediterranean climate. Summer fog finds its way through gaps in the coastal ranges to cool some inland areas, while on the same day, nearby areas untouched by fog are baking hot.

Some Bay Region microclimates experience heavy frosts in winter, while others rarely have frost at all. The same mountain ranges that separate hot inland valleys from cooling ocean breezes in summer also block the moderating effects of maritime air in winter, when inland areas can be much colder than those along the coast.

PLANT COMMUNITIES OF THE BAY REGION

The different San Francisco Bay Region microclimates are associated with natural groupings or "communities" of plants. Ecologists recognize as many as several hundred plant communities in California, but the major communities in the Bay Region can be loosely categorized into a few broad vegetation types: oak or foothill woodland, chaparral, coastal scrub, grassland, and mixed evergreen or redwood forest. Immediately adjacent to the coast are coastal dune and coastal strand types of vegetation. Riparian plant communities are found along creeks and near other water sources, both inland and near the coast.

CALIFORNIA NATIVE SYCAMORE TREES (*PLATANUS RACEMOSA*)

Plant communities may occur as relatively homogeneous areas with distinct boundaries, but more often adjacent communities intergrade with one another, forming a mosaic of overlapping communities with "ecotones" where characteristics of two or more communities are blended in various proportions. As with climate and microclimate, plant communities in California vary from north to south, but the greatest variations in the Bay Region occur from west to east, from coastal to inland.

Plant communities have evolved over time with geologic changes in climate, topography, and soils. On a shorter time scale, a series of plant communities may replace one another through a process called succession. Following landslides, fires, or land clearing for agriculture or other purposes, soil is laid bare and conditions are challenging for plant growth. A robust group of plant "pioneers" will colonize the site first. These pioneers modify conditions by loosening, shading, and cooling the soil, adding organic

matter, and generally improving conditions for the growth and establishment of other plants, which compete with and may overtake the pioneers. This process may be repeated several times over a period of years or decades, with annuals followed by short-lived perennials, then shrubs, and finally trees.

We can only speculate what plants might occur "naturally" in a given area, as vegetative cover has been altered by countless accidental events and purposeful activities over hundreds of years, even long before European settlement. The following broad vegetation types still can be found on undeveloped or lightly developed lands in the Bay Region. Knowing what vegetation types thrive in nearby regional parks and wildlands can help in selecting plants for a regionally appropriate landscape.

Blue oak (Quercus douglasii) in spring hills with mist

Oak Woodland

Oak woodland is a signature vegetation type of the San Francisco Bay Region, especially in areas of rolling hills or gently sloping terrain. Scattered oaks stand out against a background of mostly annual grasses that are green in winter and straw-colored in summer or form dense groves in the clefts of hills and in valleys.

Close to the ocean and San Francisco Bay, oak woodlands consist of coast live oak (*Quercus agrifolia*) and associated understory plants. Further inland, evergreen oaks often grow with deciduous oaks—coast live oak with valley oak (*Q. lobata*) in valley bottoms or on the coastal side of hills and mountain ranges, canyon live oak (*Q. chrysolepis*) with

California black oak (*Q. kelloggii*) in moister canyons, interior live oak (*Q. wislizenii*) with blue oak (*Q. douglasii*) in drier, inland areas.

Oak woodland plant communities may include buckeye (*Aesculus californica*) in shadier, moister areas and gray pine or foothill pine (*Pinus sabiniana*) in drier, hotter locations. Understory shrubs include manzanitas (*Arctostaphylos* spp.), toyon (*Heteromeles arbutifolia*), coffeeberry (*Rhamnus californica*), redbud (*Cercis occidentalis*), cream bush (*Holodiscus discolor*), and poison oak (*Toxicodendron diversilobum*). In addition to nonnative annual grasses, which have largely displaced native bunchgrasses in many areas, native needlegrasses (*Nassella* spp.), bromes (*Bromus* spp.), and blue wild rye (*Elymus glaucus*) share the woodland floor with herbaceous plants such as soap root (*Chlorogalum* spp.) and death camas (*Zigadenus* spp.).

Chaparral

Chaparral is characteristic of hot, dry areas at mid-elevations where winters may bring occasional frosts as well as drenching rains. Unlike desert plants, which also are adapted to heat and drought, chaparral plants must be able to withstand not only lengthy periods of dryness but sometimes soggy winter soils.

Chaparral consists primarily of closely spaced, woody, evergreen shrubs that form dense, interlacing canopies. There are few understory plants and considerable dry leaf

litter. Soils tend to be rocky and shallow, overlaying rock or subsoil that is mostly clay. An occasional oak tree may hug the hillside, nestled among rocks, low and broadly rounded by the wind.

Plants found in chaparral include manzanitas, toyon, coffeeberry, California lilac (*Ceanothus* spp.), and chamise (*Adenostoma fasciculatum*). Many chaparral plants have tough, durable leaves that are seldom shed, even in hot weather, and extensive root systems that reach widely and deeply for sources of water.

Chaparral often intergrades with oak woodland, where many of the same plants are found.

Coastal Scrub

Coastal scrub is found in a discontinuous band from coastal northern California south to northern Baja California. In northern Calfornia this vegetation type occurs on shallow, rocky soils on windy, south- and west-facing hillsides in the fog belt. The climate is strongly influenced by the ocean. Northern coastal scrub consists of small to medium-sized shrubs with scattered openings that support an understory of herbaceous plants and smaller woody shrubs. There are few if any trees.

COASTAL SCRUB

The dominant plants in northern coastal scrub are coyote brush (*Baccharis pilularis*), lupine (*Lupinus arboreus, L. albifrons*), bush monkeyflower (*Mimulus aurantiacus*), salal (*Gaulthera shallon*), silktassel (*Garrya elliptica*), blackberry (*Rubus ursinus*), poison oak, and buckwheat (*Eriogonum* spp.). Understory plants may include herbaceous annuals and perennials such as thrift (*Armeria maritima*), wallflower (*Erysimum* spp.), and California buttercup (*Ranunculus californicus*).

Coastal scrub often intergrades with adjacent coastal prairie or with chaparral, oak woodland, or riparian woodland, where these plants form part of the understory vegetation.

Grassland

Grassland occurs in two main forms in northern California: coastal prairie, which is found in a narrow strip near the Pacific Ocean, and relics of the expansive Central Valley grassland, now dominated by mostly introduced annual grasses and herbs. Grassland typically occurs in open areas within other vegetation types, particularly oak woodland and chaparral, and can be found in drylands, wetlands, forests, woodlands, shrublands, and mountain meadows.

In drier areas, open grassland includes mostly introduced annual grasses and herbs such as soft chess (*Bromus hordeaceus*), wild oats (*Avena barbata*), wild barley

(*Hordeum* spp.), annual rye grass (*Lolium multiflorum*), filaree (*Erodium* spp.), and thistles. Some native grasses and herbs also are found, including needlegrasses (*Nassella* spp.) and melic (*Melica* spp.), bulbs such as brodiaea, dichelostemma, triteleia, calochortus, and soap root, California fuchsia (*Epilobium canum*), clarkia, lupines, and poppies.

Coastal prairie is a wetter habitat than annual grassland, and, in addition to introduced annuals, typically consists of native perennial grasses and herbs, such as fescues (*Festuca* spp.), Junegrass (*Koeleria macrantha*), California oatgrass (*Danthonia californica*), bent grass (*Agrostis* spp.), reed grasses (*Calamagrostis* spp.), hair grasses (*Deschampsia* spp.), bulbs, buttercups, checkerbloom (*Sidalcea malviflora*), *Iris douglasiana*, blue-eyed grass (*Sisyrinchium bellum*), and baby blue eyes (*Nemophila menziesii*).

Redwood and Mixed Evergreen Forests

Redwood forest occupies a restricted range in the San Francisco Bay Region, confined to the coastal fog belt but some distance from the immediate coastline. Within this narrowly defined range, coast redwood (*Sequoia sempervirens*) is further restricted to cool, sheltered canyons, moist creekbanks or river bottoms, and north-facing slopes, where these magnificent trees dominate their habitats with the deep shade cast by dense canopies and a thick layer of duff covering the forest floor.

Redwoods thrive where annual rainfall is 35 to 80 inches, supplemented by as much as ten inches of fog drip in summer months. Understory is often easy to walk through: scattered shade-loving shrubs such as huckleberry (*Vaccinium ovatum*), salal, and wax myrtle (*Myrica californica*) and herbaceous plants such as sword fern (*Polystichum munitum*), wild ginger (*Asarum caudatum*), and redwood sorrel (*Oxalis oregana*).

On warmer slopes, redwood forest intergrades with mixed evergreen forest, with Douglas-fir (*Pseudotsuga menziesii*) and California nutmeg (*Torreya californica*) near the coast and California bay and madrone (*Arbutus menziesii*) further inland.

Mixed evergreen forest is drier and warmer than redwood forest, but not as hot and dry as oak woodland. These forests may occur on cooler, north-facing slopes in the same areas where south- and west-facing slopes are dominated by oak woodland. Mixed evergreen forest also may be found on canyon bottoms near riparian corridors, where its more typical evergreen components are accompanied by deciduous trees such as bigleaf maple (*Acer macrophyllum*), white alder (*Alnus rhombifolia*), and western sycamore (*Platanus racemosa*).

ABOVE: MIXED EVERGREEN FOREST
OPPOSITE: REDWOODS

PLANT ADAPTATIONS TO SUMMER-DRY CLIMATES

Vegetation types in the Bay Region have counterparts in other mediterranean climates, and many plants from these other parts of the world show similar adaptations to seasons and soils. Mediterranean-climate plants typically have characteristics that enable them to defend themselves against summer drought and to thrive in soils that are low in organic matter. These characteristics are displayed in leaves and roots, as well as in life cycles adapted to the short spring growing season and long, dry summers.

Leaves

Many mediterranean plants, such as evergreen oaks and silktassel, have thick, leathery, "sclerophyll" leaves that resist dehydration. The leaves of some sclerophyllous plants, such as some California lilacs, have a shiny, waxy coating that reflects heat and light and protects against water loss. The stomata, or small pores, through which leaves exchange gases and release water vapor to the air may be fewer or have smaller openings than those of plants from wetter regions, or they may be protected by tiny hairs or positioned in ways that reduce exposure to hot sun.

The leaves of some drought-resistant plants are held upright or may alter their

orientation in ways that minimize exposure to sunlight. Grayish green or whitish leaves and leaves with hairy surfaces reflect sunlight or diminish its effects. The leaves of some manzanitas are held edgewise or vertically or have a whitish bloom that helps deflect the full impact of the sun's heat. Chamise has narrow, needlelike leaves that minimize surface area exposed to the sun. The dense canopies of many chaparral plants shade the roots and cool the soil around them.

Some mediterranean-climate plants are drought-deciduous, dropping leaves under drought stress and growing new ones when water becomes available. California sagebrush is a drought-deciduous plant.

Other plants, such as purple sage (*Salvia leucophylla*), survive periods of dryness by producing different kinds of leaves in different seasons, the lusher and larger spring leaves dropping off and being replaced with smaller, more drought-resistant leaves in mid- to late summer.

Coast live oak sometimes bears two kinds of leaves, one adapted to sun and the other to shade. Sun-exposed leaves are small, thick, and convex; leaves in shade are flat, thin, and broad, exposing them to more light where light is less intense.

Roots

Some mediterranean-climate plants, such as coast live oak, may have both a deep taproot and a widely spreading surface root system. The taproot draws on longer-lasting sources of water deeper in the soil, while the mass of surface roots picks up transient moisture from light rains or fog drip that evaporates before it can sink into the soil.

Many plants benefit from a symbiotic relationship with mycorrhizal fungi, beneficial organisms that grow on roots and spread widely in the soil, taking up and storing nutrients leached from leaf litter during rains. The fungus releases stored nutrients slowly to plant roots, providing nourishment during dry periods when the supply available from surrounding soil has diminished. Oaks, pines, and eucalypts are examples of plants that benefit from symbiotic mycorrhizal associations.

THE SEASONS OF CALIFORNIA

Immigrants to California often say that they miss the seasons, those familiar changes that define the natural year. It's true; the four-season model of Winter, Spring, Summer, and Fall doesn't fit here, but California has its own rhythms and seasons, both dramatic and subtle.

At first it may seem that there are just two seasons in California, the rainy season and the dry, but there is another. As the weather warms and the rains taper off from mid-February to mid-June, we have four glorious months when the still-moist land explodes with color and life. The third season is Wildflower season, and wildflowers make California a place like no other on earth.

Each of California's three seasons—the rainy season, the wildflower season, and the dry season—is about four months long, and each has markers for its start and finish.

The Rainy Season

There is no calendar date for the start of the rainy season, but its onset each year is clear. The first big rain, usually in October, is when the thirsty land drinks again, becoming moist and fragrant and soon green. For California, it is New Year's Day and the first day of spring wrapped up together.

The first seedlings appear within a week of the rains, and so do the newts. The bulbs and roots come up—soap root, lace plant, buttercups, mushrooms. In December, trees and shrubs join the parade, first the pink and white bells of manzanita and then the chartreuse flowers of California bay.

NORTHERN CALIFORNIA HILLS TURN GREEN WITH WINTER RAIN

The rainy season brackets the winter solstice with four months of cool, wet weather, shorter days, and slanting light. Between storms there are clear days, days of fog, frosts, and the best sunsets. By New Year's the catkins of alder and hazelnut appear, as do the shoots of elderberry and the first pussy willows. Later in January the currants bud and bloom. By the first of February the hills are green, and the long spring that spans two seasons is half over. Buckeyes leaf out in the rain, heralding the onset of the next season.

Wildflower Season

Wildflower season unfolds in three phases: the early, wet phase; the balmy, showy phase; and the drying

er Carpet Roses

Fri 21st Feb 2003

Home » Garden Tour » Driveway Garden Tour

< Driveway Garden Border | Bergenias >

· The driveway border is home to several bright pink flower carpet roses, seen here flowering in mid-summer.

These were the first so-called Flower Carpet roses to be sold in New Zealand, and they caused a sensation. They were marketed as the perfect groundcover - which anyone who has tried to weed underneath them knows just isn't true!

Round The Bend

Summer Flowering Roses

I've always rated the **Flower Carpet roses** - their bright colour is great in my garden, and their flowering time is later then my other roses. So they nicely fill a slot in the summer rose flowering calendar.

Carolina Jasmine — (Gelsemium Sempervirens)
Rudbeckia

Bright Pink Flower Carpet Rose

'Chelsea Physic Garden 3'

My rose book says they have rambler blood running through their veins. Hmm...

*Head
Gardener.*

discuss
'Flower Carpet Roses'
in the gardening forums

<< Driveway Garden Border   ∧   Bergenias >>
                                            TOP

mooseyscountrygarden.com :
Animals I Annuals I Arches I Articles I Benches & Seats I Gardening Books I
Botanical Gardens I Bridges I Bulbs I Camellias I Chelsea Flower Show I Containers I
English Gardens I Foliage I Forums I Image Gallery I old gallery I Garden Design I
Hampton Court Flower Show I Journals I Links I Gardening Magazines I Mail I mcgTV I
News I Native Plants I Garden Paths I Perennials I Rhododendrons I Roses I Shrubs I
Succulents I Garden Tour I Weather I Welcome I © 1996-2004 eggyweb

phase. In the first phase, late February and March, the creeks are flowing, the ground is often soggy, and flooding can occur. But the storms become warmer and farther apart and are often followed by warm, moist days with puffy white clouds.

The woods are the first to bloom. Buckeyes unfold their leaves, and milkmaids and trilliums blossom. Soon come forget-me-nots, and, out in the grasslands, shooting stars. The first bumblebees appear, and, with warming nights, tree frogs sound. By the end of March, with the light now stronger, the early bloomers are already making seeds.

The second phase comes in April, with shirtsleeve days and dwindling rain. After six months of leafy growth, wildflowers burst forth in remarkable shapes and colors: poppies, larkspur, lupine, tidytips, fiddlenecks, owls' clover, mule ears. The deciduous oaks green up, birds are everywhere, and the hills are emerald green.

By May the rains have finished and the land begins to dry out. There still may be a storm or two, but the ground is getting harder, grasses are seeding, and the noses of the ridges are turning brown. Now come the bulbs: brodiaeas, onions, and mariposas—those elegant cups of yellow and lavender that bloom in drying grass.

The Dry Season

June and July is when the hardy Californians step forward and shine, those tough souls that bloom in dry heat: farewell-to-spring, milkweed, tarweeds, and, later on, asters and California fuchsias. Seeds ripen and fall, bulbs and roots rest underground, leaves wax and thicken. The creeks slow to a trickle or dry out altogether, and nature enters a hot, dry slumber.

Buckeyes say it best by browning and dropping their leaves in July. The land becomes still, and a day out in the hills in August will be suffused with quiet, a good baking, and a search for shade. It is the dormant time, much like the deep, snowy winters of other lands.

THE HILLS ARE TAWNY
GOLD IN SUMMER

In September the heat begins to lose power. One day that unmistakable yellowish light signals change. Maples yellow, rose hips and honeysuckle berries redden, and poison oak turns pink and violet. The sun moves south, and the days shorten. By October the nights can be cold, with heavy dews. Some leaves fall, seeds unhook their dormant locks, and eyes turn toward the sky. Thoughts turn to green in these final dry days, and we wait, and wait, for rain.

Glen Schneider, author
*Touching the Earth: a field guide
to East Bay nature*, in press

Life-Cycle Patterns

Summer dormancy is a common adaptation to summer-dry climates. Plants native to such climates tend to grow most vigorously in late winter and spring, when soils are moist, temperatures are moderate, and days are lengthening. Summer is a time of partial to full dormancy. Some plants lose leaves or die back to the ground with the onset of hot, dry weather. With the end of summer and the arrival of fall or winter rains, plant growth begins again.

Annuals and bulbs or bulblike plants are especially well adapted to summer-dry climates. Annuals complete their life cycle before the hottest summer weather, setting seed and dying as the soil dries out; seeds germinate and new plants appear with fall and winter rains. Bulbs, corms, and tuberous plants lose their leaves and lie dormant over the summer months as underground food storage organs, sending up new shoots only as the days shorten and rains return. If the rains do not come, seeds and bulbs may wait for a more propitious year.

GARDENING WHERE YOU ARE

CALIFORNIA POPPIES AND SKY LUPINE (*LUPINUS NANUS*) IN SPRING

Vibrantly green in winter and in summer softly subdued, natural landscapes in summer-dry climates are markedly different from those in regions with summer rainfall. The seasons seemingly are reversed: many plants lose leaves, die, go dormant, or rest at the height of summer, when elsewhere, with summer rains, the grass is at its greenest and trees, shrubs, and perennials are actively growing or in bloom.

There is a place for artfully designed oases in summer-dry climates. But the scale at which lush, green, resource-intensive landscapes are blanketing semi-arid and arid parts of the world ultimately is not sustainable. The contrived landscapes that surround so many homes and businesses in the San Francisco Bay Region stand out starkly against a background of untended wildlands. Artificially maintained and often consisting of the same few plants, such landscapes not only waste water and energy, but also disconnect us from the natural processes of the world around us. They deny the seasons and discourage or eliminate wildlife. They may even endanger human inhabitants with chemicals applied to keep plants growing and blooming where, without our interventions, they might not survive.

"Being in tune with the seasonal spirit of a place is not an abstract idea; indeed it offers the gardener a healthy dose of reality. Knowing about the water cycle . . . appreciating the diversity that adapts to seasonal patterns in endlessly imaginative forms . . . these temporal dimensions tell us where we really are."

—Francis and Reimann,
The California Landscape Garden

Compare these synthetic landscapes with those designed to work with, rather than fight, the natural conditions of climate, microclimate, and soils. The natural landscape garden celebrates the seasons of the San Francisco Bay Region. The gardener or landscape designer takes full advantage of the conditions of the site, whatever they may be—cool and foggy or hot and dry; sunny or shady; sandy, rocky, or clayey soils. A variety of plants grouped by cultural preference and

lightly maintained attracts and supports birds, butterflies, and other wildlife, which enliven the landscape with movement, color, and sound.

ONLY ROSES AND FRUIT TREES RECEIVE OCCASIONAL SUMMER WATER IN THIS COLORFUL BACKYARD

To begin planning your own summer-dry landscape, take a walk in the wildest, least cultivated park or open space in your area. Note the look and feeling of those places with topography most like your own. Go back in each season to experience the changes throughout the year. Become familiar with the soils of your area and your site. Keep a daily weather diary. Learn about plants that thrive in nearby wildlands and in gardens where butterflies and bees abound. Talk to a gardener who spends more time with a bird book than with pesticides or power tools in hand. Consult friends, neighbors, and strangers whose garden styles you admire. Join your local native or mediterranean plant society. Buy a one-gallon plant and see how it grows.

RESOURCES

Barbour, M. *et al., California's Changing Landscapes*, Sacramento, California Native Plant Society, 1993.

Dallman, P. R., *Plant Life in the World's Mediterranean Climates*, Berkeley, California Native Plant Society and University of California Press, 1998.

Francis, M. and A. Reimann, *The California Landscape Garden*, Berkeley, University of California Press, 1999.

Gilliam, Harold, *Weather of the San Francisco Bay Region*, Berkeley, University of California Press, 2002.

Chapter Two

SOME NOTES ON DESIGN

Landscape design presents special challenges where rain, if it comes at all, falls only in winter months. In the San Francisco Bay Region, these may include not only summer drought and waterlogged winter soils, but rugged topography with varied microclimates, cities and suburbs surrounded by open space, and a natural tendency toward periodic wildfires.

The benign mediterranean climate also encourages outdoor activities almost year-round, so landscapes are used for many purposes. Home gardens typically include areas for entertaining or relaxing outdoors, and many commercial and public landscapes feature spaces designed for the enjoyment of visitors or office workers. The creation of satisfying outdoor spaces is an important design goal in summer-dry climates.

LOW-WATER LANDSCAPES CAN BE INVITING YEAR ROUND

DESIGNING FOR SUMMER DROUGHT

Landscapes in summer-dry climates must be designed to deal with many months without a drop of rain. Too often the default design response is irrigation. If we take our cue from the natural areas around us, we can create private and public landscapes that are functional and attractive year round with little or no supplemental water. This doesn't mean we can't choose to have a pool or fountain, a lawn, or pots of thirsty annuals. The choice, however, should be conscious and deliberate: to add water to a landscape that could get by with none.

Two approaches to designing for summer drought are the liberal use of unwatered spaces such as pavings, decks, or lightly tended natural areas and the selection of plants that are adapted to summer-dry climates. Paved areas and decks can provide usable outdoor spaces while minimizing or eliminating the need for irrigation. Areas left largely to their own devices can provide a pleasing contrast to groomed and tended planting beds. Plantings can be designed to thrive with occasional to no summer water.

OPPOSITE: SLOPE PROVIDES GOOD DRAINAGE FOR SANTOLINA, LAVENDER, THYMES, AND LEAFY REEDGRASS (*CALAMAGROSTIS FOLIOSA*)

STEPS TO SUCCESSFUL DESIGN

It is tempting, when planning a garden, to pull out the catalogs or dash to the nursery and buy plants, but a successful landscape rarely starts that way. Just as the best houses start not with paint colors and carpet styles but with considerations of volumes and orientation on the ground—how many rooms, which direction the most public rooms should face—so, too, the best landscapes begin with deliberate planning of outdoor spaces.

Creating a plan is an essential first step. Some master designers can do this intuitively, without drawn plans, without written lists of needs and functions. The rest of us are better off if we go through the process of writing down our wants and needs and at least roughly sketching out our ideas for a design that will meet them. As you think about the project, trying out various ideas in your imagination, the design will evolve gradually from a loosely defined concept to a detailed plan.

"Good garden design is essentially simple and fit for its purpose. Great gardens . . . show in addition a subtle and apparently instinctive ability to link with the house they adjoin and the environment in which they are placed."

—David Stevens,
The Garden Design Sourcebook

Time spent planning is time well spent. You will be better able to anticipate potential problems and resolve details on paper. Your understanding of the project will grow, and this will help when the time comes to build. If your landscape will be installed by someone else, it's important to have detailed construction drawings, as they will form the basis of your agreement with the contractor.

Designing is best done with a budget in mind. While you may not want to limit your choices prematurely, costs usually become an important factor in decisions about construction, and budget can provide a reality check as the design proceeds.

Step 1: Study the Site. Start by looking at existing conditions. Even a newly graded lot will have physical characteristics or features that you will need to consider in creating a successful landscape. Views, topography, sun and shade, prevailing winds, soils and drainage patterns, surrounding structures, boundaries, and vegetation—all of these present both challenges and opportunities. A successful landscape is one that takes advantage of, and fits comfortably within, the natural and man-made conditions of the site.

Step 2: Consider Uses and Define Spaces. Think about

how the landscape will be used and how each use might be accommodated. Set priorities, but don't feel compelled to choose among them at this stage. Where might the various areas of use be located? How will each space be enclosed or defined? How might these areas be related and differentiated? How will you move from one area to another? Wherever possible, don't just sketch it on paper. Try it out on the ground. Access and circulation can make or break a landscape plan, whether residential or commercial. That private spot for hammock or bench may be too close to the street for quiet reflection or comfortable conversation.

Step 3: Develop a Plan. Begin drawing up a plan. Sketch out several versions and compare them. Think about materials and forms. How, specifically, will you address those challenges and opportunities you identified? How will your wants and needs be met? Will that private space be formed by walls or hedges? Will that slope be terraced or planted to control erosion? What shape, size, and material will that space for outdoor entertaining be? How wide this path, how tall that wall, how far that view?

Now it's time to think about plants. When selecting plants, it's usually best to start with the largest, most enduring elements, such as trees and large shrubs, which will form the "backbone" of your landscape. Next select some smaller and perhaps shorter-lived plants for accent, fill, color, and seasonal interest. Some of these plants may be partly or fully summer-dormant, so your overall planting scheme should be attractive and functional without them. If your planting plan has a strong underlying structure, it will be satisfying at all times of year.

Step 4: Finalize Your Plan. Synthesize and refine your ideas. Usually this means simplifying. Does your plan try to do too much? Are there uses that can be eliminated or combined? Are there too many features, spaces, materials, or shapes? This is the time when difficult choices must finally be made—the gazebo or the greenhouse, the vegetable garden or the basketball court, the grand stairway of granite slabs or the more subdued approach of concrete pavers on sand.

Even with a final plan in hand, it's best to remain open to the possibility of minor adjustments, even during construction. Wall heights or path widths may be increased or reduced. You may decide to substitute materials—for reasons of cost or availability, or simply because, once underway, you decide that an alternate approach would be more satisfying. Don't forget, the product of all your thoughtful planning is not the design as it appears on paper. The proof is on the ground.

Unwatered Spaces

The composition of patios, decks, paths, and other "hard" spaces can serve as a framework for the entire landscape design. There are many choices of materials—flagstone, wood or composite decking, bricks, concrete or adobe pavers, cobbles, gravel, decomposed granite, wood chips, even tumbled glass. Each material has its own advantages and disadvantages. Each has its ecological costs in production and transportation. Recyled materials such as broken concrete or used bricks can be attractive and environmentally sound, especially if they are reused on the same site or nearby.

Functional spaces may consist of only one or two materials for a simple, unified design. For a more lively effect, a number of materials can be used in creative combinations. The

ABOVE: STEPS LEAD UP PLANTED HILLSIDE TO WILDLANDS RIGHT: DECOMPOSED GRANITE PATIO AND FLAGSTONE PATH BELOW: VINE-COVERED ARBOR PROVIDES SHADY RETREAT

degree of variety should support the overall style of the project: casual, whimsical, formal and stately, or whatever mood you desire. Keep in mind that too much of a single material can be dull, while too many shapes and materials can be distracting to the eye and unsettling to the mind—hardly the desired effect for a relaxing outdoor space. Finding the right combination of tranquil simplicity and intriguing detail is central to good landscape design.

Pavings should be porous and open to the soil below whenever possible. The quantity and quality of stormwater runoff from roofs, roads, and parking lots is an increasingly important issue in urban and suburban areas. Porous pavings reduce runoff to storm drains and natural watercourses while helping to filter out waterborne pollutants before runoff reaches creeks and the bay. Bricks or paving stones on sand with planted or unplanted spaces between the pavers are an attractive and ecologically friendly alternative to poured concrete or other impervious materials.

Low-Water Plantings

In the San Francisco Bay Region, as in other mediterranean climates, natural landscapes are green in winter, bursting with color in spring, and mostly subdued or

dormant in late summer and fall. Plants native to or naturalized in local wildlands and untended open spaces have adapted to this seasonal pattern. Plants in designed landscapes can do the same.

There are dry-adapted plants that flower brilliantly in summer, but spring is when it really happens here, and winter is when it starts. Summer in the San Francisco Bay Region, when many plants rest or go dormant, is a little like winter in areas of snow and sleet. Residents of colder climates don't expect flowers or even leaves in winter; they appreciate and feature the striking silhouettes of bare branches and gray bark among their hardy evergreens. Here we can appreciate and feature the magnificent golds, gray-greens, and rusty colors of summertime.

Plan to celebrate the vibrancy of new leaves and flowers in winter, when colder lands are sleeping under a blanket of snow. Revel in the rush of bloom in spring and early summer, then kick back and take pleasure in that quiet time when summer-wet parts of the world are experiencing their high points. Summer dormancy is a fact of life in mediterranean climates. Design for it. Enjoy it.

For a pleasing counterpoint to the dry summer garden, create a small oasis of lush color in an entry courtyard or backyard patio. Add a simple fountain or pool to provide the sounds and sight of water in a shady spot, a welcome reprieve from the bright sunlight and baking heat of late-summer afternoons.

DESIGNING FOR WINTER WET

Winter in the Bay Region can bring dramatic rainstorms and another set of challenges for the gardener. Many mediterranean and native California plants prefer good drainage, and some demand it. These plants may grow naturally on rocky outcrops or on sloping terrain where winter rains seep beneath the root zone or are carried away by seasonal watercourses. Many urban and suburban properties don't provide this natural drainage, especially if the site is flat and the soil is mostly clay.

If your soil is a heavy clay, you may decide to limit your choices to plants that thrive in clay soils. Or you may choose to install some artificial means of improving drainage such as terraces, raised beds, earth mounds, or swales. Raised beds and earth mounds are good solutions for poor drainage and can add visual interest to an otherwise flat landscape. Terraces not only serve as raised planters, but also help to control erosion and slow runoff on sloping terrain. Swales are wide, shallow, summer-dry streams or watercourses, vegetated or lined with cobbles and boulders, that slow the flow of water on sloping land. Swales and dry streams can be designed to direct water away from plants that won't survive in saturated soil and toward plants that benefit from some extra water. Be sure to consult a licensed professional before making any changes to your landscape that may affect site drainage. Ponding of water near foundations and oversaturation of unstable or compacted soils can have catastrophic consequences.

ABOVE: BOARDWALK OVER BACKYARD POND WITH SEDGES

Raised Beds

If your soil is a heavy clay, amended topsoil can be added when making raised beds and terraces. Raised planting beds should be open to the ground below, so plant roots can reach deeply into cooler soil where some moisture may be retained. When constructing raised beds and terraces, it is important to mix any imported or amended soil with existing site soil to form a gradual transition between the layers. Otherwise, plant roots may never venture into the heavier soil beneath, and plants will need more summer water. Also, water may not drain freely into lower levels of soil, and the beds may become waterlogged in rainy winters.

Free drainage can be further enhanced by constructing terrace walls with porous

RIGHT: HILLSIDE GARDEN WITH UNDULATING RETAINING WALLS
BELOW: TERRACED HERB GARDEN

materials such as dry-stacked rock or broken concrete. If your walls are poured concrete or mortared rock, be sure to provide for sufficient drainage by placing drain rock and perforated drain line behind the wall.

Earth Mounds

Earth mounds or berms are another effective means of improving drainage while featuring special plants and adding visual interest to the landscape. As with raised beds and terraces, imported or amended soils should be mixed thoroughly with existing site soil to create a gradual transition between the layers. Groups of large and small boulders set into the mounds make an attractive foil for leaves and flowers and give roots a cool place to run.

EARTH MOUND GIVES VISUAL INTEREST AND SOME PRIVACY FROM STREET

Containers

Good drainage can be provided in large ornamental pots. Plants in containers generally should be considered a high-water choice, since most will need almost daily summer water except in shade or right along the foggy coast. Make sure the container has at least one good-sized drainage hole, then put a piece of broken pottery or fine mesh screen over the hole before filling with potting soil.

Small, summer-dormant bulbs vulnerable to rodents and delicate ephemerals easily lost in open ground may be best grown in pots. These can be moved out of the limelight in their down season. Large containers with a specimen shrub or combination of flowering plants also can provide dramatic accents and an architectural or artful quality—a frame for a floral picture.

DESIGNING WITH MICROCLIMATE

Most sites will have more than one microclimate, as there usually will be spots that are in sun all day and others that receive some shade. In areas of varied topography, and near buildings, the differences are magnified.

Microclimate is important to landscape design both for people and for plants. Our own enjoyment of the outdoors will depend on how thoughtfully we locate and shelter areas for recreation and relaxation. If a patio is exposed to cold winds or hot sun, it

TRANSITIONS

The designed landscape can be both a work of architecture and an expression of nature, standing between the urban built environment and the surrounding countryside.

Gardens, parks, and planned open spaces are human habitat. Built of terraces, walls, benches, shelters, and other cultural artifacts, they offer safety and comfort and enhance our experience of the outdoors. At the same time, they can be wild places, rich in biodiversity and ecological value for many species, places for us to renew our connections with nature. If well designed, our landscapes can offer us the joyous experience of moving back and forth between civilization and the natural world.

Skillful handling of transitions is central to successful design. One approach is to begin with the functions, forms, and materials of the building, extending them outward, then allowing them to give way gradually to more organic, natural qualities.

The style and materials of the building set the tone for the landscape immediately around it. Interior floor tile may be continued into a patio or courtyard just outside, and exterior wall materials might be repeated in benches and landscape walls nearby. South- or west-facing windows can be shaded by a vine-covered arbor that merges with the building. The result is a geometric, transitional space: part indoors and part outside.

Moving further from the building, structure can begin to soften and become more naturalistic. Paths flow out into the landscape, leading the eye toward unknown destinations. Materials become more rustic, straight lines more irregular, and plants begin to spill over built edges.

WATER-LOVING
PLANTS AND ARBOR
ADJACENT
TO HOUSE

If the landscape is large enough, there may be a series of open spaces, each with its own qualities of size, shape, and materials. Spaces open and close in sequence, and the wild character becomes stronger as we move away from the building. This comfortable progression into a more naturalistic place might be punctuated by occasional architectural or sculptural elements that recall the cultural world we are leaving behind.

The effect is enhanced if the plants reflect this gradual transition from formal to natural, from architectural to wild. Plantings next to the building may be in rectangular beds and ceramic containers, featuring old favorites from parts of the world with climates unlike our own. Highly visible and limited to small areas, they may be relatively high in water and maintenance needs.

Moving away from the building, we see more plants from mediterranean areas of the world in more natural and lower-maintenance arrangements. Plantings then gradually become more Californian, including species that will establish themselves and thrive with little help from the gardener.

And finally, in remote areas, we may choose to keep existing native vegetation and plant only local species, taking our cue from the plant communities that occur naturally in the region — for example, coyote brush, California sagebrush, and monkeyflowers on a sunny slope in the fog belt or oaks, toyon, and sun-loving bunchgrasses on a hot, dry, inland hillside. Native insects, birds, and small mammals will recognize their ancient foods, and congregate in surprising numbers. Here, in the furthest reaches of the site, we might sit for a while on a simple bench or among a cluster of large rocks to enjoy our wild surroundings and reflect on our place in the world. In good time, we will make the return trip to civilization, rested and rejuvenated.

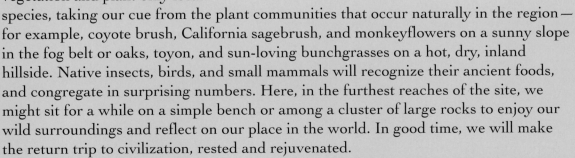

TOP: FLAGSTONE PATH AND CONTAINER PLANTING EASE TRANSITION TO WILD GARDEN BOTTOM: WILD GARDEN WITH BENCH

Michael Thilgen, Landscape Architect
Oakland, California

TOP: SUCCULENT GARDEN
WITH MULCHED PATHS
ABOVE: A SUNNY
MEADOW OF MEXICAN
FEATHER GRASS
(*NASSELLA TENUISSIMA*)

probably won't be used, no matter how extraordinary the view.

Plants also respond to microclimate, establishing themselves and growing where their needs are met, sulking or dying where they're not. The concept of "zoning" by plant needs and microclimate is central to planting design, as well as to the design of efficient irrigation systems. As you consider what to plant where, start with the growing conditions in each zone or microclimate. Soil type, exposure to cold or drying winds, and amount and timing of sun and shade will determine which plants will do well in a particular zone and the amount of water they will need to thrive there.

Group plants by the amount of sun they prefer as well as their needs for water. If you include in a group of drought-tolerant, sun-loving plants even one plant that needs a lot of water in full sun, you'll have difficulty watering all of the plants appropriately.

If you choose to install an irrigation system, whether sprinkler or drip, automatic or manually controlled, make sure that the system is designed to irrigate the different planting zones separately. Irrigation systems should be designed in conjunction with plantings. It is difficult to design an efficient irrigation system for a landscape that has been designed without thought for how it will be watered.

Microclimates and Plant Communities

Another way to design with microclimates is to organize your plantings around the concept of plant communities. In designed landscapes as in natural ones, variations in soil type, topography, and microclimate combine to make conditions that favor some species and discourage others. If your site is a sunny, west-facing slope, you might choose plants that grow in California's coastal scrub, chaparral, or grassland communities. If you have an area that is shaded by a building or a grove of mature trees, consider shrubs and perennials that grow in valley and foothill woodlands. If your landscape will include a small oasis of high water use, this is a good place for riparian plants that grow naturally in wetlands or seasonally damp places.

PINK-FLOWERED ARMERIA WITH PURE WHITE FLOWERS OF SNOW-IN-SUMMER (*CERASTIUM TOMENTOSUM*)

You can expand your plant palette to include plants from other mediterranean climates by learning about their preferred conditions and grouping them accordingly. In South Africa's Western Cape, central Chile, southwestern Australia, and the Mediterranean Basin, there are natural plant communities that correspond roughly to those of the San Francisco Bay Region.

Blending the science of ecology with the practice of horticulture, we can learn to create landscapes that evoke the natural qualities of the site while minimizing environmental impacts and maintenance needs.

DESIGNING FOR THE WILDLAND INTERFACE

It is our great fortune in the Bay Region that cities and suburbs are surrounded by regional parks, watershed land, rangelands, and other undeveloped open spaces. In this setting, the views are often spectacular and one can hike easily from public roads to many miles of scenic trails.

In many suburban areas, home gardens are visited regularly by opossums, raccoons, deer, and other wildlife that depend on us to retain open corridors through which they can move from one area to another. Eagles and hawks soar overhead, and numerous smaller birds periodically visit urban and suburban parks and gardens to feed and nest. Countless small mammals, snakes and lizards, and insects—including the universally favored butterflies—bring life to our gardens and help maintain the ecological balance necessary for a healthy, sustainable landscape.

The price of our proximity to natural areas is a shared responsibility to protect the integrity of the ecosystems around us. We can choose to be stewards of the natural landscape, even while gardening within it. One way we can protect natural ecosystems is to leave the landscape as close as possible to the condition in which we find it, perhaps editing lightly by removing unwanted plants and shaping others. If you have even a small area of natural landscape, consider leaving it that way. If you add plants, try to include a diversity of species, especially local natives, known to be favored by birds and beneficial insects. If you garden within a wildlife corridor, leave some open, unfenced areas through which wildlife can travel. If you live near a creek or where water is not far below the surface, take special care in selecting landscape plants, avoiding those with a tendency to take over in damp areas.

Fire Safety

Another price of living near wildlands is the likelihood of some day experiencing a disastrous wildfire. In summer-dry climates fire is a regularly expected natural event. Prior to our public policy of fire suppression, most acreage in lowland and mid-elevation California burned every ten to fifty years. The most destructive fires occur in hilly areas, which, because of the views and surrounding open space, is where much suburban development has occurred.

Although some plants may burn more readily than others, landscape design and maintenance are far more important than plant selection in protecting against fire. Maintaining lightly and conserving native shrubs to provide habitat must be balanced against the need to minimize fuel load in areas prone to wildfires.

Two primary principles guide firewise landscape design: fuel reduction and interruption of the "fire path"—the horizontal or vertical continuity of fuel. Fuel

includes anything that burns—not only landscape trees and shrubs, but buildings, fences or arbors, stacked firewood, and adjacent wildland vegetation. Avoid any arrangement of fuels that facilitates movement of fire along the ground or from the ground up into the tree canopy.

Ideally, in fire-prone areas, no vegetation over a few inches tall should be planted within six to ten feet of any building or under a raised deck or overhang. Traditional "foundation plantings," with trees and large shrubs next to windows and walls, should be avoided in fire-prone areas.

Fuel load should be minimized within at least thirty feet of the house or other structure. This is a good place for a patio of concrete pavers, brick, paving stones, decomposed granite, or gravel mulch. Plantings should be mostly groundcovers and low-growing shrubs. Trees, if any, should be small and well groomed. Choose plants that will grow to a size appropriate for their location so that pruning is not required to maintain desired spacing. Because healthy plants are more fire resistant than plants struggling to survive, select

and locate plants with regard for their needs for sun, shade, water, and soil type, as well as their tolerance of heat and frost.

Further away from the building, larger shrubs or trees can be planted in widely spaced "islands" or groups separated by areas of low groundcovers that break up the path of fire. The taller the plants, the more widely they should be spaced. Walkways can help separate planting areas and simplify maintenance.

CEANOTHUS 'JOYCE COULTER' (LEFT) AND *C.* 'CONCHA' (RIGHT) WITH *SALVIA SONOMENSIS* GROUNDCOVER AND REDBUD BEHIND

RESOURCES

Beidleman, Linda and Eugene Kozloff, *Plants of the San Francisco Bay Region: Mendocino to Monterey*, Berkeley, University of California Press, 2001.

Conran, Terence, and Dan Pearson, *The Essential Garden Book*, New York, Three Rivers Press, 1998.

East Bay Municipal Utility District, *Firescape: landscaping to reduce fire hazard*, Oakland, CA, 2003.

Keator, Glenn, *Plants of the East Bay Parks*, Boulder, CO, Roberts Rinehart, 1994.

Smithen, Jan, *Sun Drenched Gardens: the Mediterranean style*, New York, Harry N. Abrams, 2002.

Stevens, David, *The Garden Design Sourcebook: the essential guide to garden materials and structures*, London, Conran Octopus, 1999.

Thompson, J. William and Kim Sorvig, *Sustainable Landscape Construction: a guide to green building outdoors*, Washington, D.C., Island Press, 2000.

Chapter Three

PLANT CATALOG

This chapter features a catalog of photographs and descriptions of more than 650 plants that, given the right conditions, do well in the dry summer, wet winter climate of the San Francisco Bay Region. They should do as well in other mediterranean climates, as many of them hail from parts of the world with a summer-dry, winter-wet seasonal pattern. The chart, Plants at a Glance, summarizes the information provided in the text.

Criteria for inclusion of plants in this book are:

- prefer or thrive with moderate to little or no summer water;
- are relatively pest- and disease-free;
- are attractive year-round with little maintenance (summer dormancy qualifies);
- are available in nurseries or from specialty suppliers, botanic gardens, or native plant sales.

Invasiveness in wildlands was initially a disqualifying consideration for inclusion in this book. However, most nonnative plants—and a few of our finest natives—are considered to be at least potential invaders in some areas. Eliminating all potential invaders would have severely restricted the number and variety of plants featured in this book.

CAREX MORROWII
'AUREA-VARIEGATA'

Almost all plants are invasive somewhere. Experience has shown that plants once considered not to be invasive in the San Francisco Bay Region are beginning to pop up in local wildlands. In the future, there undoubtedly will be more. As gardeners and landscapers, as stewards of the land, we all have a responsibility to be alert for invasive potential. If we live or garden near wildlands, that responsibility increases immeasurably.

Potential invasiveness in the garden or in the wild is indicated in the text, where currently known. Don't plant these plants near wildlands, and watch out for them in cultivated landscapes. Root them out if they seem to be taking over in your garden. Invasive plants not only crowd out natives and disrupt natural ecosystems—both plants and animals—but add to the overall wildland fuel load and increase the frequency and intensity of disastrous wildfires.

Just because a plant is included in this book doesn't mean that it may not, in the future or in particular natural ecosystems, become an invasive wildland weed. A beautiful native lupine, *Lupinus arboreus*, has invaded some coastal dunes in northern California. California pepper (*Schinus molle*), a magnificent nonnative tree planted since the 1830s in mission gardens, is invading riparian landscapes in parts of southern

OPPOSITE: *ALOE BUHRI* (YELLOW), *ALOE SAPONARIA* (ORANGE), *ALOE STRIATULA* (FOLIAGE), AND PROTEA (RED)

California. We've tried to eliminate from this book plants known to invade wildlands in the Bay Region, but only time will tell. A seemingly innocent exotic plant, or even a particularly rugged native, may come to be widely known as an invasive pest in time. It is our individual and collective responsibility to remain watchful, informed, and aware.

SOME FUNDAMENTALS

OPPOSITE: *Sedum* 'Autumn Joy' with *Carex secta* and Artemisia

Because almost nothing can be said to apply to all plants all the time, horticultural reference books are full of qualifiers. One plant is said to grow from a foot to three feet tall and wide, depending on soil, sunlight, and water. Another plant is said to tolerate drought, but only near the coast or where protected from afternoon sun. Reference books and nursery catalogs differ radically in their assessment of a particular plant's requirements—this plant needs "regular" water, it needs "little" water, it "tolerates drought" or it doesn't. The fact is, the needs and characteristics of most plants differ, sometimes widely, under different conditions.

To complicate the matter further, the plant you purchase with a label attached may behave quite differently from a plant obtained from another source with the same label. It's not just that plants are sometimes labeled incorrectly. Plants of the same species grown from individual plants adapted to different parts of the world, state, or county may look quite different and have different needs for sun, water, and

soils. It's best to proceed slowly and observe. How does this plant perform on this site? Does it tolerate "full sun" in this situation? Unless you have personal experience with a particular plant from a particular source in a particular neighborhood—or know someone who does—try one out before planting a whole hillside.

The same caution applies to every aspect of the plant descriptions in our Catalog. One person's "grayish green" leaves may look "bluish green" to another. Is that flower "bright yellow" or "golden yellow"—or could that be a touch of red? Plant descriptions in this book are based on a rough consensus among local gardeners and growers we consulted and major reference books and nursery catalogs. Your experience may differ.

COLORFUL BORDER ALONG SIDEWALK SHARES GARDEN WITH PASSERSBY

The information provided here covers plant names, both scientific and common, climate zones, plant type, and cultural preferences or requirements for sun or shade, drainage, and water. Sizes given are approximate and vary with site conditions.

PLANT NAMES

Scientific names consist of a genus, or generic name, and a specific epithet (often incorrectly called the "species name"). Together, the genus and the specific epithet make up the species name. Often the species name includes categories below the level of the species, such as subspecies (abbreviated "ssp.") and variety (abbreviated "var."). Cultivars are cultivated varieties of species or hybrids selected or bred for particular characteristics. Cultivar names are capitalized, not italicized, and enclosed in single quotes, as in *Achillea millefolium* 'Rosea'. If the cultivar cannot be attributed to a single species, the specific epithet may be omitted, as in *Achillea* 'Coronation Gold'.

The scientific names of plants are important because they tend to identify the plant in question with some precision and clarity. Scientific names are more reliable and more universally accepted than are the multiple "common" or vernacular names applied to plants, which differ from one region, supplier, or gardener to another. But scientific names do change, and at any given time there may be disagreement among botanists and taxonomists about the correct scientific name of a plant.

The sources we used for scientific names of plants include the online Jepson Interchange, a regularly updated reference of accepted names of plants native to or naturalized in California. Other sources include the *Sunset Western Garden Book*, the online Integrated Taxonomic Information System, and the Royal Horticultural Society's online Plant Finder. On occasion, these sources disagree. To assist the reader, we have tried to include the various synonyms and alternate names in the index. Nursery plant names may differ from those provided here.

CLIMATE ZONES

With permission from Sunset, we have adopted the zone concept from *Sunset Western Garden Book* because that book is one of the most widely used references for plants grown in western North America. The Sunset zones in the San Francisco Bay Region include Zones 7, 9, 14, 15, 16, and 17. Other zones are indicated in the plant descriptions for the convenience of readers who garden outside the Bay Region. Where a plant is not included in *Sunset Western Garden Book*, the zone designation is listed as not available (N/A).

Sunset zones give a general idea of climates in the Bay Region, and you can locate your city fairly accurately on the zone map. However, it is important to understand that each of these zones contains considerable variations in microclimate. Local terrain can affect amount of coastal influence, as well as orientation to the sun. South-facing slopes receive more solar heat than flat land, while north-facing slopes receive less. Hillsides seldom are as cold in winter as hilltops above them or lowland areas below. Even within a single site, there may be cold pockets and warm, protected areas with microclimates where different plants will grow. Sunset describes the zones of the San Francisco Bay Region as follows.

Zone 7: Hot summers and mild but pronounced winters bring sharply defined seasons without severe winter cold or humidity. In the San Francisco Bay Region, these are hilltop and ridgetop areas that are too high (and too cold in winter) to be included in milder Zones 15 and 16. Typical winter lows range from 23 to 9 degrees F.

CLIMATE ZONES FOR THE SAN FRANCISCO BAY REGION (ADAPTED FROM *SUNSET WESTERN GARDEN BOOK*, 2001)

Zone 9: High summer daytime temperatures and almost constant sunshine during a long growing season. Winter cold is sufficient for the dormancy requirements of some plants, and heat-loving plants perform at their best. Tule fogs (dense fogs that rise from the ground on cold, clear nights) are common during winter months. Winter lows range from 28 to 18 degrees F.

Zone 14: Inland areas with some ocean influence, which moderates both winter and summer temperatures. This zone includes both mild-winter, maritime-influenced areas and cold-winter inland areas, accommodating both plants that need winter chill and those that need summer heat. Lows range from 26 to 16 degrees F., with record lows from 20 to 11 degrees F.

PHORMIUM
'CREAM DELIGHT'

Zone 15: Areas influenced by marine air about 85 percent of the time, by inland air 15 percent of the time, and almost constant afternoon wind in summer. Cold-winter areas in this zone lie in lowland basins, on hilltops above thermal belts, or far enough north that plant performance dictates a Zone 15 designation. Many plants recommended for Zone 15 are not recommended for Zone 14 mainly because they must have a moister atmosphere, cooler summers, and milder winters. Zone 15 does receive enough winter chill to favor plants not recommended for the warmer winter Zones 16 and 17. Lows range from 28 to 21 degrees F., with record lows from 26 to 16 degrees F.

Zone 16: Benign climate in thermal belts and on hillsides in the coastal climate area. One of northern California's finest horticultural climates, with more summer heat than in Zone 17 and warmer winters than in Zone 15. Like Zone 15, this zone has afternoon wind in summer. Lows range from 32 to 19 degrees F., with record lows from 25 to 18 degrees F.

Zone 17: Mild, wet, almost frostless winters and cool summers (typical highs from 60 to 75 degrees F.) with frequent fog or wind. Heat-loving plants may not flower or fruit reliably, but mild winters support many plants that cannot tolerate cold, and many plants are in bloom year-round. Lows range from 36 to 23 degrees F., with record lows from 30 to 20 degrees F. Highest summer temperatures average 97 degrees F., while adjacent highest temperatures are 104 to 116 degrees F.

PLANT TYPE

There often is as much disagreement about whether a plant is a tree or a shrub, a woody perennial or a perennial subshrub—even sometimes whether a plant is deciduous or evergreen—as there is about everything else in the plant world. Plant type in this book follows the lead of *Sunset Western Garden Book*. If a plant is listed as an evergreen shrub in that book, it is listed as an evergreen shrub here. The definitions are roughly as follows.

OPPOSITE: *RUBUS PENTALOBUS* AND AN UPRIGHT ROSEMARY EDGE STEPS LEADING DOWN TO GRAVEL PATIO

Annual: Herbaceous plant that germinates, grows shoots and leaves, flowers, sets seed,

and dies within a single year or less. An annual plant may seem to be perennial if it self-sows in place, coming up with new plants year after year.

Biennial: Herbaceous plant that takes two growing seasons to complete its life cycle; usually blooms in its second year. Many biennials will produce offshoots or self-sow or both, seeming to be perennial in mild climates.

Perennial: Herbaceous or partially woody plant that lives for more than two and often for many years. Some perennials are treated as annuals because they look their best for only one year or do not survive cold winters.

Shrub: Woody plant that lives for many years, usually multi-trunked and often with foliage almost to the ground, typically but not always smaller than a tree.

Tree: Woody plant that lives for many years, often but not always single-trunked, typically but not always larger than a shrub. Shrubbiness can be a maintenance issue: the search for small trees for

urban yards has led many shrubs to be grown as "standards" with a single trunk, but stems growing from the base must be regularly removed to maintain this form.

Fern: Flowerless, seedless plant with leaf-like fronds and reproducing by spores.

Grass: Perennial or annual tufted herbaceous plant, usually growing from rhizomes or stolons, with linear leaves and often showy plumes of small, inconspicuous flowers.

Palm: Single or sometimes multi-trunked, treelike plant that does not form true wood and has a crown of distinctively divided leaves.

Vine: Flexible woody or semi-woody shrub that sprawls, climbs, clings, or twines.

Deciduous: Plants that lose their leaves at the end of the growing season. In mild-winter areas, deciduous plants may lose their leaves much later. Some plants are deciduous when exposed to drought.

Evergreen: Plants that retain most of their leaves year-round, but shed older leaves periodically or continuously. Plants that lose many but not all of their leaves at the end of the growing season are described as semi-evergreen or semi-deciduous.

CULTURAL PREFERENCES

Preferences or requirements for sun or shade, drainage, and summer water are relative and interdependent. A plant that thrives in full sun along the coast with no supplemental water may die in full sun in hot, interior locations or survive there only with copious amounts of water. The conditions recommended for plants in this book assume at least the following:

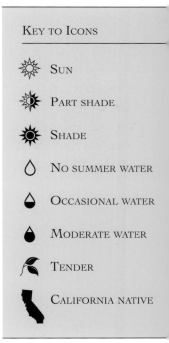

KEY TO ICONS

☀ SUN

☀ PART SHADE

☀ SHADE

◊ NO SUMMER WATER

◖ OCCASIONAL WATER

● MODERATE WATER

🌿 TENDER

⬟ CALIFORNIA NATIVE

- Plants that prefer coastal conditions are planted near the coast. A sun-loving coastal plant in an inland garden probably will need at least afternoon shade.

- The previous winter and spring have provided "normal" amounts of rain. If plants enter summer in droughty soil, they will need more supplemental water.

- Plants are already well established. All plants need some water and protection from hot sun when they're first planted and as they mature, developing strong stems and branches and fully efficient root systems. Establishment usually takes at least one growing season, often two or more.

- When water is applied, plants receive a deep, thorough soaking. With a daily five-minute sprinkling, even drought-tolerant plants may never get beyond their dependence on supplemental water. Shallow, frequent watering discourages plants from sending roots deep into the soil.

- Soil is mulched to reduce evaporation and discourage weeds, and plants that need it receive protection from the hottest afternoon sun.

- Drainage is at least reasonably good. Some plants will tolerate soggy soils and standing water, but most of those included in this book will not. Dig a test hole and fill it with water. If water is still standing in the hole an hour or so later, you may need to take steps to improve drainage. If "perfect drainage" is required, there should be no standing water after a few minutes.

Sun/Shade

Preferences for sun or shade suggest the relative amount of sun a plant requires or will tolerate with the amount of water indicated.

Full sun: Unobstructed sunlight from morning until evening. Few plants will tolerate full sun in hot, interior locations without at least moderate water.

Afternoon shade: Assumes enough sun throughout the day for a sun-loving plant to thrive, but with protection from the hottest afternoon sun. Most plants prefer some afternoon shade in hot, interior locations.

Part shade: Filtered sunlight. Many plants do well in at least part shade.

Full shade: Little or no direct sun. Plants that require shade may grow best on the north side of a building or wall or underneath the evergreen canopy of a tree or large shrub.

Water Needs

Water needs suggest the relative amount of supplemental water a plant requires in rainless summer months. Sometimes a low-water plant will look better with moderate water, at least temporarily, but applying more water than a plant needs often will shorten its life or kill it. Watch plants for signs of drought stress and dig around in the

ABOVE: Flowering quince (*Chaenomeles*)

soil to see how dry it is. Don't assume that yellowing leaves mean more water is needed; as often as not, the problem is too much water with inadequate drainage.

Moderate: Less than regular summer water; tolerates some drying of the top few inches of soil; may need water every week to ten days away from the coast or every two weeks in areas with maritime influence.

Occasional: Deep soaking every three to four weeks. This regime works for many plants included in this book, except in the hottest weather.

Infrequent: Deep soaking once or twice during the hottest and driest months of the year; applies to California native and Mediterranean plants that are adapted to long dry periods.

None: No water required beyond what is naturally available in normal rainfall years; applies only to the most drought-adapted plants and to those that are dormant in summer. Note that some plants, such as native bulbs, require a dry summer dormancy. You probably can give most summer-dormant plants an occasional squirt, but it can kill some plants, and it's usually just a waste of water.

Coastal/Inland

The Catalog descriptions and Plants at a Glance indicate plants that do best with, or require, coastal influence, as well as those that sulk, mildew, or fail to bloom well except in inland areas with summer heat. This doesn't mean that you can't grow a plant inland if it's said to prefer coastal conditions or vice versa. If you can provide similar conditions on your site, it's worth a try. Note that some plant genera contain both species that prefer coastal conditions and others that prefer inland climates.

BERKELEY SEDGE (*CAREX TUMULICOLA*) WITH *HEUCHERA MAXIMA* AND PACIFIC COAST HYBRID IRIS BEHIND

Coastal: Can indicate that a plant may grow only near the coast or that it may do best in a more temperate climate. Some plants, for example, are quite intolerant of frost even though they might thrive in heat.

Inland: Some plants need heat to perform, while others require a period of cold temperatures to flower or fruit. For such plants, interior locations with greater temperature ranges are preferable to the more temperate zones.

OTHER CHARACTERISTICS

Native Plants

For our purposes here, native plants are those occurring naturally within the boundaries of the state of California prior to significant alteration of their natural habitats by human intervention.

There are other definitions. Native may be defined in terms of a particular site or community of plants in the immediate area. Native also may be defined in terms of larger biogeographical regions that span political boundaries of states and nations. For example, the California Floristic

Province encompasses mediterranean-climate areas of California, southwestern Oregon, and northwestern Baja California.

Naturally occurring hybrids and some cultivars of native plants may be considered native if they have been selected and propagated from native species. The question becomes more complex when considering deliberately crossed hybrids or cultivars of uncertain parentage. Many plants offered commercially fall into this category.

If you're interested in growing plants that are truly native to your area, join the local chapter of your native plant society, visit regional botanic gardens, check to see what grows in nearby, untended wildlands (watch out for invasive wildland weeds), and get to know people who are knowledgeable about local native plants.

Native to Oakland is different from native to Walnut Creek, Concord, or Antioch, and so on. Some plants are adaptable and can make the switch, but others cannot. Wherever you live or garden, there's a whole world of intricate detail on plants with locally specific needs and adaptations awaiting you. Success in the landscape may depend on your willingness to learn about and attend to those details.

Plants at a Glance and the Catalog both flag genera that include at least one native species. Note that a genus also may include other plants not native to California.

Summer Dormancy

Some plants have adapted to summer drought with a life cycle that includes growth of roots, leaves, and flowers from fall through spring and dying back to the ground in the heat of summer.

Summer dormancy may be partial; some plants lose leaves or turn brown in summer, while others slow down and stop growth but retain their usual color. Some summer-dormant plants can't tolerate any summer water without rotting; others accept a little; a few, with good drainage, don't seem to be affected.

Fast Growth

Fast-growing plants are those that get off to a fast start and reach maturity quickly. However, fast-growing may mean short-lived, so be sure to include some slower-growing, longer-lived plants in your landscape. Fast-growing, short-lived plants are good temporary fillers while slower-growing plants are taking shape.

Fast-growing also may mean rampant or aggressively spreading, requiring frequent pruning or cutting back to keep plants from overtaking paths, structures, or nearby plants.

OPPOSITE: LEAVES FORM A NATURAL MULCH IN SUNNY OPENING AT WOODLAND EDGE

FOLLOWING SPREAD: *SANTOLINA ROSMARINIFOLIA* (GREEN) AND *S. CHAMAECYPARISSUS*

Bloom Time

Season of bloom is indicated only in relative terms. A plant said to flower in "early spring" will tend to flower earlier than a plant described as flowering in "late spring to early summer," but early spring in one garden may arrive a month or more earlier or later than in a garden a few miles away.

PLANT CATALOG

Abelia x *grandiflora*
(glossy abelia)

ZONES 4-24. EVERGREEN SHRUB.
4-8' x 4-6'.

Fine-textured shrub with gracefully arching branches, glossy green leaves that turn bronzy green or red in fall, and pendulous clusters of small, white to lilac-pink, slightly fragrant, tubular to bell-shaped flowers in summer and fall. Attractive to hummingbirds and butterflies. Usually ignored by deer. Full sun to part shade, occasional

water; moderate water in hot locations. Prune lightly to control size and shape; shearing destroys the fountainlike habit. Hybrid of two species native to China.

'Edward Goucher', 3-5' x 3-5', has lilac-pink flowers with orange throats. 'Sherwoodii', 3-4' x 5', dense and compact, has smaller leaves that turn purplish in cold weather. 'Confetti' has small green leaves with creamy white or pink-tinged margins.

Acacia (acacia)

ZONES VARY. EVERGREEN OR DECIDUOUS SHRUBS
AND TREES. SIZE VARIES.

Fast-growing, short-lived, somewhat tender shrubs and small trees with green to gray-green leaves and bright to pale yellow or creamy white flowers in late winter to early spring. Full sun, good drainage, occasional deep watering. Prolific seed producers; some (e.g., *A. longifolia*, *A. melanoxylon*) are invasive. Attractive to birds. Ignored by deer. Most plants offered commercially are native to Australia.

A. baileyana, Bailey acacia, 20-30' x 20-40', rounded, widespreading, evergreen tree with

weeping branches, ferny, bluish gray leaves, and golden-yellow flowers in late winter. 'Purpurea' has purplish new growth. Zones 7-9, 13-24.

A. cultriformis, knife acacia, 8-15' x 8-15', graceful, evergreen, multi-stemmed small tree or shrub with drooping, gray-green leaves and bright yellow flowers in early spring. Zones 13-24.

A. glaucoptera, clay wattle, 3-5' x 4-6', sprawling evergreen shrub with small, overlapping, bluish green or gray-green, pointed leaves, purplish red in new growth, and deep yellow flowers in spring. Zones N/A.

ACANTHUS MOLLIS WITH *ALYOGYNE HUEGELII* IN BLOOM BEHIND

A. pravissima, ovens wattle, 12-20' x 12-20', adaptable, upright, evergreen shrub or small tree with small triangular, gray-green leaves, bronzy or reddish new growth, and bright yellow flowers in late winter, aging to coppery brown. Zones 12-24.

A. redolens, prostrate acacia, 2-4' x 10-15', low, mounding, evergreen shrub with narrow, gray-green, leathery leaves and yellow flowers in spring. Good for large areas on dry slopes. Zones 8, 9, 12-24. 'Low Boy' is under 1' tall.

A. smallii, 10-35' x 15-25', is deciduous, with finely divided gray-green leaves on thorny branches and small, yellow flowers in spring. Native to southwestern U.S. Zones 8, 9, 12-24.

A. stenophylla, shoestring acacia, 30' x 20', upright evergreen tree with long, narrow, gray-green leaves, and creamy yellow flowers in late winter and spring. Zones 8, 9, 12-24.

Acanthus mollis (bear's breech, acanthus)

ZONES 5-24. PERENNIAL. 2-4' x 3-4'.

Dramatic, undemanding plant for dry shade, noted for ability to survive almost any conditions. Large, deeply lobed, shiny, dark green leaves and tall, long-lasting spikes of white, rose, or purplish flowers beneath green or purple bracts in late spring or summer.

Spreads by seeds and rhizomes; difficult to eradicate; best planted where it can be confined. Grown dry, leaves wither in summer heat; cut back hard and wait for plants to leaf out again with winter rains. Can be kept fairly green in a cool, shady spot with occasional deep soakings. Remove flower spikes after flowering to control reseeding. Flowers attractive in dried or fresh arrangements. Native to the Mediterranean.

Achillea (yarrow)

ZONES 1-24. PERENNIALS.
SIZE VARIES.

Sturdy, dependable Mediterranean perennials that thrive in hot, dry climates. Ground-hugging mats or mounds to upright, sometimes rangy plants with silvery gray to green, feathery or ferny, aromatic leaves. Flattish clusters of summer flowers in a wide range of colors that change subtly with age. Mid-season flowers feature a pleasing combination of shades. Long-lasting fresh or dried. Full sun, reasonable drainage, moderate to occasional water. Remove spent flowers and trim back occasionally to keep plants neat and prolong blooming. Attractive to butterflies.

A. clavennae, silvery yarrow, spreading mat 4-12" x 1-2', with finely cut, silvery gray leaves and white flowers summer to fall.

A. filipendulina, fernleaf yarrow, mounding to 3' x 3', deep green to gray-green, fernlike leaves and bright yellow flowers on tall stems in summer.

A. x *kelleri*, small, dense hummocks, 6-12" x 12-18", with silvery gray leaves and white flowers with yellow centers in summer.

A. millefolium, common yarrow, 12-30" x 2-4', has medium-green or grayish green leaves and white or cream flowers on tall stems in summer and fall. 'Island Pink' has dark green leaves and rich pink flowers.

LEFT: *ACHILLEA MILLEFOLIUM* 'ISLAND PINK' BELOW: *A. MILLEFOLIUM* BOTTOM: *A.* 'MOONSHINE'

A. x *taygetea*, 12-18" x 12-18", forms large clumps of gray-green leaves and has bright yellow flowers that fade to pale yellow in summer and fall.

A. *tomentosa*, woolly yarrow, 6-12" x 18", has gray-green, finely divided leaves and yellow flowers in summer.

A. 'Coronation Gold' has silvery gray leaves and intense golden yellow summer flowers. 'Moonshine' has deep yellow flowers.

Aeonium (aeonium)

ZONES 15-17, 20-24. SUCCULENT PERENNIALS. SIZE VARIES.

Symmetrical rosettes of fleshy, waxy leaves, generally at the ends of upright, branched, succulent stems, and conical clusters of bright yellow to creamy yellow, star-shaped flowers in spring or early summer. Tender. Full sun along coast, part shade inland, excellent drainage, infrequent deep watering. Plant on mounds in sandy or gravelly soil to avoid winter rot. Native to the Canary Islands, northern Africa, and the Mediterranean. Many species; most plants offered are cultivars.

A. *arboreum*, 3' x 3', has many thick stems topped by rosettes to 6" across and conical clusters of golden yellow flowers. Leaves of 'Zwartkop' are dark purple, almost black.

A. *canariense*, 12-18" x 18-24", forms large rosettes of bright green leaves on short, branching stems and golden yellow flowers in spring. Zones N/A.

A. *haworthii*, pinwheel, 1-2' x 18"-2', has gray-green leaves

TOP: *AEONIUM ARBOREUM* 'ZWARTKOP' ABOVE: *AEONIUM CANARIENSE* 'MINT SAUCER' RIGHT: AEONIUMS IN MIXED BORDER

and white or creamy yellow flowers. Leaves of variegated forms are edged with red, pink, or cream.

SILVERY GRAY BARK OF BUCKEYE (*AESCULUS CALIFORNICA*) IN SPRING WITH YELLOW-FLOWERED SEDUM

Aesculus californica (California buckeye)

ZONES 3-10, 14-24. DECIDUOUS TREE OR SHRUB. 15'-20' x 30'.

Boldly textured, rounded small tree or large shrub, often multi-trunked and much broader than tall. Gray bark turns silvery in age. Large, palmately compound, rich green leaves in late winter or early spring, turning brown in summer. Showy, spikelike clusters of fragrant, white to rose flowers make a striking display in early spring. Attractive to butterflies and bees. Large, leathery, pear-shaped pods hang from bare branches into winter and are attractive in arrangements.

Full sun along coast; part shade inland. Native and endemic to California. Grows naturally in shady, dry woodlands or along streams in sun. Quite drought tolerant when properly sited, but gardeners should be prepared for early browning of leaves.

Aethionema (stonecress)

ZONES 1-9, 14-21. PERENNIALS. 6-10" x 8-12".

AETHIONEMA SCHISTOSUM

Fussy and shortlived but lovely plants for sunny spots where excellent drainage can be provided. Low-growing mounds of gray-green to bluish leaves and small, rose-pink or bright pink flowers in spring and early summer. Not for hot interior gardens. Dislike wet soil, especially in winter. Native to the Mediterranean and Asia Minor.

A. grandiflorum is a lax shrublet with narrow, gray-green leaves and bright pink flowers.

A. schistosum is smaller, with pink flowers in early spring.

Agapanthus (lily-of-the-Nile)

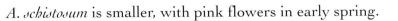

ZONES 6-9, 12-24. PERENNIALS. SIZE VARIES.

AGAPANTHUS 'PETER PAN'

Reliable performers so commonly grown that some gardeners dismiss them as ordinary, but few plants give so much for so little. Dense, compact, symmetrical clumps of strap-shaped, glossy green leaves and upright stalks topped by spherical

clusters of funnel-shaped blue, blue-violet, or white flowers in summer. Good for formal effects in home gardens and low-maintenance commercial plantings. Deer may munch the flowers.

TOP: *AGASTACHE RUPESTRIS*
BOTTOM: *AGASTACHE* 'APRICOT SUNRISE' WITH PURPLE CONEFLOWER.

Full sun to part shade, reasonable drainage, occasional water. Some afternoon shade in hot locations. Dig and divide when plants become crowded. Bold flowers long-lasting in arrangements.

Two evergreen species and many named cultivars. *A. orientalis* has pale blue flowers on strong stems up to 4-5' feet tall. *A. africanus* has smaller leaves and shorter flower stems; flowers are deep blue. Native to South Africa. 'Peter Pan', 1' x 1', is smaller in all respects, with narrow leaves and blue flowers on 18" stems. 'Rancho White', 12-18" x 12-18", has bright white flowers. 'Storm Cloud' has deep violet-blue flowers on tall stems.

Agastache (agastache, hyssop)

ZONES VARY. PERENNIALS. SIZE VARIES.

Compact, well-branched, shrubby perennials with aromatic, green to grayish green leaves and upright spikes of tubular flowers midsummer to fall. Flower color ranges from violet or purple to pink, blue, orange, red, and white. Attractive to butterflies, hummingbirds, and bees. Flowers open in succession, extending the show for many weeks; good in arrangements, fresh or dried.

Best in well drained soils and full sun to part shade with occasional deep soakings. Some tolerate drought when established, especially in coastal gardens. Short-lived in heavy clay soils, but self-sow, with often beautiful results.

A. aurantiaca, orange hummingbird mint, 3' x 2', has orange flowers and gray-green leaves. Native to Mexico. Zones 3-24.

A. cana, Texas hummingbird mint, 2' x 2', has light green leaves and rose-pink to red-violet flowers. Native to Texas and New Mexico. Zones 2-24.

A. foeniculum, anise hyssop, 3' x 2', with blue-purple flowers and

BELOW: *AGAVE PARRYI*
BOTTOM: *AGAVE
DESMETTIANA* 'VARIEGATA'
WITH EUPHORBIA AND
PHORMIUM BEHIND
OPPOSITE: *AGAVE AMERICANA*
WITH *STIPA GIGANTEA*

licorice-scented leaves, is more tolerant of winter wet than some other species. Native to north-central North America. Zones 1-24.

A. mexicana, Mexican giant hyssop, 2-3' x 1', has lemon-scented, pink to crimson flowers on 12" spikes spring to fall. Native to Mexico. Zones 3-24.

A. rugosa, Korean hummingbird mint, 3-4' x 18"-2', has purplish blue flowers. Native to Korea. Zones 4-24.

A. rupestris, licorice mint, 2' x 2', is a willowy plant with narrow, gray-green, anise-scented leaves and salmon-orange flowers. Native to southern Arizona, northern Mexico. Zones 1-24.

'Apricot Sunrise', 3' x 2', has gray-green leaves and bright orange flowers that fade to light orange. 'Blue Fortune', 4' x 2', has powder blue to purple-blue flowers. 'Summer Breeze', 3' x 2', has lavender-pink flowers and gray-green leaves and is quite tolerant of dryness. 'Tangerine Dreams', 2' x 2', has deep orange flowers. 'Tutti Frutti', 3-4' x 2', has dark gray-green leaves and lavender-pink or purplish red flowers.

Agave (agave)

ZONES VARY. SUCCULENT PERENNIALS. SIZE VARIES.

Rosettes of green to grayish green, somewhat succulent, strap-shaped leaves from the center of which eventually forms a massive stalk with side branches bearing creamy white to greenish yellow flowers. After flowering, the rosette dies, and is replaced by offsets or "pups" that become new plants. Full sun with afternoon shade in hottest areas, excellent drainage, little water.

A. americana, century plant, 6' x 10', has large, bluish green, toothed leaves with sharp terminal spines and yellowish green flowers on a 15-20' stalk. Native to Mexico. Zones 10, 12-24.

A. desmettiana, 2-3' x 2-3', has smooth, arching, toothless leaves and pale yellow flowers on a 7-10' stalk. Native to Cuba. 'Variegata' has green leaves with creamy yellow margins. Zones N/A.

A. filifera, threadleaf agave, 2' x 2', forms a dense rosette of glossy, dark green leaves edged with white and long threads on the margins. Native to Mexico. Zones 12-24.

A. parryi, 3' x 3', compact rosette of light green to gray-green, semi-succulent leaves with sharp terminal spines; at maturity develops a 5-15' stalk with pink buds opening to greenish yellow flowers. Native to southwestern U.S. and Mexico. Zones 2, 3, 6-24.

A. shawii, Shaw's agave, 18"-2' x 5', has handsome, deep blue-green to gray-green leaves tipped with sharp spines and reddish, hooked teeth along the margins. Native to southern California and Baja California. Zones N/A.

ALBIZIA JULIBRISSIN

Albizia julibrissin (silk tree)

ZONES 4-23. DECIDUOUS TREE. 40' X 60'.

Widespreading, flat-topped, often multi-trunked tree with ferny, yellow-green leaves appearing late in spring and dropping early in fall. Fluffy, pinkish red flowers in summer. Best planted where flowers can be viewed from above. Does best with summer heat. Full sun, moderate to occasional water. May be invasive. Native to Asia.

Allium (wild onion)

ZONES VARY. PERENNIALS FROM BULBS. SIZE VARIES.

Wild onions have grasslike leaves and roundish, compact or loosely spreading clusters of lilac to purple, pink, blue, white, or yellow flowers on leafless stems in spring or early summer. Flowers attractive in fresh or dried arrangements. All aboveground portions of the plant wither after flowering. Full sun to part shade, good drainage, dry summer dormancy. Ignored by deer. Hundreds of species, native throughout the northern hemisphere, and many cultivars. Those listed are California natives.

A. amplectens, narrow-leaf onion, has rose, purple, pink, or white flowers. Zones N/A.

A. haematochiton, red-skinned onion, 6-10" tall, has dark green leaves and compact umbels of white to pale rose flowers with darker midveins in spring to early summer. Zones N/A.

A. hyalinum, glassy onion, has large, open umbels of white to pink-tinged flowers. Zones N/A.

A. serra, jeweled onion, has rose-pink flowers in tight umbels. Zones N/A.

A. unifolium, one-leaf onion, has dense clusters of large, showy, rose-pink, lavender, or white flowers over a long period in spring and summer. Zones 3-9, 14-24.

ALLIUM UNIFOLIUM

Aloe (aloe)

ZONES 8, 9, 12-24. SUCCULENT SHRUBS AND PERENNIALS. SIZE VARIES.

Rosettes of fleshy, pointed, green or gray-green leaves and spikes or clusters of tubular or oblong red, orange, or yellow flowers on tall stems in late winter to late spring. Most are somewhat tender. Sun along coast, afternoon shade in hot locations, excellent drainage, occasional water. Attractive to hummingbirds and bees. Native to South Africa.

A. arborescens, tree aloe, 6-8' x 5-6', much-branched shrub with loose rosettes of gray-green leaves with toothed margins and upright spikes of deep orange, red, or pure yellow flowers in winter. Quite hardy near coast.

A. aristata, 8-10" x 8-10", stemless rosettes of softly toothed, green leaves with small white spots and loose spikes of red-orange flowers in winter.

ALOE ARBORESCENS

A. ferox, bitter aloe, 3-5' x 3-5', has gray-green or blue-green leaves with reddish marginal teeth and tall, dense spikes of bright orange flowers in late summer to fall. Eventually forms a trunk 6-8' tall with old leaves forming a "skirt" below the single rosette.

A. striata, coral aloe, 2' x 2', stemless aloe with blue-green leaves with smooth, pinkish margins and showy, flat-topped clusters of coral-red flowers in winter. Tolerant of drought and frost with good drainage.

Alstroemeria (Peruvian lily)

☀ ☀ ZONES 5-9, 14-24. PERENNIALS. 3-4' x 2-3'.

◖◖

ALSTROEMERIA
'THE THIRD HARMONIC' IN
COASTAL GARDEN

Deciduous or evergreen, upright perennials with loose clusters of brilliantly colored flowers resembling miniature lilies or azaleas on tall, leafy stems in summer. Long-lasting in arrangements. Most prefer full sun in cooler areas, afternoon shade inland. Best near coast. Good drainage. Somewhat tender.

Deciduous plants produce leaves in late winter and early spring, followed by flowers in early to midsummer as leaves begin to die back. Plants go dormant after flowering and need no summer water. Self-sow and naturalize in mild climates. Ligtu hybrids and Dr. Salter's hybrids are available with flowers in orange, peach, salmon, yellow, red, or creamy white, all with contrasting speckles and stripes of darker colors.

Evergreen plants are mostly hybrids or cultivars of *A. aurea*, a vigorous grower native to South America. Plants multiply by underground tuberous roots and withstand some drought but prefer moderate water during growth and bloom. Can be invasive. 'The Third Harmonic' is especially vigorous, forming thickets of stems up to 4' tall with many large, bright orange flowers.

Alyogyne huegelii (blue hibiscus)

ZONES 13-17, 20-24. EVERGREEN SHRUB.
5-10' X 5-10'.

Tender, somewhat gawky shrub with rough-textured, dark green leaves and large, tropical-looking, lilac to deep purple flowers almost year-round. Tip prune regularly to control legginess. Full sun, moderate to occasional water. Native to Australia. 'Santa Cruz' has deep lilac-blue flowers. 'White Swan' has white flowers.

Amaryllis belladonna (belladonna lily, naked lady)

ZONES 4-24. PERENNIAL FROM BULB. 1-2' X 1-2'.

Robust clumps of shiny, dark green, strap-shaped leaves in winter, dying back in summer, when nothing appears aboveground. In the dry heat of fall, large, fragrant, lilylike flowers rise up on leafless, reddish brown stems 18 to 30" tall. Flowers usually light pink, but some forms are deep rose, purple-rose, scarlet, or white. Long-lasting in arrangements.

Nearly indestructible, blooming year after year and persisting for decades with no attention from the gardener. Unperturbed by poor soil, summer heat and drought, or winter wet. Full or part sun, no water in summer. Bulbs resent disturbance and take a year or so to become reestablished and flower again. Native to the southwestern Cape region of South Africa and naturalized in mild-winter areas of North America.

Anagallis monelli (blue pimpernel)

ZONES 4-9, 12-24. PERENNIAL OR BIENNIAL.
18" X 18".

Vigorous, bushy or sprawling Mediterranean native of weedy origins with intensely blue flowers from late spring to summer. Full sun and a sheltered location for best display, occasional water. Short-lived but self-sows freely. 'African Sunset' has bright blue flowers with a yellow eye. 'Skylover Blue' has dark blue flowers with a pinkish eye.

ALYOGYNE HUEGELII

AMARYLLIS BELLADONNA

ANAGALLIS MONELLI

Anchusa (bugloss, alkanet)

ZONES VARY. ANNUALS, BIENNIALS, PERENNIALS. SIZE VARIES.

ANCHUSA AZUREA

ANDROPOGON GERARDII

Annual, perennial, or biennial herbs grown for their cobalt blue to purplish blue summer flowers. Narrow leaves and tall stems are coarsely hairy. Full sun to part shade, good drainage, moderate water. Reseeds readily, and not easily pulled. Cut back after flowering to neaten and control reseeding. Attractive to bees. Some species are weedy-looking and can be invasive: *Anchusa arvensis* and *A. officinalis* are noxious weeds in some parts of the world.

A. azurea, Italian bugloss, 2-4' x 2', Mediterranean perennial usually offered as named cultivars. 'Loddon Royalist' has bright blue flowers on plants about 3' tall. 'Blue Heaven' is 2' tall and quite drought tolerant; its flowers are gentian blue. 'Dropmore' has gentian blue flowers on sturdy 3'-4' stems. Zones 1-24.

A. capensis, Cape forget-me-not, 12-18" x 8-12", is a vigorous spring-flowering biennial with bright blue flowers. Best grown as an annual in summer-dry gardens, where it dies back after forming seed. Native to South Africa. 'Blue Bird' is a compact, bushy plant with brilliant blue flowers. Zones 6-24.

Andropogon gerardii (big bluestem)

ZONES 1-9, 14-24. PERENNIAL GRASS. 3-5' x 3'.

Clumping warm-season grass with narrow, bluish green leaves turning coppery in fall and flower spikes with a purplish tinge. Full sun to light shade, moderate to occasional water. Tolerates drought. Native to the midwestern U.S.

Anemone coronaria (windflower, poppy-flowered anemone)

ZONES 4-24. PERENNIAL FROM TUBER. 12" x 8-12".

Summer-dormant Mediterranean native with finely divided, mostly basal, green leaves and red, pink, purple, white, or red flowers in spring. Sun to part shade, no water. Dislikes heavy clay. Plants offered usually are hybrids: those called De Caen are single-flowered; those labeled St. Brigid are double or semi-double.

ANEMONE CORONARIA

Anigozanthos

(kangaroo paw)

ZONES 15-24. PERENNIALS. SIZE VARIES.

Strap-shaped, evergreen leaves and branching spikes of velvety, tubular flowers in yellow, orange, red, green, pink, or various combinations in spring and summer. Attractive to hummingbirds. Long-lasting cut flower. Sun, excellent drainage, periodic deep watering. Short-lived, somewhat tender; may need replacement after wet winters. Cut back in winter and keep as dry as possible to control fungus rots. Native to Australia.

A. flavidus, 2-4' x 2-3', the largest and hardiest of the kangaroo paws, has shiny, dark green leaves and pale greenish yellow flowers on tall, reddish stems. Many hybrids and selections with pink, red, or orange flowers. 'Pink Joey' has salmon-pink flowers. 'Bush Ranger' has red-orange flowers and tolerates more drought than others.

A. rufus, 1-3' x 1-3', has gray-green leaves and dark red flowers.

A. 'Red Cross' is a vigorous hybrid with rich burgundy flowers with a distinct bright yellow blotch at the base. *A.* 'Regal Claw' has double-headed clusters of orange and red flowers.

ANIGOZANTHOS HYBRID WITH LAVENDER

Anisodontea x *hypomandarum*
(Cape mallow)

ZONES 14-24.
EVERGREEN SHRUB.
4-6' x 4'.

Easy, fast-growing, short-lived, upright shrub with small, lobed, bright green leaves and pink, purple, or magenta flowers almost year-round. Tender in hard frosts. Full sun, occasional water. Tolerates clay. Ignored by deer. 'Tara's Pink' has clear pink flowers and larger leaves. 'Tara's Wonder' has deep rosy pink flowers and dark green leaves.

ANISODONTEA
X *HYPOMANDARUM*
'TARA'S PINK'

Arbutus (arbutus)

ZONES VARY. EVERGREEN SHRUBS AND TREES. SIZE VARIES.

Dark green, finely toothed leaves, pendulous clusters of white flowers tinged pink, and round yellow fruits maturing to bright red. Flowers from the current year are borne with both yellow and red fruits in fall to winter, giving a striking multi-colored display. Peeling older bark reveals shiny, reddish new bark beneath. Attractive to birds. Prefers acidic soils; tolerates clay. Full sun to part shade, good drainage, occasional deep watering.

OPPOSITE: *ARBUTUS UNEDO*
BELOW: *A. UNEDO* 'ELFIN
KING'

A. andrachne, Grecian strawberry tree, 15-30' x 15-30', slow-growing, shrubby tree native to the Mediterranean. Zones 8, 9, 14-24.

A. unedo, 15-30' x 15-30', strawberry tree, is an adaptable, long-lived, multi-stemmed shrub or tree. Heavy fruiting. Native to Europe. 'Elfin King' is a dwarf form to 6' tall. Zones 4-24.

A. 'Marina', 25-40' x 30', is a large multi-stemmed tree or shrub, usually pruned to a single-stemmed tree, with rosy pink flowers and cinnamon-red new bark. Excellent specimen tree, coastal or inland. Zones 8, 9, 14-24.

Arctostaphylos (manzanita)

 ZONES VARY. EVERGREEN SHRUBS. SIZE VARIES.

Prostrate mats to treelike, multi-trunked shrubs with smooth, cinnamon-red to mahogany or reddish brown bark, leathery green to gray-green leaves, and nodding clusters of urn-shaped, pale pink to white flowers in late winter or early spring. Red fruits in late summer or fall resemble tiny apples.

Most of the fifty or so species of manzanita are endemic to California. All require good to excellent drainage, and some do well only in coastal areas or at mid- to high elevations. Do not fertilize or overwater, especially in clay soils. Attractive to bees, butterflies, and birds. Most plants offered are named cultivars.

TOP: *ARCTOSTAPHYLOS UVA-URSI* 'POINT REYES'
MIDDLE: *A. PURISSIMA*
BOTTOM: *A. DENSIFLORA* 'SENTINEL'

A. densiflora, Vine Hill manzanita, is an upright shrub with reddish bark, small, glossy, green or grayish green leaves, and white or pale pink flowers. 'Howard McMinn', 5-7' x 6-10', has medium green leaves, dark red bark, and profuse pink flowers. Prefers coastal conditions, but thrives inland with occasional summer water. Accepts pruning and a wider range of soils and watering regimes than most other manzanitas. 'Sentinel', 6-8' x 5', is an upright shrub with gray-green leaves, dark purplish bark, and light pink flowers. Can be trained as a small tree. Zones 7-9, 14-21.

A. edmundsii, Little Sur manzanita, 6-12" x 4-6', with green to grayish green leaves, new growth bronzy green, and pinkish white flowers. Prefers coastal conditions, some shade, occasional water. 'Carmel Sur', 12" x 6', makes a tidy, flat groundcover with gray-green leaves and pink flowers. Zones 6-9, 14-24.

A. hookeri, Monterey manzanita, 18"-4' x 4', forms broad carpets or dense mounds of dark green leaves and white to light pink flowers. Full sun to part shade, coastal conditions, occasional water. 'Monterey Carpet', 1' x 10-12', forms a dense mat with pinkish white flowers. 'Wayside', 4' x 8', is a mounding shrub with pale pink flowers; tolerant of many soils. Zones 6-9, 14-24.

A. manzanita, common manzanita, 6-15' x 8-12', erect, treelike shrub with smooth, peeling, dark reddish brown bark, glossy green leaves, and white or pale pink flowers. 'Dr. Hurd' is tolerant of a fairly wide range of soils and watering regimes. Zones 4-9, 14-24.

A. pajaroensis 'Warren Roberts', 4-8' x 10', is an upright shrub with deep rose-pink flowers and large, bluish green leaves that are dark bronzy red in new growth. Best near coast. Excellent on clay slopes. Zones 14-24.

A. pallida, Oakland Hills manzanita, 6-12' x 6-8', is an upright shrub with bristly, oval, overlapping leaves and white flowers. Zones N/A.

A. pungens, Mexican manzanita, 3-6' x 3-6', upright shrub with dark green to gray-green leaves and white flowers. Zones N/A.

A. purissima, Lompoc manzanita, 3-10' x 4-12', nearly prostrate to erect shrub with strongly overlapping, shiny, bright green leaves, red new growth, deep red bark, and profuse white flowers. Prefers sandy soils and coastal conditions. Zones N/A.

A. tomentosa, woolly leaf manzanita, 2-5' x 2-3', upright, openly branched shrub with gray-green leaves and white flowers; twigs are downy when young. Zones N/A.

A. uva-ursi, 1-2' x 10-15', forms dense, fine-textured mats of glossy green leaves that turn bronzy red in fall and white flowers tinged with pink. Prefers full sun, excellent drainage, and coastal conditions. Effective on slopes or cascading over a wall. 'San Bruno Mountain', 4-8" x 6', needs some summer water, even along the coast. 'Point Reyes', 1-2' x 10', takes full sun along coast, part shade inland. 'Wood's Compact', 12-18" x 3', is fairly drought resistant in shade or part shade. Zones 1-9, 14-24.

A. 'Greensphere', 4' x 4', slow-growing, formal-looking shrub with dark green leaves, smooth, red bark, and white flowers, forms a dense, dark green, almost perfectly round sphere. Sun or part shade. Zones N/A. *A.* 'Emerald Carpet', 12-18" x 3-6', with dark glossy green leaves and light pink flowers, makes a neat groundcover, sun to part shade, occasional summer water. Zones 6-9, 14-24. *A.* 'Pacific Mist', 2-3' x 6-8', is a fast-spreading, tall groundcover with narrow, gray-green leaves and white flowers. Good for clay slopes. Zones 7-9, 14-24.

ABOVE: *A. PAJAROENSIS*
BELOW: *A. HOOKERI* BARK

Arctotis (African daisy)

☀️
💧
🌿

ARCTOTIS HYBRID

ZONES VARY. ANNUALS AND PERENNIALS. SIZE VARIES.

Short-lived, tender annuals and perennials with lobed, rough, green to gray-green leaves and large, daisylike flowers in late winter into summer. Full sun, good drainage, moderate water. Native to South Africa. Many hybrids with white, pink, purple, yellow, or orange flowers, usually with darker centers. Ignored by deer.

A. acaulis, 12" x 12", perennial with large yellow or orange flowers with purplish centers on tall stems. Zones 5-9, 14-24.

A. venusta, 1-2' x 12-18", annual with gray-green leaves and white flowers with deep blue centers. Zones 1-24.

BELOW: *ARISTIDA PURPUREA*

Aristida purpurea (purple three-awn)

☀️
💧💧
🌿

ZONES N/A. PERENNIAL GRASS. 1-3' x 1-2'.

Densely tufted, fine-leaved, perennial bunchgrass with tall, purplish flower stalks that loosely splay out, reflecting sunlight off the angular seedheads in summer and fall. Full sun, reasonable drainage, occasional to no water. May reseed and spread, but usually not aggressively. Native to midwestern and southwestern North America, including California.

Armeria maritima
(thrift, sea pink)

☀️
💧
🌿

ZONES 1-9, 14-24. PERENNIAL. 4-8" x 6-12".

Compact, slowly spreading mounds of narrow, bluish green, grassy leaves and small, round heads of rose-pink or white flowers in spring and early summer. Good drainage, sun, occasional to little water along coast. Not for hot interior gardens. Good seaside plant. The variety *californica* is native to coastal bluffs of California. 'Alba' has white flowers.

ARMERIA MARITIMA

Artemisia (artemisia, wormwood)

☀ ZONES VARY. EVERGREEN SHRUBS AND PERENNIALS. SIZE VARIES.

◊◊ Grown for their intricately divided, aromatic, grayish white or
silvery green foliage; the tiny, white or yellow flowers are
insignificant. Pleasing backdrop for other plants. Full sun,
excellent drainage, occasional water. Cut shrubs back hard
and divide perennials in fall or early spring. Ignored by deer.

A. arborescens, 3-6' x 4-6', evergreen shrub or woody perennial
with silvery gray, finely divided leaves. Best along coast.
Native to the Mediterranean. Zones 7-9, 14-24.

A. californica, California sagebrush, 2-5' x 4-5', evergreen shrub
with finely divided grayish leaves. Endemic to coastal
California and the Channel Islands. 'Canyon Gray', 1' x 4',
forms a ground-hugging mat or cascades nicely over a wall.
Zones 7-9, 14-24.

A. caucasica, silver spreader, 6" x 2', evergreen shrub with
silvery gray-green leaves. From the Caucasus Mountains in
Turkey, it needs excellent drainage, but tolerates heat and cold. Zones 2-11, 14-24.

TOP: *ARTEMISIA CALIFORNICA*
MIDDLE: *A. PYCNOCEPHALA*
'DAVID'S CHOICE'
BELOW: *A. 'POWIS CASTLE'*
WITH *SALVIA LEUCANTHA*

A. pycnocephala, sandhill sage, 2' x 3', short-lived, woody perennial with silvery white or
gray leaves. Native to coastal California, in the garden it usually needs replacement
every few years. 'David's Choice' is a low-growing selection to about 1' tall. Zones 4, 5,
7-9, 14-17, 19-24.

A. tridentata, big sagebrush, 4-15' x 3-10', upright evergreen shrub with aromatic, hairy,
gray-green leaves. Full sun, no water. Native to the Great Basin of the western U.S.
Zones 1-3, 6-11, 14-24.

A. 'Powis Castle', 3' x 6', is a mounding perennial grown for its lacy, silvery gray,
aromatic foliage; it seldom blooms. Zones 2-24.

Asclepias (milkweed, butterfly weed)

ZONES VARY. PERENNIALS. SIZE VARIES.

Upright to sprawling perennials with hairy stems and leaves and showy flowers in spring or summer. Seed pods split open when ripe to release silky-tailed, wind-dispersed seeds, attractive in arrangements. Die back to the ground in winter, appearing again in late spring. Full sun, good drainage, moderate to occasional water. Attractive to butterflies. Ignored by deer.

A. speciosa, showy milkweed, 2-4' x 1-3', has grayish green leaves and purplish rose and white flowers in late spring. Easy and more drought tolerant than *A. tuberosa*. Native to western North America, including California. Zones N/A.

A. tuberosa, butterfly weed, 3' x 2', has narrow green leaves and clusters of brilliant orange flowers in summer. Native to eastern North America. Zones 1-24.

Aster (aster)

ZONES VARY. PERENNIALS. SIZE VARIES.

Stalwarts of the traditional perennial border, most asters need regular garden water. A few somewhat less showy species tolerate dryness, even some drought. Full sun to part shade, moderate to occasional water. Attractive to butterflies.

TOP: *ASCLEPIAS TUBEROSA*
MIDDLE: *A. SPECIOSA*
RIGHT: *ASTER ERICOIDES*

A. chilensis, California aster, 2-3' x 18"-3', has erect stems and pale blue, violet, or white flowers with yellow centers in summer. Full to part sun. Dormant in late summer without water; returns with winter rains. Native to coastal California. Zones N/A.

A. ericoides, heath aster, is a bushy plant, 1-3' x 1-3', with narrow leaves and a profusion of small, white, pink, or pale blue daisylike flowers in late summer. Native to eastern North America. 'Blue Star' and 'Pink Star' are more compact and tidier than the species. Zones 1-10, 14-24.

Asteriscus maritimus (Mediterranean beach daisy)

ZONES 9, 15-24. PERENNIAL. 6-12" X 4'.

Prostrate evergreen groundcover with green or gray-green leaves and brilliant yellow, daisylike flowers in spring and summer or almost year-round. Full sun to part shade, little to moderate water. Good seaside plant. Native to the Mediterranean. Usually offered as 'Gold Coin'. Shear to improve appearance and to promote bloom.

ASTERISCUS MARITIMUS 'GOLD COIN'

Atriplex (saltbush)

ZONES VARY. EVERGREEN SHRUBS. SIZE VARIES.

Tough plants grown for their dense, gray-green foliage, which can be sheared. Full sun, infrequent water. Tolerate drought, heat, wind, and alkaline, saline, or heavy clay soils. Adapted to seaside. Not for the well-kempt garden, but good habitat plants, providing food and cover for wildlife.

A. canescens, four-wing saltbush, 3-6' x 4-8', is widely distributed in dry regions of western North America. Zones 1-3, 7-24.

A. lentiformis, big saltbush, 6-8' x 4-8', is native to western central California south to northwestern Mexico. Zones 3, 7-14, 18-19.

ATRIPLEX LENTIFORMIS

Babiana (baboon flower)

☀ ☼ ZONES 4-24. PERENNIALS FROM CORMS. 6"-1' x 1'.

○ Mostly summer-dormant corms with fans of narrow, ribbed or pleated, hairy leaves and blue, lilac, purple, red, or white flowers in spring or early summer. Flowers long-lasting in the garden and in arrangements. Full sun to light shade, good drainage, no water in summer. Cut back after foliage dies. Somewhat tender. Corms loved by rodents. Native to South Africa. Many species and hybrids.

TOP RIGHT: *BABIANA STRICTA* **BOTTOM LEFT:** *B. STRICTA* WITH *CHAMAECYPARIS LAWSONII* 'LUTEA'

B. rubrocyanea, 6-8" tall, has large, deep blue-purple flowers with crimson centers.

BACCHARIS PILULARIS AS LARGE-SCALE GROUNDCOVER

B. stricta, to 1' tall, has royal blue or purplish pink flowers. Many named hybrids. 'Blue Gem' has intense blue-violet flowers. 'Snowdrop' has pure white flowers. 'Dark Mood' has flowers of deep maroon.

Baccharis pilularis (coyote brush)

ZONES 5-11, 14-24. EVERGREEN SHRUBS. SIZE VARIES.

Adaptable shrub or groundcover for dry-summer climates. Small, shiny green leaves kept fresh and green with periodic cutting back in late winter. Upright forms are 3-5' x 4-5'; groundcover forms are 1-2' x 6'. Full sun, little or no water near coast; may benefit from monthly summer watering in hot interior gardens. Tolerant of drought, salt spray, alkaline soils. Native to coastal California and Oregon. Attractive to butterflies; good habitat plant. 'Pigeon Point' is a fast-spreading groundcover to 1' x 10-15'. 'Twin Peaks' has smaller, dark green leaves and grows more slowly.

Baileya multiradiata (desert marigold)

 Zones 1-3, 7-23. Perennial. 12-18" x 1-2'.

 Sprawling, low-maintenance perennial with softly woolly, gray-green leaves and bright yellow, daisylike flowers on tall stalks from spring to fall. Thriving in full sun and reflected heat, this desert plant needs little supplemental water, except in the hottest months. Short-lived, but self-sows readily. Needs good drainage. Attractive to butterflies. Remove spent flowers to prolong bloom. Native to California, the southwestern U.S., and northern Mexico.

BAILEYA MULTIRADIATA

Ballota pseudodictamnus (false dittany)

Zones 2, 3, 6-9, 14-24. Perennial. 2' x 3'.

Shrubby perennial with greenish white stems, grayish green, downy leaves, and small, white or pale pink, tubular flowers in summer. Mediterranean native. Full sun, good drainage, moderate to occasional water. Cut back to renew in late winter or early spring. Ignored by deer.

BALLOTA PSEUDODICTAMNUS

Banksia
(banksia)

ZONES 15-24.
EVERGREEN SHRUBS.
SIZE VARIES.

Somewhat tender Australian shrubs with deep green leaves, most with silvery undersides. Unusual and showy, round or cylindrical spikes of densely packed, tiny flowers, mostly in fall and winter. Striking in fresh or dried arrangements, flowers range in color from gold, orange, and red to lime green, tan, or brown. Fruits hard and coblike. Not for beginners. Full sun, perfect drainage; moderate to occasional water. Usually dislike salt spray. Attractive to birds and other wildlife.

B. ericifolia, heath banksia, 10-15' x 6-12', has dark green, needlelike leaves

and reddish orange flowers in fall and winter. Accepts salt spray.

B. menziesii, 8-15' x 10', has grayish green leaves and pinkish or red-maroon flowers with touches of gold and silvery gray. Dwarf forms sometimes available.

B. speciosa, showy banksia, 10-18' x 10-25', has long, narrow leaves with distinctively toothed margins and white flowers opening to greenish yellow.

ABOVE: *BANKSIA ERICIFOLIA*
LEFT: *B. SPECIOSA*

Berberis (barberry)

ZONES VARY. EVERGREEN AND DECIDUOUS SHRUBS. SIZE VARIES.

Tough, spiny shrubs with glossy, dark green to grayish green leaves, masses of small, waxy, bright yellow to yellow-orange flowers in spring and summer, and orange or red berries in fall and winter. Can be sheared, but best grown as informal hedge or specimen plants. Full sun to part shade, most soils, moderate to occasional water. Attractive to birds. Ignored by deer.

B. darwinii, Darwin barberry, 5-8' x 4-6', evergreen shrub with dark green, hollylike leaves, abundant yellow-orange flowers spring through summer, and blue-black berries in fall. Native to Chile. Zones 5-9, 14-24.

B. x *stenophylla*, rosemary barberry, 6-10' x 10-12', evergreen shrub with narrow, spiny-tipped leaves and yellow-orange flowers in spring. Compact cultivars include 'Irwinii', 2-4' x 3-5', with deep yellow flowers, and 'Corallina Compacta', 1-2' x 1-2', with coral red buds opening to bright orange flowers. Zones 4-9, 14-24.

B. thunbergii, Japanese barberry, 4-6' x 4-6', graceful, upright, deciduous shrub with deep green leaves that turn yellow, orange, and red in fall and bright red berries in winter. Many named cultivars. 'Atropurpurea', red Japanese barberry, 3' x 4', has purplish red leaves and yellow flowers. 'Aurea', 2-3' x 3-4', has yellowish green leaves. 'Rose Glow', 4-6' x 4-6', has bronzy new leaves mottled with pink. Zones 2-24.

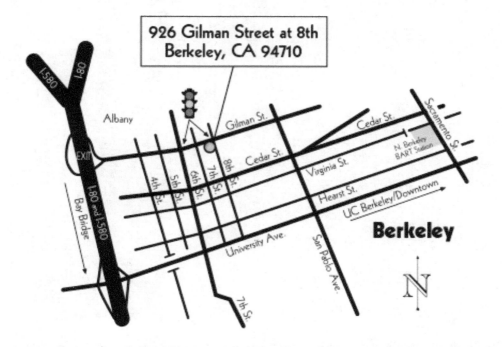

We're Easy to Find:

Take the Gilman Street offramp from I-80/I-580 and drive East (towards the hills) 7 blocks to 8th Street.

Turn right on 8th. Our entrance is on 8th Street. There is plenty of parking right by our door.

Our Hours Are:

Tuesday - Friday, 10am - 6pm
Saturday, 10am - 2pm

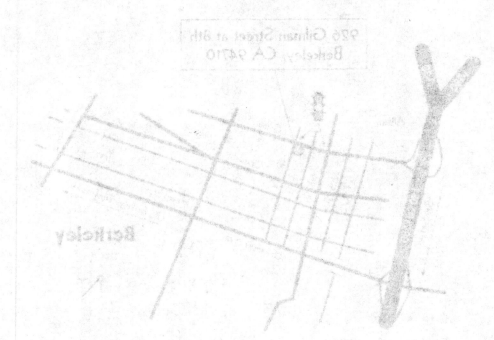

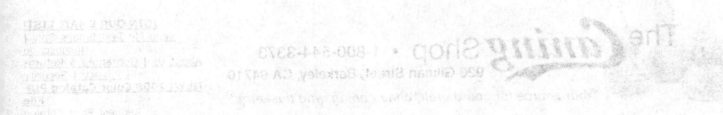

The Caning Shop

926 Gilman Street, Berkeley CA 94710 • 1-800-544-3373

Map to the Caning Shop

JOIN OUR EMAIL LIST!
Send Me Text Emails Only |
Unsubscribe
About Us | Guarantee & Returns
| Privacy | Security
**NEW! 2008 Color Catalog PDF
File**
Request Print Catalog
Classes | Map

Home   -> SHOP ENTRANCE <-   Search   Browse   🛒 View Shopping Cart

Map to the Caning Shop

BACK
Coreopsis
Ivy Geraniums
Nandina's

Lobelia - In Front of Pink Geraniums

Hebe Veronica lake — Camellia Area

Laminum

Coral Bells

5 Nandina

Gazania - Day Break — Petunia

Karen Off Fri & Sun

Bergenia (bergenia)

☼ ☀ ZONES 1-9, 12-24. PERENNIALS. 12-18" x 18-24".

💧 Slowly spreading clumps of large, glossy, rounded or heart-shaped, green leaves with wavy edges, some turning bronzy red or burgundy in fall. Clusters of small, pale pink to ruby red or white flowers atop stout, reddish stems in late winter or early spring. Not tolerant of hot sun or wind. Best along coast or in cool shade of the woodland garden, where they thrive with moderate watering and will survive with less. Color in winter, bold texture in summer. Large leaves highly attractive to deer. Native to China.

B. cordifolia, heartleaf bergenia, with rosy pink to purplish pink flowers in spring and leaves tinged with purple, especially in winter. Most cold- and heat-tolerant bergenia.

B. crassifolia, winter-blooming bergenia, with rose, lilac, or purplish flowers in late winter.

Many hybrids, including 'Bressingham White' with white flowers, 'Silver Light' with white flowers aging to pale pink, and 'Evening Glow' with dark red flowers.

ABOVE: *BERGENIA CRASSIFOLIA* IN WINTER BLOOM WITH LILYTURF (*LIRIOPE* SP.)

Beschorneria (Mexican lily, amole)

 ZONES 8, 9, 12-24. PERENNIALS. 2' X 4'.

 Stemless rosettes of green or gray-green, sword-shaped leaves like those of a yucca but spineless and more pliable. Dramatic specimen plants with striking summer flowers on tall stems. Sun or light shade, moderate to occasional water. Attractive to hummingbirds. Native to Mexico.

B. septentrionalis, false red agave, 3' x 3', has green leaves and fuchsia-red flowers tipped with emerald green.

B. yuccoides, Mexican lily, 2' x 4', has gray-green leaves and green, bell-shaped flowers surrounded by pinkish red bracts in early summer on coral pink, branching stems.

RIGHT: *BESCHORNERIA YUCCOIDES* BELOW: *BOUGAINVILLEA* AS GROUNDCOVER

Bougainvillea (bougainvillea)

ZONES 12-17, 19, 21-24. EVERGREEN VINES. 15-30'.

Tropical and subtropical South American vines, tender but widely grown in areas of occasional frost because of the spectacular beauty of the papery bracts in summer. May lose leaves in cold weather. Vigorous, fast-growing, respond well to pruning. Stems

have needlelike thorns and must be tied to supports until basic form is established. Plants flower best when kept on the dry side. Full sun, moderate to occasional water. Can be grown as groundcover.

'Barbara Karst' has bright red bracts, crimson blue in light shade; blooms young and thrives in heat. 'California Gold' has golden yellow bracts. 'Cherry Blossom' has rich rose-red bracts with white centers. 'Raspberry Ice' is a low, spreading form with variegated green leaves with creamy yellow margins and bright pink bracts. 'San Diego Red', with orange-red to rose-red bracts, is fairly cold-hardy, with large, dark green leaves and a long period of bloom.

BOUTELOUA GRACILIS

BRACHYCHITON POPULNEUS

Bouteloua gracilis (blue grama)

ZONES 1-3, 7-11, 14, 18-21. PERENNIAL GRASS. 12-18" X 1'.

Warm-season bunchgrass with narrow, grayish green leaves that turn purplish and then tan in late summer or fall. Highly ornamental reddish purple flowers in summer grow on one side of tall spikes. Full sun, good drainage, little to no water. Fine choice for naturalized areas, native plant gardens, unmowed meadows, or as a coarse, drought-tolerant, mowed turf. Does not thrive in shade or wet, poorly drained soils. Tolerates no summer water, greening up quickly with fall rains. Native to central and western North America and Mexico.

Brachychiton populneus
(bottle tree)

ZONES 12-24. EVERGREEN TREE. 30-50' X 30'.

Fast-growing tree with glossy green leaves that flutter in the breeze, giving a glittering effect, and a distinctive trunk, wide at the base and tapering above, especially when young. Small, greenish, bell-shaped flowers in spring, followed by woody, boat-shaped seedpods. Good shade tree for larger landscapes. Full to part sun, moderate water. Does best with some heat. Native to Australia.

Brachyscome (Swan River daisy, cutleaf daisy)

ZONES VARY. ANNUALS AND PERENNIALS. SIZE VARIES.

BRACHYSCOME MULTIFIDA

Softly mounding, short-lived plants with finely divided, feathery leaves and prolific displays of daisylike blue, white, or lavender flowers from early spring to summer. Full sun to part shade, good drainage, moderate to occasional water. Good filler, edging, accent. Native to Australia.

B. iberidifolia, Swan River daisy, 8-12" x 6-10", cascading annual with gray-green leaves and lavender to pinkish blue flowers with yellow centers. At its best in cool weather. Zones 1-24.

B. multifida, cutleaf daisy, 12" x 3', mounding perennial with lavender, pink, or white flowers with yellow centers. Shear after flowering. Zones 14-24.

Hybrid perennials include 'New Amethyst' with small dark purple flowers in spring through fall, 'City Lights' with light lavender-blue flowers, and 'Strawberry Mousse' with bright pink flowers.

Brahea (brahea)

ZONES VARY. PALMS. SIZE VARIES.

Fan palms with creamy white flowers followed by small, round fruits on long, pendulous stalks. Full sun, good drainage, moderate to occasional water. Native to Mexico.

B. armata, Mexican blue palm, 30' x 20', slow-growing with silvery blue leaves and dramatic show of creamy white flowers that hang well below the leaves. Old leaves form a "skirt" if not removed. Zones 10, 12-17, 19-24.

B. edulis, Guadalupe palm, 20-30' x 15-20', has shiny green leaves and yellow flowers. Old leaves fall, not forming a skirt. Zones 12-24.

Brodiaea (brodiaea)

ZONES VARY. PERENNIALS FROM CORMS. SIZE VARIES.

Summer-dormant corms with a few grasslike leaves and loose clusters of tubular or funnel-shaped, waxy flowers on leafless stems from early spring to early summer. Full sun to part shade, good drainage, no water. Leaves often die back before flowers appear. Diminutive plants; mass for best effect. Protect from rodents. Native to western North America and Baja California.

B. californica, California brodiaea, tallest and showiest of the brodiaeas, as well as the most common. Pale lavender or violet to blue flowers on 2' stems in late spring. Zones N/A.

B. elegans, harvest brodiaea, thrives in sun and heat; lavender-blue to blue-purple flowers on 2' stems late spring to midsummer. Zones 2-9, 14-24.

B. minor, dwarf brodiaea, has lavender blue to dark blue flowers on 6" stems. Zones 7-9,14-17, 19-24.

B. terrestris, earth stars, less than 3" tall, has bright blue-lavender flowers often resting on the soil. One of the best low-growing brodiaeas for the garden. Zones N/A.

TOP: *BRAHEA EDULIS*
BOTTOM: *BRODIAEA MINOR*

Buddleja (butterfly bush)

 ZONES 2-24. EVERGREEN OR
DECIDUOUS SHRUBS. SIZE VARIES.

Upright, multi-stemmed shrubs with
dark green to gray-green leaves,
usually grayish white and softly hairy
beneath, and spikes of small, fragrant
lilac to purple flowers. Attractive to

RIGHT: *BUDDLEJA*
'LOCHINCH' BELOW:
BUDDLEJA DAVIDII

butterflies and
bees. Ignored by
deer. Full sun,
good drainage,
moderate to
occasional water.
Can be invasive.
Best in hot
climates. Prune in
early spring to
promote bloom.
Native to China
and Japan.

B. alternifolia,
10-12' x 10-12',
deciduous shrub
with arching,
willowy branches
and small clusters
of lilac flowers in
spring.

B. davidii, 4-10' x
4-10', fast-growing, semi-evergreen shrub with small, fragrant, rosy lilac to deep purple
flowers in summer. *B.* 'Lochinch', 8' x 6', has gray leaves and purple flowers.

Bulbinella floribunda (bulbinella)

 ZONES 14-24. PERENNIAL. 1-2' x 1-2'.

Vigorous, clumping, summer-dormant perennial with
narrow, bright green, grasslike leaves and upright,
dense spikes of glowing yellow, orange, or white
flowers in early spring. Full sun to part shade, good
drainage, no water. Native to South Africa. Sometimes
confused with another South African plant, *Bulbine
frutescens*, which has fleshy or succulent leaves, is not

BULBINELLA FLORIBUNDA summer-dormant, and needs regular water.

84 . . .

Calamagrostis (reed grass)

☀ ☼ ZONES 2-24. PERENNIAL GRASSES. SIZE VARIES.

💧💧 Cool-season bunchgrasses with varying cultural preferences, reed grasses all prefer good drainage, most do best in cooler areas, and some prefer moist soils. Not for hot interior gardens. Water until well established. Those listed will accept some dryness near coast.

C. x *acutiflora*, feather reed grass, 2-4' x 18"-2', upright, graceful, with leaves tinged red in fall and winter. Narrow plumes of pale pink flowers rise well above the leaves in late spring, aging to golden tan in summer and fall. Full sun to part shade, moderate water. 'Karl Foerster' has bright green leaves to 3' tall and flowering stems to 5' in summer. 'Overdam' has leaves with creamy margins. Part shade, moderate water.

C. foliosa, leafy reed grass, 1-2' x 1-2', has bluish green leaves that turn golden tan in fall, and tall, arching, feathery flower panicles in summer. Native to north coastal California; grows well in coastal gardens in the Bay Region. Full sun, good drainage, moderate to occasional water.

ABOVE: *CALAMAGROSTIS* X *ACUTIFLORA* 'KARL FOERSTER' WITH *LAVANDULA ANGUSTIFOLIA*

Calamintha (calamint)

ZONES 1-9, 14-24. PERENNIALS. 12-18" x 12-18".

Mounding, bushy herbs with aromatic, mintlike leaves and masses of dainty, pale blue to lilac or white flowers. Full sun to part shade, good drainage, moderate to occasional water. Low maintenance, compact, and heat-tolerant, calamints accept more dryness than most other plants in the mint family. Bloom late summer, when many summer-dry plants are dormant. Native to the Mediterranean.

C. grandiflora, large-flowered calamint, bears pink flowers over a long summer-to-fall season. 'Variegata' has green leaves marked with white.

C. nepeta, calamint, forms a dense, green to gray-green mat with upright, branching stems and lilac pink to blue or white flowers in late summer.

Callirhoe involucrata (poppy mallow, wine cups)

ZONES 1-3, 7-14, 18-24. PERENNIAL. 6-12" x 2-3'.

Mat-forming perennial mallow with deeply lobed,

green leaves and large, purplish red, carmine-rose, or magenta flowers all summer. Good groundcover; effective spilling over walls. Full sun near coast, part shade in hot locations, good drainage, occasional water. Native to central and southern U.S.

Callistemon (bottlebrush)

ZONES VARY. EVERGREEN SHRUBS. SIZE VARIES.

Bottlebrushes are native to moist areas, but tolerate drought once established and combine well with other low- to moderate-water plants. Flowers have prominent stamens in colorful, brushlike spikes. Full sun to light shade, occasional to little water. Tender in prolonged freezes. Attractive to hummingbirds, butterflies, and bees. Native to Australia.

C. citrinus, lemon bottlebrush, 6-12' x 8-12', has bright red flowers in summer and fall and narrow, medium green, leathery leaves with a citrus fragrance, bronzy red to silvery pink new growth. Can be trimmed lightly as an informal hedge or screen or trained as a small tree. Zones 8-9, 12-24. 'Splendens', 6' x 6', has brilliant red flowers. 'White Anzac' is a low, wide-spreading form with pure white flowers aging to creamy white.

C. viminalis, weeping bottlebrush, 20' x 15', has narrow, light green leaves, reddish new growth, and bright red flowers from late spring to summer. Pendulous branches lend a weeping effect. Attractive trained as a single- or multi-stemmed tree. Protect from wind. Zones 6-9, 12-24. 'Captain Cook' and 'Little John' are dwarf varieties about 3-6' x 4-5'.

C. 'Canes Hybrid', 8-10'x 6-8', has soft pink flower spikes and gray-green leaves, pink-tinged when young, on weeping branches. Can be pruned to umbrella-shaped tree. Zones N/A.

CALLISTEMON VIMINALIS

Calocedrus decurrens (incense-cedar)

ZONES 2-12, 14-24. EVERGREEN TREE. 80' X 15'.

Long-lived, large conifer for parks and larger landscapes. Shiny, scalelike, fragrant leaves are held in flattened sprays. Upright, symmetrical, and pyramidal form. Tolerant of shade in youth. Gray bark flakes off, maroon beneath. Full sun to part shade, good drainage, occasional water. Native to hot, dry sites in the mountains from southern Oregon to northern Mexico.

CALOCEDRUS DECURRENS

Calocephalus brownii

(cushion bush)

ZONE 16, 17, 19, 21-24. EVERGREEN SHRUB. 2-3' x 3'.

Mounding, wiry-textured plant with tiny, threadlike, silvery white leaves and small, yellow, buttonlike summer flowers. Best along coast; may freeze inland. Tolerates wind and salt spray. Full sun, excellent drainage, little to no water. Native to Australia.

CALOCEPHALUS BROWNII

Calochortus (calochortus)

ZONES 1-9, 14-24. PERENNIALS FROM BULBS. 6"-2'.

Thin, upright or basal leaves emerge in spring, often dying back by the time flowers appear. Lovely flowers are upright or nodding, bell-shaped or bowl-shaped, and range from white or yellow to lavender, lilac, dark rose, wine red, deep red, or vermilion, with contrasting tints or lines in the center and a scattering of silky hairs. Sun to part shade or afternoon shade, excellent drainage, no water. Many calochortus are difficult to grow, but a few adapt readily to gardens with no summer water and protection from rodents. Native to western North and Central America. Most are native to California.

C. albus, white globe lily, has nodding white flowers on 1-2' stems in spring; woodland plant best in filtered sun or part shade.

LEFT: *CALOCHORTUS SUPERBUS* BELOW: *CALOCHORTUS* 'VIOLET QUEEN'

C. luteus, gold nuggets, has bright yellow flowers on unbranched stems 1-2' tall, sometimes marked with reddish brown, in late spring. Thrives in heat, tolerates clay. 'Golden Orb' has golden yellow or bright canary yellow flowers with a brown central spot.

C. superbus, superb mariposa, has creamy white or yellow to rose or deep lavender flowers with darker centers in late spring or early summer.

Calothamnus villosus (silky net bush)

ZONES N/A. EVERGREEN SHRUB. 4-6' x 6'.

Erect, spreading Australian native with deep red or rosy red flowers resembling one-sided bottle brushes in late winter to spring and fine, needlelike, dark green to grayish green leaves. Good foliage plant. Tolerates wind, salt spray. Full sun to part shade, good drainage, occasional to little water. Prune lightly after flowering to shape.

ABOVE: PINKISH RED
NEW GROWTH OF
CALOTHAMNUS VILLOSUS

Calylophus (sundrops)

CALYLOPHUS HARTWEGII

ZONES 1-3, 6-16, 18-24. PERENNIALS. SIZE VARIES.

Winter-dormant perennials with bright green to gray-green linear leaves covered with large yellow flowers in spring and early summer. Full sun or light shade, reasonably drained soil, moderate to occasional water in hot weather. Attractive to butterflies. Native to midwestern and southwestern North America and northern Mexico.

C. drummondianus, Drummond's sundrops, 12-18" x 2', has narrow green leaves and intense yellow flowers in spring and early summer.

C. hartwegii, Hartweg's sundrops, 12-18" x 2', has bright green leaves and lemon-yellow flowers. The variety *lavandulifolius*, lavender-leaf sundrops, has gray-green leaves.

C. serrulatus, tooth-leaved calylophus, 6-12" x 2-3', prairie plant with slender, finely toothed, green leaves and bright yellow flowers.

Campsis radicans (trumpet vine, trumpet creeper)

ZONES 1-21. SEMI-DECIDUOUS VINE. 30-40'.

Rampant vine with clusters of large, orange and scarlet tubular flowers summer to fall. Full sun to part shade, moderate to occasional water. Attractive to hummingbirds. Climbs by aerial roots on stems; rapidly covers trellises, arbors, walls, or trees. Less aggressive when kept on the dry side. Cut back hard to control and renew. Native to southeastern United States.

LEFT: *CAMPSIS RADICANS*
BELOW: *CAREX TUMULICOLA*

Carex (sedge)

ZONES VARY. PERENNIALS. SIZE VARIES.

Clumping, mostly evergreen, grasslike plants found worldwide, usually in moist situations. A few are content with moderate to occasional water, especially in coastal locations. Some are invasive and difficult to control. Those listed below tolerate some dryness in part shade and make fine specimens, fillers, edgings, or rough turf. Native to many parts of the world.

C. buchananii, leather leaf sedge, 18"-2' x 12-18", slender, upright sedge with rusty bronze or coppery brown foliage. Full sun to part shade. Native to New Zealand. Zones 2-9, 14-24.

CARPENTERIA CALIFORNICA

C. flagellifera, weeping brown sedge, 2' x 2', graceful, fountainlike tussock of fine-textured, reddish brown foliage with orange tones. Full sun to part shade. Native to New Zealand. Zones 4-9, 14-24.

C. texensis, Catlin sedge, Texas sedge, 4-6" x 6-8", small, matlike sedge with dark green leaves. Part shade to full shade. Good mowed or unmowed turf. Native to central and southwestern North America. Zones N/A.

C. tumulicola, Berkeley sedge, 1-2' x 1-2', clump of thin, arching, dark green foliage. Part sun to part shade. Good rough turf. Tends to self-sow. Native to western North America, including California and the Bay Region. Zones N/A.

Carpenteria californica

(bush anemone, carpenteria)

ZONES 5-9, 14-24. EVERGREEN SHRUB. 6' x 4'.

Lovely, refined, multi-stemmed shrub, not always easy in cultivation, but well worth a try. Glossy green, leathery leaves and stunning, lightly fragrant, white flowers with yellow centers in late spring. Part shade in hot interior climates, full sun near coast. Accepts regular garden watering with excellent drainage, but looks best with moderate to occasional water. Native to the foothills of the Sierra Nevada, where it grows along seasonal creeks in granitic soils. 'Elizabeth', a selected wild form, is more compact, with smaller, more abundant flowers.

Caryopteris (bluebeard, caryopteris)

ZONES VARY. DECIDUOUS SHRUBS. SIZE VARIES.

Woody subshrubs with aromatic, green or grayish green leaves and clusters of light blue to deep blue flowers in late summer and fall. Striking in mass or combined with

CARYOPTERIS X *CLANDONENSIS* 'DARK KNIGHT'

ornamental grasses and perennials. Full sun, excellent drainage, moderate to occasional water. Attractive to butterflies and bees. Ignored by deer. Plants die back in winter and leaf out again in spring. Native to Asia.

C. x *clandonensis*, blue mist, 2-4' x 2-4', mounding shrub with gray-green leaves and flowers in tight clusters on one side of the stem. 'Blue Mist', 2-3' x 2-3', has pale blue flowers. 'Longwood Blue', 3' x 3', has silvery gray leaves and violet-blue flowers. 'Dark Knight', 2' x 3', has silvery gray leaves and darker purple flowers. Zones 2-9, 14-24.

C. incana, bluebeard, 3-5' x 4-5', has downy, gray-green, leaves and lavender or dark blue-purple flowers encircling the stem. 'Bluebeard' has intensely purple flowers. Zones 4-9, 14-24.

Casuarina (she-oak)

ZONES 8, 9, 12-24. EVERGREEN TREES. SIZE VARIES.

Fast-growing trees with pendulous branches, long, wiry twigs that resemble pine needles, and conelike fruit. Tolerant of extreme conditions, including salt spray, boggy soils, alkaline or saline soils, drought, frost, wind. Full sun, occasional water. Native to Australia.

C. littoralis, black she-oak, 30' x 20', small, rounded tree with dusty green needles. Prefers sandy or stony soils.

CASUARINA LITTORALIS

C. stricta, mountain she-oak, 25' x 20', forms a dense crown and has grayish green foliage.

Ceanothus (wild lilac)

ZONES VARY. EVERGREEN SHRUBS. SIZE VARIES.

Spring-blooming, evergreen shrubs, from widespreading ground-huggers to medium-height mounds to tall, upright shrubs that can be trained as small trees. Showy clusters of tiny flowers are pale to brilliant blue, white, lavender, occasionally pinkish rose. Wonderful plants for untended areas of larger gardens, most perform better and live longer with some neglect. Some fail to thrive inland with summer water; others require cool, foggy summers to do well. Excellent drainage is a must. Sun to part shade; little to no summer water. Fast-growing, but often short-lived. Deer regularly munch all but those with the tiniest leaves. Most are native to western North America including California.

C. arboreus, tree lilac, 15-20' x 10-15', fast-growing with dark green leaves and medium-blue flowers. Zones N/A.

C. griseus var. *horizontalis* 'Yankee Point', 3' x 10', fast-spreading, evergreen groundcover with large, dark green leaves and dark blue flowers. Best along coast. 'Carmel Creeper' 18-30" x 10-15', has glossy green leaves and light blue flowers. Zones 5-9, 14-17, 19-24.

C. leucodermis, chaparral whitethorn, 6-12' x 6-12', has rigid, spiny, pale green branchlets maturing to grayish white and pale blue to white flowers in dense clusters. Zones N/A.

C. thyrsiflorus, blueblossom, prostrate to erect evergreen shrub with small, shiny, bright green leaves and clusters of pure white flowers. Best along coast. 'Snow Flurry', 8' x 12', has white flowers. Zones 5-9, 14-24.

C. 'Dark Star', 6' x 8', with small, dark green, evergreen leaves, makes a spectacular display of cobalt blue flowers. Zones 5-9, 14-24.

C. 'Ray Hartman', 15' x 15', vigorous shrub with large, medium-green leaves and masses of gray-blue flowers opening from pinkish burgundy buds. Zones 5-9, 14-24.

TOP LEFT: *Ceanothus thyrsiflorus* 'Snow Flurry'
TOP RIGHT: *C. thyrsiflorus* MIDDLE: *C. griseus* VAR.
horizontalis 'Yankee Point' BOTTOM: *C. leucodermis*
WITH MANZANITA IN FOREGROUND AND REDBUD BEHIND

OPPOSITE: *Ceanothus* 'Ray Hartman'

CEDRUS DEODARA

Cedrus (cedar)

ZONES VARY. EVERGREEN TREES.
SIZE VARIES.

Tall, deep-rooted, drought
tolerant trees for parks and
large gardens with plenty of
room for low branches to
spread. Full sun, good drainage,
moderate to occasional water.

C. atlantica, Atlas cedar, 60-80' x
30-40', slow-growing,
widespreading, large tree,
pyramidal in youth, flat-topped
with broad, horizontal branches
in age. Bluish green foliage.
Heat tolerant. Native to North
Africa. Zones 3-10, 14-24.
'Glauca' has silvery blue foliage.
'Glauca Pendula' is a weeping
form; needs staking and training
to shape.

C. deodara, deodar cedar, 80' x
40', with medium to light green
foliage, is a graceful, refined,
soft-textured tree with
pendulous branch tips and top.
Native to the Himalayas, it is
the fastest growing cedar. Zones
3-10, 14-24. 'Pendula' is
prostrate or cascading if given
support.

Celtis (hackberry)

ZONES VARY. DECIDUOUS TREES.
SIZE VARIES.

Tough, deep-rooting, fast-
growing trees that don't raise
paving and accept heat, wind,
and dry, alkaline soils. Good, low-maintenance street trees. Fruit attractive to birds.
Some fall color. Spring flowers inconspicuous; small, hard fruits. Full sun to part
shade, moderate to occasional water.

C. australis, European hackberry, 40-60' x 35-50', rounded canopy, dark green leaves,
and smooth, light gray, warty bark. Native to eastern Mediterranean. Zones 8-16,
18-20.

C. occidentalis, common hackberry, 50' x 40', rounded canopy with spreading, sometimes pendulous branches and bright green leaves. Native to eastern North America. Zones 1-24.

C. sinensis, Chinese hackberry, 40' x 40', rounded canopy and wavy-edged, glossy green leaves. Native to eastern Asia. Zones 8-16, 18-20. 'Green Cascade' is a weeping variety that can be trained to drape over an arbor or form a living archway.

Cerastium tomentosum

(snow-in-summer)

ZONES 1-24. PERENNIAL. 6" x 3'.

Low-growing spreader with whitish gray leaves and bright white flowers in early summer. Short-lived but fast-growing. Can look bedraggled at off-times of year, but worth growing for the lovely spring and summer display. Excellent among rocks or cascading over walls. Full sun to light shade, excellent drainage, occasional water. Cut back hard after flowering or replace when plants decline. Native to Europe and western Asia.

Cercis (redbud)

ZONES VARY. DECIDUOUS SHRUBS OR TREES. SIZE VARIES.

C. canadensis, eastern redbud, 25-35' x 25-35', rounded tree with large, rich green leaves and rosy pink flowers in spring. Full sun to part shade, moderate water. Native to eastern North America. 'Forest Pansy', with large, deep purple leaves, needs some shade and extra water in hot locations. Zones 1-24.

C. occidentalis, western redbud, 12-20' x 12-20', multi-trunked, small tree or large shrub with brief but brilliant display of magenta flowers in early spring, appearing before bright green to blue-green, heart-shaped leaves. Magenta seedpods turn reddish purple and are held through winter. New branches are wine-red; older bark is smooth and silvery gray. Slow to moderate growth. Responds well to pruning during winter dormancy. Full sun to part shade, good drainage, infrequent water. Tolerant of clay soils. Flowers best with some winter chill. Native to California, Arizona, and Utah. Zones 2-24.

C. siliquastrum, Judas tree, 25' x 25', shrubby tree with large green leaves and rose-pink to purplish flowers in spring. Full sun, moderate water. Native to Europe and western Asia. Zones 3-19.

ABOVE: *CERCIS OCCIDENTALIS*

Cercocarpus betuloides
(birchleaf mountain mahogany)

ZONES 3-5, 7-10, 13-24. EVERGREEN
SHRUB OR TREE. 5-12' X 5-12'.

Erect, open, slow-growing shrub or
small tree with smooth, gray bark,
reddish gray branches, green to grayish
green, softly hairy leaves, and tiny
yellow flowers followed by tailed fruits
that add to the overall silvery quality in
fall. Tolerates heat, drought, and clay
or serpentine soils. Full sun, little to no
water. Native to southwestern Oregon,
California, and northern Baja
California.

Chaenomeles (flowering quince)

ZONES 2-23. DECIDUOUS SHRUBS. SIZE
VARIES.

Broadly spreading shrubs with clusters
of flowers resembling tiny apple
blossoms on usually thorny branches in
late winter, before new leaves appear.
Flowers range from pure white to pale
pink to coral, red, or scarlet. Striking in
arrangements. Glossy, dark green
leaves. Greenish yellow, round fruit.
Contorted growth habit and gray bark
give winter interest. Full sun to part
shade, any soils, occasional water.
Suckers form a dense, impenetrable
thicket; good habitat plant. Native to
Asia. Most plants offered are cultivars.

'Apple Blossom', 6' x 8', has pink and
white flowers. 'Cameo', 3' x 5', nearly
thornless with peach-pink double
flowers. 'Coral Sea', 6-8' x 6-8', has
coral-pink flowers. 'Hollandia', 6-8' x
6-8', has large red flowers. 'Jet Trail',
2-3' x 3', nearly thornless with pure
white flowers. 'Nivalis', 6-8' x 6-8',
has pure white flowers. 'Texas
Scarlet', 3' x 3', nearly thornless with
orange-red flowers.

CERCOCARPUS BETULOIDES

CHAENOMELES 'CORAL SEA'

Chamaerops humilis (Mediterranean fan palm)

ZONES 4-24. PALM. 10-20' x 10-20'.

Variable, slow-growing, small palm with a shrubby habit, usually multi-trunked, with rigid and erect, fan-shaped fronds of green, bluish green, or gray-green leaves on long petioles. Small, bright yellow flowers cluster at base of leaf petioles. One of the most cold-tolerant palms. Full sun, good drainage, moderate water. Good seaside plant. Native to the western Mediterranean.

BELOW: *CHAMELAUCIUM UNCINATUM* 'PURPLE PRIDE'

Chamelaucium uncinatum
(Geraldton waxflower)

ZONES 8, 9, 12-24. EVERGREEN SHRUB.
6-8' x 6-8'.

Tender shrub with an open habit, light green, softly needlelike, aromatic leaves, and loose sprays of late winter to spring flowers. Flowers pink, white, purple, or bicolored and long-lasting in arrangements. Full sun, good drainage, occasional deep watering. Prune after flowering. Native to Australia.

'Purple Pride' has dark green leaves that densely line the dark red stems and large, rosy purple flowers. 'Eric John' is more compact, with shorter leaves and pink flowers. 'Lady Stephanie' has light rose-pink flowers aging to deep pink.

Chilopsis linearis (desert willow)

ZONES 7-14, 18-23. DECIDUOUS SHRUB OR TREE. 15-30' x 10-20'.

Large shrub to small, multi-trunked tree with long, narrow, willowlike leaves and scented, pink to lavender, purplish, burgundy, or sometimes white trumpet-shaped flowers in spring and summer. Attractive to hummingbirds and butterflies. Long, cylindrical seedpods persist on bare branches through winter. Full sun, good drainage, infrequent deep watering. Tolerates cold and prefers heat, even reflected heat. Best inland. Native to California, the southwestern U.S., and northern Mexico.

CHILOPSIS LINEARIS

x *Chitalpa tashkentensis* (chitalpa)

ZONES 3-24. DECIDUOUS TREE. 20-30' x 20-30'.

Fast-growing tree with long, narrow, green leaves and clusters of trumpet-shaped, pink, white, or lavender flowers in late spring to fall. Full sun, good drainage, occasional to little water. Tolerates heat. 'Pink Dawn' has showy lavender-pink flowers with yellow throats. 'Morning Cloud' has white flowers.

x *CHITALPA TASHKENTENSIS*

Choisya ternata (Mexican orange)

 ZONE 6-9, 14-24. EVERGREEN SHRUB. 6-8'x 6-8'.

CHOISYA TERNATA

Fast-growing shrub with shiny, bright green leaves and clusters of fragrant, white flowers in late winter or early spring. Full sun to part shade, good drainage, moderate to occasional water. Prune anytime to shape. Good informal hedge. Native to Mexico. Ignored by deer.

Chondropetalum tectorum (Cape rush)

ZONES 8, 9, 14-24. PERENNIAL. 4-6' x 4-6'.

Tufted, reedlike plant with tough, wiry, green stems. Attractive tan-brown bracts. Well behaved in the garden, it can be grown wet or dry. Sun to part sun, good air circulation, moderate to occasional water. Selective removal of brown stems will

CHONDROPETALUM TECTORUM WITH CISTUS

keep the plant neat; do not cut back entire plant, as cut stems will not regrow. Native to South Africa, it occurs naturally in damp areas but accepts a long dry season.

Cistus (rockrose)

 ZONES 6-9, 14-24. EVERGREEN SHRUBS. SIZE VARIES.

Low, mounding groundcovers to tall shrubs shrubs with showy, crinkled, papery flowers borne in succession over a long bloom period in spring and early summer. Full sun, excellent drainage, little or no water. Good choice for

CISTUS LADANIFER 'BLANCHE' WITH EUPHORBIA

large-scale informal planting on slopes. Tolerate salt spray, wind, heat, and drought, but short-lived if watered where drainage is less than perfect. Tip prune to shape; some do not resprout from old wood. Native to the Mediterranean. Ignored by deer.

C. x *aguilarii*, 6' x 6', upright with narrow, wavy-edged, slightly sticky, dark green leaves and large white flowers with a crimson blotch at the base of each petal. 'Maculatus' has unusually large flowers; does not tolerate pruning.

C. x *hybridus*, white rockrose, 3-5' x 3-5', has reddish stems, medium green, wavy-edged leaves, and crimson-tinged buds opening to pure white flowers. Tolerates heavy soils better than most rockroses.

C. incanus, pink rockrose, 3-4' x 4-6', has grayish green leaves and bright pink flowers.

CISTUS INCANUS

C. ladanifer, crimson spot rockrose, 3-5' x 3-4', has dark green leaves and pure white flowers with a crimson spot at the base of each petal. 'Blanche', 4-8' x 4-6', has especially large flowers.

C. salviifolius, sageleaf rockrose, variable height and spread, prostrate to upright, with white flowers, nodding in bud, and hairy leaves. 'Prostratus', 2-3' x 6', makes an excellent mounding groundcover on slopes.

C. x *skanbergii*, 2-3' x 3-4', upright plant with gray-green leaves and pale pink flowers.

C. 'Sunset', 3' x 3', has soft, gray-green leaves and vivid magenta flowers.

Clarkia (clarkia)

ZONES 1-24. ANNUALS. SIZE VARIES.

Annuals with with pink, white, purple, or red, single or double flowers from late spring

CLARKIA AMOENA 'AURORA'

until hot days arrive. Showy in mass and long-lasting in arrangements. Full sun to part shade, good drainage, no water. Tolerate alkaline soil, clay, sand, seaside conditions, but most need heat to bloom well. Sow seeds in fall. Native to western North and South America, especially California.

C. amoena, farewell-to-spring, godetia, 18-30" x 12-18", has cup-shaped, slightly flaring, pink or lavender, single or double flowers.

C. concinna, red ribbons, 18" x 1', has luminous, deep pink to lavender or red flowers with deeply three-lobed, ribbonlike petals.

C. pulchella, 12-18" x 1', has reddish stems, sparse leaves, and flowers with deeply three-lobed petals in lavender, pink, red, or white.

C. rubicunda, 1' x 1', has rosy pink to lavender, bowl-shaped flowers with bright red or purplish red at the base of the petals. Easy, with long blooming season.

C. unguiculata, mountain garland, 18-30" x 12-18", upright, with white, rose-pink, or purple flowers. 'Salmon Queen' has fully double, apricot-colored flowers.

☀ ☀ *Clivia miniata* (clivia)

ZONES 12-17, 19-24. PERENNIAL. 18" x 12-18".

Lovely plant for dryish shade with broad, green, straplike leaves and bright orange or

red-orange, funnel-shaped flowers, mostly in spring, on sturdy stalks above the leaves. Lights up dark places. Frost tender, but usually recovers. Part to full shade, good drainage, moderate to occasional water. Solomone Hybrids have yellow flowers. Native to South Africa.

Clytostoma callistegioides (violet trumpet vine)

ZONES 8, 9, 12-24. EVERGREEN VINE. 25'.

Robust, woody-stemmed vine with glossy, dark green leaves and showy lavender, trumpet-shaped flowers with purple veins in spring and summer. Full sun or part shade, most soils. Blooms best with heat. Rampant grower in fertile soil with regular water; better behaved and flowers well if kept on the dry side. Not for small gardens. Supports itself with tendrils on rough or uneven surfaces. Tops may freeze, but the plant usually survives. Prune in winter to shape and control. Native to South America.

Colchicum (autumn crocus, meadow saffron)

ZONES 2-10, 14-24. PERENNIALS FROM CORMS. 4-12" x 6".

Fall- or spring-flowering plants with broad strap leaves and delicate flowers that resemble crocus. Spring-flowering kinds bloom with their leaves; fall-flowering kinds usually produce leaves in spring. Full sun or light shade, excellent drainage, no summer water. Free-flowering and easy. Native to the Mediterranean and central Asia. Many species and cultivars.

Coleonema (breath of heaven)

ZONES 7-9, 14-24. EVERGREEN SHRUBS. SIZE VARIES.

Short-lived but lovely, erect and wispy shrubs prized for their bright green, needlelike, fragrant foliage and masses of tiny, pink or white, star-shaped flowers in winter and spring. Full sun to part shade, good drainage, moderate water. Somewhat tender. Tolerate shearing. Attractive to butterflies and bees. Ignored by deer. Native to South Africa.

C. album, white breath of heaven, 3-5' x 3-5', has pure white flowers. Good coastal plant. Tolerates salt spray and wind.

C. pulchrum, pink breath of heaven, 5' x 5-6', has pink flowers. 'Compacta' is smaller with denser foliage and lighter pink flowers. 'Sunset Gold', 18" x 4', has yellow-green foliage.

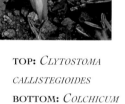

TOP: *CLYTOSTOMA CALLISTEGIOIDES*
BOTTOM: *COLCHICUM*

COLEONEMA PULCHRUM
'SUNSET GOLD'

Collinsia heterophylla
(Chinese houses)

 ZONES 1-24. ANNUAL. 1-2' x 1'.

Easy annual with 1-2' tall stems bearing tiers of lavender or purple and white spring flowers that resemble snapdragons. Light shade or sun, good drainage, no water. Prefers cool locations such as north-facing slopes or under trees. Reseeds and naturalizes where content. Native to California.

COLLINSIA HETEROPHYLLA WITH *LAYIA PLATYGLOSSA* (YELLOW) AND *NEMOPHILA MENZIESII* (BLUE)

Coprosma (coprosma)

ZONES VARY. EVERGREEN SHRUBS. SIZE VARIES.

Spreading or mounding shrubs with glossy, deep green or variegated leaves and small white flowers followed by clusters of shiny, fleshy, orange berries. Best near coast. Tolerate sea spray, drought, and wind, but not prolonged frosts. Full sun to part shade along coast, part shade inland, good drainage, moderate water. Can spread by seed. Prune to maintain form. Native to New Zealand.

C. x *kirkii*, 1-3' x 4-6', horizontal branching habit and narrow, yellow-green leaves; makes a good groundcover and spills over walls. 'Variegata' has sage-green leaves with creamy white margins. 'Black Cloud' has dark bronzy green, almost black, leaves. Zones 14-24.

C. repens, mirror plant, 8' x 6', has dark green to light green, exceptionally shiny leaves. Zones 14-24.

C. 'Coppershine', 4-6' x 3-6', upright, vase-shaped, has green leaves with bronzy margins. Zones 8, 9, 14-24.

COPROSMA X KIRKII 'VARIEGATA'

Coreopsis (coreopsis)

ZONES 1-24. PERENNIALS AND ANNUALS. SIZE VARIES.

 Vigorous and easy but short-lived plants with yellow, deep golden, maroon, or orange flowers in summer. Full sun to part shade, good drainage, occasional water. Accept heat, salt spray, drought, neglect. Attractive to butterflies and birds. Deadhead to promote rebloom and control self-sowing. Most are native to eastern and southern United States.

COREOPSIS GRANDIFLORA 'SUNRAY'

C. grandiflora, 1-2' x 3', perennial with dark green leaves and bright yellow single flowers on tall stems in summer. Native to Texas. 'Sunray' is more compact, with yellow-orange double flowers. Zones 2-24.

C. tinctoria, annual coreopsis, 18"-3' x 12-18", has narrow green leaves and vivid yellow, orange, red, maroon, or bicolored single or double flowers. Dwarf varieties available.

C. verticillata, threadleaf coreopsis, 2-3' x 12-18", perennial with finely divided leaves and bright yellow flowers summer to fall. 'Moonbeam' has pale yellow flowers. 'Zagreb' has golden yellow flowers.

Correa (Australian fuchsia)

ZONES 14-24. EVERGREEN SHRUBS. SIZE VARIES.

Small, tubular, creamy white, greenish yellow, rose, scarlet, or crimson flowers hang gracefully from branch ends in winter. Small, grayish green to glossy dark green leaves. Dense and spreading, plants range from almost prostrate to upright. Full shade

CORREA 'DAWN IN SANTA CRUZ'

to full sun, fast drainage, moderate to occasional water. Good for dry shade in cooler locations. Tolerate alkaline soils. Attractive to birds and butterflies. Ignored by deer. Native to Australia.

C. alba, 8' x 8', has leathery, dark gray-green leaves and white, almost star-shaped flowers.

C. backhousiana, 4' x 5', has tubular chartreuse or creamy white flowers and leaves with upper surfaces glossy, rusty hairs beneath.

C. pulchella is a variable species, generally 2-3' x 4-5', with pale pink, orange, or red flowers and dark green leaves with gray-green undersides. Greener than other correas and flowers later. 'Pink Flamingo' has salmon-pink flowers. 'Mission Bells' has dark pink or red flowers.

C. reflexa is a variable species, ranging from nearly prostrate to erect and 4' tall, compact to open habit, leaves from rough-hairy to smooth, and flowers yellow-green to crimson red with yellow tips.

C. 'Dusky Bells', 2-3' x 6-8', is a densely branched, mounding shrub with carmine-pink to deep red flowers and dark green leaves. 'Ivory Bells' is more upright, with creamy white flowers opening from yellowish tan buds.

Cosmos (cosmos)

ZONES 1-24. PERENNIALS AND ANNUALS. SIZE VARIES.

COSMOS SULPHUREUS 'SUNNY RED'

Masses of white, pink, orange, yellow, or crimson, daisylike flowers in late summer and fall. Attractive to birds. Somewhat floppy habit; may need staking or support from nearby plants. Full sun, moderate water. Native to Mexico. May be invasive.

C. bipinnatus, 3-6' x 2', annual with finely divided leaves and large flowers in white, pink, purple, or crimson with yellow centers.

C. sulphureus, yellow cosmos, 6' x 2', annual with yellow to orange flowers.

Cotinus coggygria (smoke tree)

ZONES 2-24. DECIDUOUS SHRUB OR TREE. 10-15' x 10-15'.

Upright, loosely spreading, multi-stemmed shrub that can be trained to a single trunk. Rounded to oval leaves are dull bluish green to purple, on some plants turning yellow, orange, or reddish in fall. Dense clusters of tiny, greenish white to pink-purple flowers in spring. Masses of billowy hairs on spent flowers in summer lend a striking smoky effect, especially from a distance.

Slow-growing and a bit rangy as a specimen. Excellent color and textural contrast in

mixed shrub plantings. Full sun to part shade, excellent drainage, infrequent water. Best in poor, rocky soils; short-lived in rich soils. Native to southern Europe and Asia. 'Purpureus' has purple leaves that gradually turn green, and richer purple flowers. 'Royal Purple' has dark purple, almost black, leaves and purplish pink flowers. 'Pink Champagne', 4-8' x 6-8', has green leaves that turn salmon orange in fall.

COTINUS COGGYGRIA 'PINK CHAMPAGNE' WITH DEER GRASS (*MUHLENBERGIA*)

Cotoneaster (cotoneaster)

☀️ ☀️ ☀️ ZONES VARY. EVERGREEN OR DECIDUOUS
💧 SHRUBS. SIZE VARIES.

Low groundcovers to tall, upright shrubs of fountainlike habit with graceful, arching branches. Though beautiful and useful shrubs, some of the large cotoneasters (e.g., *C. lacteus*) can be invasive in irrigated gardens and have spread into wildlands in some parts of coastal California.

COTONEASTER DAMMERI
'LOWFAST'

. . . 109

Low-growing, trailing or mounding cotoneasters are excellent, fine-textured groundcovers in sun or shade, especially on slopes, and have not proved invasive. Dense enough to discourage weeds, they also slow erosion by rooting as they spread. All have attractive leaves, tiny but abundant white or pinkish spring flowers, and orange or red berries in fall or winter. Sun to shade, reasonable drainage, occasional to little water. Native to Asia.

C. dammeri, bearberry cotoneaster, 8-12" x 8-10', evergreen with glossy green leaves and bright red berries. Effective cascading down slopes or over walls. Zones 2-24. 'Coral Beauty', 6" x 12' has shiny green leaves and coral pink berries. 'Lowfast' is about 1' tall.

C. horizontalis, rock cotoneaster, 2-3' x 15', is briefly deciduous; leaves turn orange-red before dropping. Needs room to spread. Zones 2-11, 14-24.

C. microphyllus, rockspray cotoneaster, 2-3' x 6', evergreen shrub with tiny, dark green leaves and red berries in fall. Hugs the ground and drapes over walls. Zones 2-9, 14-24.

Crassula (crassula)

ZONES 8, 9, 12-24. SUCCULENT PERENNIALS. SIZE VARIES.

CRASSULA MULTICAVA

Tender, succulent plants for mild-winter areas. Shelter from frost, protect from hot sun. Need excellent drainage, occasional water. Many species, most from South Africa. Many named cultivars.

Crataegus (hawthorn)

ZONES 2-12, 14-17. DECIDUOUS TREES. SIZE VARIES.

Showy in flower and fruit, some with fall leaf color, these deciduous, often multi-trunked, shrubby trees offer year-round interest and good habitat value. Best planted where they can be left to their own devices, as dense twigs and sharp thorns make working in or around them hazardous. Attractive to birds, bees, and other wildlife. Full sun, reasonable drainage, occasional water. Tolerant of drought, compacted or poor soils, reflected heat, salt spray. Potentially invasive.

C. crus-galli, cockspur thorn, 20-30' x 20-35', horizontal, spreading habit, with prominent thorns and glossy, dark green leaves that turn orange or red in fall. Red fruits persist into winter. The variety *inermis* is thornless and smaller than the species. Native to eastern North America.

C. phaenopyrum, Washington thorn, 25' x 25', masses of spring flowers, good orange, scarlet, or burgundy fall color, shiny red-orange fruit in winter. Native to southeastern U.S.

Crocosmia (crocosmia)

ZONES 5-24. PERENNIALS FROM CORMS. SIZE VARIES.

Reliable, easy South African natives with irislike leaves and small, brightly colored flowers in summer. Full sun to part shade, little or no water. Long-lasting cut flowers are creamy white to orange or scarlet. Attractive to hummingbirds. Invasive in damp areas, cultivated or wild.

C. x *crocosmiiflora,* montbretia, 3' x 12-18", with bright red-orange flowers on 3-4' stems. Naturalizes readily.

C. masoniorum, 2-3' x 12-18", with vivid orange to orange-scarlet flowers on 3' stems that arch over at the top.

CROCOSMIA 'LUCIFER'

Many named and unnamed hybrids. 'Lucifer' has fiery red flowers. 'Solfatare' has bronzy green leaves and yellow flowers. 'Emily McKenzie' has deep orange flowers with maroon and yellow markings in the center.

Crocus (crocus)

 ZONES 1-24. PERENNIALS FROM CORMS. 3" x 3".

Blooming in late fall (*Crocus goulimyi, C. ochroleucus, C. pulchellus, C. sativus, C. speciosus, C. zonatus*) or early spring (*C. chrysanthus, C. sieberi, C. tomasinianus, C. vernus*), crocus have narrow, grasslike leaves and low, cup-shaped, white, yellow, lilac, or rich purple flowers that open in sun, close on cloudy days. Sun to part shade,

CROCUS 'PICKWICK'

BELOW: *CUPRESSUS ARIZONICA* 'BLUE ICE' WITH *CERCIS CANADENSIS*

good drainage, no summer water. Best massed in drifts; wonderful among grasses. Native to the Mediterranean.

Cupressus (cypress)

ZONES VARY. EVERGREEN TREES. SIZE VARIES.

Tough, hardy, cone-bearing trees with scalelike foliage and reddish, often shredding bark. Tolerate extremes of drought, heat, cold, wind, and soils. Full sun, reasonable drainage, occasional water.

C. arizonica, Arizona cypress, 40' x 20', variable tree with green to gray-green to bluish gray leaves. Fast-growing. Good screen or windbreak. Native to Arizona. Zones 7-24. 'Blue Ice' has intensely silver-blue foliage.

C. sempervirens, Italian cypress, 50-60' x 8-10', slow-growing columnar classic of Mediterranean landscapes. Zones 4-24; best in 8-15, 18-21. 'Glauca' has blue-green foliage. 'Monshel' is 8-20' x 3'.

Cyclamen (wild cyclamen)

ZONES 2-9, 14-24. PERENNIALS FROM TUBERS. 4-6" X 4-10".

Delightful summer-dormant perennials with rounded or heart-shaped, usually variegated basal leaves in late fall or early winter. Smaller and more delicate-looking than florists' cyclamen (which are tender cultivars of *C. persicum*) and more tolerant of garden conditions. Long-lasting flowers with charmingly reflexed petals are pale to deep pink, magenta, or white. Shade to part sun, good drainage, no water. Native to Europe and Asia.

C. coum has pale pink or white to dark magenta flowers in winter and deep green leaves marbled with darker green or silvery markings; some have silvery green leaves.

C. hederifolium has ivylike green leaves with silvery white markings and pure white, pink, or deep pink flowers in fall; some have silvery green leaves.

Cynoglossum

(hound's tongue)

ZONES VARY. PERENNIALS AND BIENNIALS. SIZE VARIES.

Short-lived perennials with summer flowers that resemble forget-me-nots. Self-seed readily; can be invasive in irrigated gardens. Shade to part sun, water needs vary.

C. amabile, Chinese forget-me-not, 18"- 2' x 1', biennial with softly hairy, grayish green leaves and dense clusters of sky-blue flowers on strong stems. Part sun, moderate water. 'Blue Showers' grows 2-3' tall. Native to east Asia. Zones 1-24.

C. grande, western hound's tongue, 2' x 1', perennial with blue flowers with white centers. Part to full shade, little or no water. Native to Oregon and California. Zones 4-9, 14-24.

Dasylirion wheeleri (desert spoon, sotol)

ZONES 10-24. EVERGREEN SHRUB. 3-5' X 4-5'.

DASYLIRION WHEELERI
WITH YELLOW-FLOWERED
AEONIUM AND BARREL
CACTUS

Rounded clump of long, narrow, bluish green leaves with hooked teeth along the margins. Eventually develops a short trunk and a 10-15' tall stalk from the center of the clump bearing small white flowers. Good specimen or accent. Full sun to light shade, excellent drainage, little or no water. Native to the southwestern U.S. and northwestern Mexico.

Dendromecon (bush poppy)

ZONES VARY. EVERGREEN SHRUBS. SIZE VARIES.

Showy, bright yellow flowers in spring and summer and deep green to gray-green leaves. Full sun, excellent drainage, little to no water. Not easy, but rewarding. Attractive to butterflies and bees. Good habitat plants.

DENDROMECON HARFORDII

D. harfordii, island bush poppy, 6-10' x 6-10',

rounded or spreading shrub with glaucous, deep green leaves and brilliant yellow flowers that cover the plant in spring and summer. Native to the Channel Islands. Zones 7-9, 14-24.

D. rigida, bush poppy, 4-8' x 4-6', open branched shrub with narrow, gray-green leaves, pale, shredding bark, and bright yellow flowers. Native to California. Zones 4-12, 14-24.

Deschampsia (hair grass)

ZONES 2-24. PERENNIAL AND ANNUAL GRASSES. SIZE VARIES.

Clump-forming, cool-season ornamental grasses with golden flowerheads in spring to late summer. Best in part shade, with moderate water, and where summers are not too hot.

D. cespitosa, tufted hair grass, 1-2' x 2', forms clumps of narrow, dark green leaves and greenish gold flowers on 4' tall stems. Native to California.

D. danthonioides, annual hairgrass, 4-18" x 12", is an extremely fine-textured, clumping grass topped in summer by airy panicles of silver flowers that sway in the slightest breeze. Native to western North America and South America. Full to part sun, moderate water.

DESCHAMPSIA CESPITOSA

D. flexuosa, crinkled hair grass, 12-18" x 12", perennial grass with tufts of yellow-green leaves and purplish to silvery flowerheads. Thrives in dry shade as well as part sun with some moisture. Native to many parts of the world.

Dianthus (pink)

ZONES 1-24. PERENNIALS AND ANNUALS. 6-12" X 6-12".

Mats or tufts of narrow, grasslike, gray-green, blue-green, or dark green leaves and single or double white, pink, or red flowers with a spicy fragrance in spring or summer.

Most pinks need full to part sun, good to excellent drainage, and regular water, though none appreciates overwatering. Those below are perennials and take moderate to occasional water.

DIANTHUS GRATIANOPOLITANUS 'GRANDIFLORUS' WITH LOBULARIA MARITIMA

D. carthusianorum has narrow, grasslike leaves and magenta flowers on 2' stems in summer. Moderate water.

D. deltoides, maiden pink, forms a loose mat of dark green leaves and has fragrant, white or pink summer flowers, often with contrasting centers. Moderate water in part-day shade. Native to Europe and Asia. 'Nelli' has intense scarlet flowers.

DICHELOSTEMMA CAPITATUM

D. gratianopolitanus, cheddar pink, 6" x 1-2', makes a dense groundcover with bluish gray leaves and fragrant, single pink flowers in spring. 'Grandiflorus' has darker pink flowers.

Dichelostemma
(dichelostemma)

ZONES N/A. PERENNIALS FROM CORMS. SIZE VARIES.

Summer-dormant corms with grasslike leaves and open or tight clusters of red, pink, or blue-purple, tubular flowers in spring. Attractive to hummingbirds. Excellent drainage, sun, no water. Effective in meadow plantings. Native to the western U.S. and Mexico, especially northern California.

D. capitatum, blue dicks, has purple bracts and blue-violet, funnel-shaped flowers on 2' stems. Naturalizes easily where content.

D. congestum, ookow, has lavender-blue flowers in tight clusters. Good cut flower. Effective in drifts.

D. ida-maia, firecracker flower, has bright red, green-tipped, pendulous flowers. Prefers some shade.

D. multiflorum, wild hyacinth, has showy clusters of soft lavender or lilac flowers. Thrives in sun and heat.

Dietes (fortnight lily)

ZONES 8, 9, 12-24. PERENNIALS FROM RHIZOMES. 2 -3' x 2- 3'.

Easy, common, but rewarding evergreen perennials with irislike leaves and numerous flowers on strong stems in spring and summer. Sun or part shade, occasional to no water. Ignored by deer. Native to Africa.

DIETES IRIDIOIDES

D. bicolor has pale yellow flowers with dark brown spots on 3' tall stems. Graceful and more open than *D. iridioides*. 'Lemon Drop' has ivory white flowers with yellow blotches. 'Orange Drop' has ivory flowers with orange blotches.

DIMORPHOTHECA SINUATA

D. iridioides has large, white flowers with gold and lavender markings on sturdy 3' stalks. Remove dead leaves any time of year; leave old stalks, which flower again.

Dimorphotheca (African daisy)

ZONES 1-24. ANNUALS. SIZE VARIES.

Masses of cheery, daisylike flowers in late winter and early spring open in sun and close in the evening or on overcast days. Flowers are white or vibrant shades of orange or yellow with darker centers. Adapted to dry-summer climates where winters are mild. Full sun, good drainage, occasional to no water. Attractive to butterflies and bees. Native to South Africa.

D. pluvialis, 4-16" x 12", has coarsely toothed, green leaves and white flowers with brownish yellow centers and violet undersides.

D. sinuata, 4-12" x 12", has narrow, green leaves and bright orange and yellow flowers. Self-seeds. No summer water. Invasive in parts of southern California. 'Salmon Queen' has salmon or apricot flowers.

Distictis buccinatoria (blood-red trumpet vine)

ZONES 8-9, 14-24. EVERGREEN VINE. 15-30'.

Fast-growing vine with masses of red-orange, tubular or trumpet-shaped flowers with yellow throats in summer. Tender. Best along coast. Full sun to light shade, good drainage, moderate to occasional water. Native to Mexico. 'Rivers' has mauve to purple flowers with yellow to orange throats.

DISTICTIS BUCCINATORIA

Dodonaea viscosa (hop bush)

ZONES 7-24. EVERGREEN SHRUB. 10-15' x 10-15'.

Fast-growing, upright shrub with willowlike leaves and deceptively delicate appearance. Flowers insignificant, but papery seedpods are attractive. Good screen or hedge. Can be trained as small tree. Full sun to part shade, occasional water. Tolerates wind, heat, poor soil, but may suffer from prolonged frosts. Ignored by deer. Native to Australia and the southwestern U.S. 'Purpurea' has striking bronzy or wine-colored leaves streaked with green and pinkish tan seed pods.

RED SEEDPODS OF
DODONAEA VISCOSA

Dryopteris arguta (California wood fern)

ZONES 4-9, 14-24. FERN. 30" x 4'.

Reliable California native fern for dry shade. Bright green, triangular shaped fronds grow in graceful clumps, often wider than tall. Has a soft, ruffled look. Best near coast. Deciduous in drought and heat. Thrives in clay soil with some organic content. Shade, little to no water. Ignored by deer.

DRYOPTERIS ARGUTA

Dudleya (dudleya)

ZONES VARY. SUCCULENT PERENNIALS. SIZE VARIES.

Ground-hugging succulents with rosettes of gray-green leaves that appear to be covered with chalky powder and small yellow flowers in spring or summer. Best along coast. Full sun with afternoon shade to bright shade, excellent drainage, no water. Shelter from hard rain and frost. Attractive to hummingbirds.

D. brittonii, 1-2' x 30", rosettes of tapered leaves covered in white, waxy powder and yellow flowers on reddish stalks in summer. One of the easier dudleyas to grow. Native to Baja California. Zones 16, 17, 21-24.

D. caespitosa, 12" x 16", clumping rosettes of narrow, gray-green leaves and golden yellow flowers. Native to coastal cliffs of southern California. Zones 9, 14-17, 19-24.

D. farinosa, powdery dudleya, 6-12" x 12", with gray to green, red-tipped leaves and yellow flowers. Native to northern California and southern Oregon. Zones 5, 7, 14-17, 19-24.

D. pulverulenta, chalk dudleya, 16" x 16", has broad, gray-green to blue-gray leaves and red flowers. Native to southern California. Zones N/A.

Dymondia margaretae (silver carpet)

ZONES 15-24. PERENNIAL. 1-3" x 2'.

Wonderful little groundhugger that quickly creates an icy green carpet of small, narrow leaves, dark green above and cottony white below, topped by bright yellow, daisylike flowers in summer. Effective among stepping stones. Full sun to part shade, good drainage, moderate to occasional water. Best near coast, but grows in all but the coldest areas. Native to South Africa.

Echeveria (echeveria)

ZONES VARY. SUCCULENT PERENNIALS. SIZE VARIES.

Rosettes of succulent green or gray-green leaves, often edged or marked with contrasting colors, and clusters of nodding, bell-shaped flowers on tall, often branched, stems. Some are tender. Most need afternoon shade in hot climates. Excellent drainage, moderate to occasional water. Native to Mexico.

Echinacea purpurea (purple coneflower)

ECHINACEA PURPUREA

ZONES 1-24. PERENNIAL. 2-3' x 2'.

A natural for wildflower gardens and mixed borders, this lovely perennial forms slowly spreading clumps of dark green leaves with serrated edges and rosy pink, daisylike flowers in summer. Good for cutting; long-lasting in arrangements. Attractive to butterflies. Full sun, moderate water. Native to central and eastern North America.

Echium (echium)

ECHIUM CANDICANS

ZONES VARY. PERENNIALS, BIENNIALS, SHRUBS. SIZE VARIES.

Soft, gray-green, hairy leaves and spikelike clusters of blue-purple or

pink flowers. Attractive to bees, hummingbirds, and butterflies. Full sun, good drainage, little or no water. Short-lived but reseed. Good seaside plants, but may be invasive in coastal wildlands. Ignored by deer. Native to the Canary Islands.

E. candicans, pride of Madeira, 4-6' x 6-10', is a big, bold, fast-growing shrub for full sun, with tall spikes of iridescent violet-blue flowers in spring. Drought and wind tolerant. Will not take hard pruning; tip prune only to shape and remove spent flower stalks. Zones 14-24.

E. wildpretii, tower of jewels, biennial with a rosette of silvery gray leaves from which arises, in the second year, a 6-10' tall spike of dark pink to rose-red flowers in late spring. Dies after flowering but reseeds readily. Zones 15-17, 21-24.

Elaeagnus (elaeagnus)

ZONES 4-24. EVERGREEN SHRUBS. SIZE VARIES.

Large, adaptable, densely foliaged shrubs for screens and hedges. Olive-green to dark green leaves and fragrant but inconspicuous flowers. Vigorous and fast-growing. Full sun to part shade, good drainage, little water. Tolerate wind, seacoast conditions, heat, cold, poor soils, and drought. Ignored by deer. *E. angustifolia*, Russian olive, is highly invasive in gardens and in wildlands in California and the Northwest.

TOP: *ELAEAGNUS PUNGENS* 'MACULATA' BOTTOM: *ELYMUS GLAUCUS*

E. x ebbingei, 10-15' x 10-15', is spineless, with dark green leaves, silvery beneath, intensely fragrant, tiny, white flowers and rosy red fruit.

E. pungens, silverberry, 10-15' x 10-15', is dense and twiggy with spiny branches and olive-green leaves that are rusty brown beneath. Accepts shearing and pruning. Native to China and Japan. 'Fruitlandii' has large leaves with prominent silvery specks. 'Maculata' has leaves with a yellow spot in the center. 'Marginata' has leaves edged with silver. 'Variegata' has leaves edged in creamy yellow.

Elymus glaucus (blue wild rye)

ZONES N/A. PERENNIAL GRASS. 1-2' x 2'.

Variable cool-season bunchgrass valued for its tough constitution. Narrow, bright green to grayish green leaves in loose, short-lived tufts and bristle-tipped flowers on erect, 2-3' spikes in late spring. Self-sows readily, and spreads by rhizomes. Can be invasive. Good for revegetation and stabilizing slopes. Full to part sun, occasional to little water. Native to western North America, including California.

ENCELIA FARINOSA

Encelia (encelia)

ZONES VARY. EVERGREEN SHRUBS. 3-4' x 3-4'.

Tender, fast-growing, short-lived shrubs with large, yellow, daisylike flowers in spring. Full sun, good drainage, little or no water.

E. californica has bright green leaves and large, yellow flowers with brown centers. Native to coastal southern California and northwestern Mexico. Zones 7-16, 18-24.

E. farinosa, brittlebush, has silvery gray-green leaves and masses of yellow flowers on tall stalks above the leaves. Drought-deciduous. Native to California and deserts of the southwestern U.S. Zones 8-16, 18-24.

Engelmannia peristenia (Engelmann's daisy)

ZONES N/A. PERENNIAL. 2-3' x 2'.

Basal clump of large, gray-green leaves and generous display of bright yellow, daisylike flowers in summer to fall. Full sun, good drainage, moderate to occasional water. From southwestern U.S. and northern Mexico.

Epilobium (California fuchsia)

ZONES VARY. PERENNIALS. SIZE VARIES.

Sprawling perennials or subshrubs with narrow, silvery gray to gray-green leaves and loose clusters of brilliant orange to scarlet, tubular flowers in

summer and fall. Full sun to part shade, good drainage, occasional to no water. Cut back after bloom to renew. Attractive to hummingbirds, butterflies, and bees. Native to western North America and northern Mexico.

E. canum, 1-2' x 4', upright or sprawling subshrub with gray leaves and scarlet flowers. Zones 2-11, 14-24. 'Everett's Choice' has a trailing habit, gray-green leaves and reddish orange flowers. 'Solidarity Pink' has pale pink flowers.

E. septentrionale, 8-12" x 2-3', mat-forming with gray-green leaves and bright scarlet or red-orange flowers. Needs afternoon shade and some water in hot interior locations. Zones 5-7, 14-17, 19-24. 'Select Mattole' has silvery, almost white, foliage that mounds as it spreads and scarlet-orange flowers. 'Wayne's Silver' is a low groundhugger with silvery foliage.

Epimedium (epimedium)

ZONES 2-9, 14-17. PERENNIALS. 8-18" x 18".

Low-growing, evergreen or deciduous woodland plants with leaves divided into heart-shaped leaflets on thin, wiry stems. New growth usually bronzy or reddish, turning green, then bronzy again in fall. Delicate-looking sprays of flowers in spring and summer. Wonderful plants for dry shade. Spread slowly by underground stems. Best with moderate to occasional water, but survive drought in shade. Cut back in winter to renew.

E. alpinum, evergreen, to 12" tall, has dark red and yellow flowers. Native to southern Europe.

E. grandiflorum, bishop's hat, deciduous, to 12" tall, has large red, pale violet, and white flowers. Native to China and Japan. 'Rose Queen' has dark rose to crimson flowers with white tips. 'White Queen' has silvery white flowers.

E. pinnatum, 8-12" tall, briefly deciduous, has reddish brown leaves with green veining and yellow flowers. Native to Iran.

E. x rubrum, 10-12" tall, semi-evergreen, has green leaves edged with pink and yellow or white flowers with crimson centers.

E. x versicolor, 12-18" tall, briefly deciduous or partly deciduous, usually with yellow flowers.

Erigeron (fleabane)

ZONES VARY. PERENNIALS. 8"-2' x 18"-3'.

Fast-growing, easy-care perennials with profuse, long-

ERIOBOTRYA JAPONICA

lasting displays of pink, lavender, or violet, daisylike flowers with yellow centers in spring to fall. Full sun, good drainage, occasional water. Attractive to butterflies. Ignored by deer.

E. glaucus, seaside daisy or beach aster, 12" x 18", has blue-green leaves and showy lavender flowers. Native to coastal California and Oregon. Zones 4-6, 15-17, 22-24. 'Wayne Roderick', 8" x 12", seems to tolerate hotter locations.

E. karvinskianus, Santa Barbara daisy, 10-18" x 2-3', has white flowers with a pink tinge on trailing stems. Good inland as well as along coast. Aggressive spreader, but easily pulled. Native to Mexico. Zones 8, 9, 12-24.

Eriobotrya (loquat)

Zones vary. Evergreen shrubs or trees. Size varies.

Versatile, somewhat formal-looking shrubs or trees with large, bold, leathery leaves. Respond well to pruning and can be espaliered. Full sun or part shade, good drainage, moderate to occasional water. Native to China.

E. deflexa, bronze loquat, 15-20' x 10-15', rounded shrub with large, pointed leaves, coppery bronze when new, turning dark green, and clusters of fragrant, creamy white flowers in spring. Small fruits attractive to birds. Zones 8-24.

E. japonica, 15-30' x 15-30', a larger and coarser tree, often multi-trunked, with branches low to the ground and peeling bark. Leaves deeply veined, leathery, glossy, dark green above, downy and rust-colored beneath. Clusters of creamy white, fragrant flowers followed by pale yellow fruit. Zones 6-24.

Eriogonum (wild buckwheat)

Zones vary. Perennials. Size varies.

Compact, rounded, shrubby perennials with dense, rounded clusters of tiny flowers,

showy in mass and long-blooming. Excellent in dried arrangements. Full sun, good drainage, occasional water. Good wildlife plants. Attractive to butterflies and bees. Tolerate heat, wind, drought, salt spray. Native to western U.S., especially California.

E. fasciculatum, California buckwheat, 2-3' x 4', has narrow, green or gray-green leaves and flowers in spring to fall that open light pink and turn white. Zones 7-9, 12-24.

E. grande var. *rubescens*, red-flowered buckwheat, 1-2' x 1-2', has upright branch tips, gray-green leaves, and rosy red flowers in summer. Zones 5, 14-24.

E. umbellatum, sulfur buckwheat, 2' x 2', has bright yellow flowers in summer that fade to yellow-orange or rust. Zones 1-24.

Eriophyllum (woolly sunflower)

ZONES N/A. PERENNIALS. 6"-3' x 18"-5'.

Short-lived, shrubby perennials with finely divided, gray-green leaves and vivid yellow flowers on slender stalks in late spring to summer. Full sun, good drainage, little to no water. Short-lived but reseed. Native to dry, exposed sites in California and the western U.S. Ignored by deer.

ABOVE: *ERIOGONUM GRANDE* VAR. *RUBESCENS* IN LATE SUMMER BELOW: *ERIOPHYLLUM CONFERTIFLORUM*

E. confertiflorum, 1-2' x 1-2', with green to gray-green leaves and bright yellow flowers. Prefers summer dryness; accepts some water with excellent drainage.

E. lanatum, 1-3' x 1-3', matting to mounding, variable in size, with silvery gray, aromatic leaves and golden-yellow flowers on strong, thin stems in early summer. 'Pointe' forms a dense, woolly mat covered with hundreds of brilliant yellow flowers.

Erysimum (wallflower)

Zones vary. Perennials. Size varies.

Widespread in temperate regions, these short-lived perennials vary widely in habit. All have narrow green or gray-green leaves and spikelike clusters of small, usually fragrant flowers. Full sun to part shade, good drainage, moderate to occasional water.

E. capitatum, coastal wallflower, 12-18" x 6-12", has narrow green leaves and dense, rounded clusters of orange, red, yellow, or sometimes white flowers in spring to mid-summer. Native to western North America. Zones N/A.

E. concinnum, Pt. Reyes wallflower, 12" x 10", has gray-green leaves and creamy white to pale yellow, fragrant flowers in spring. Native to coastal California and Oregon. Zones N/A.

E. linifolium, alpine wallflower, 8-12" x 8-12", forms a small mound of grayish green leaves and spikes of pale violet flowers in summer. Native to the Mediterranean. Zones N/A.

ERYSIMUM LINIFOLIUM

E. 'Bowles Mauve', 2' x 3', has vibrantly lavender-purple flowers. Needs periodic replacement. Zones 4-6, 14-17, 22, 23.

Escallonia (escallonia)

Zones 4-9, 14-24. Evergreen shrubs. Size varies.

Neat, dense, fast-growing, glossy-leaved shrubs with clusters of long-blooming white, pink, or red flowers. Excellent informal hedge, better artfully clipped than sheared. Full sun to part shade, good drainage, moderate water inland, occasional water near coast. Tolerate wind and salt spray. Somewhat tender, but usually recover from short freezes. Give these shrubs space to spread. Native to South America.

ESCALLONIA RUBRA

E. bifida, white escallonia, 8-10' x 8-10', has

large, dark green leaves and white flowers in clusters at branch ends. Can be trained as a small tree.

E. x *exoniensis*, pink escallonia, has deep green leaves and bright pink to pink-tinted white flowers. 'Fradesii', 5-6' x 5-6', has small, dark green, shiny leaves and a profusion of pinkish rose flowers.

E. rubra, red escallonia, 6-15' x 6-15', upright with shiny, dark green leaves and deep pink to red flowers. 'C.F. Ball' is smaller, and 'Ingramii' has larger flowers.

E. 'Newport Dwarf', 2-3' x 3-4', dense and compact, has light green leaves and rose-red flowers.

Eschscholzia californica (California poppy)

ZONES 1-24. PERENNIAL. 6-12" x 6".

Bright orange to golden or pale yellow, cup-shaped flowers spring to summer and bluish green, finely divided leaves. Full sun, good drainage, no water. Self-sows and naturalizes on open hillsides. Native to California and Oregon. State flower of California. Many selections and cultivars with flowers ranging from pink, rose, or purplish red to creamy white.

Eucalyptus (eucalyptus)

ZONES 5, 6, 8-24. EVERGREEN TREES AND SHRUBS. SIZE VARIES.

Large group of long-lived trees and shrubs with aromatic, blue-gray to gray-green leaves and attractive, flaking or peeling bark. Some have showy flowers. Some are tender in prolonged freezes, but usually survive. Full sun, occasional to no water. Attractive to butterflies and hummingbirds. Thrive in low-nutrient soils. Native to Australia. Don't plant blue gum (*E. globulus*); its immense size and copious peeling bark make it impossible to maintain for fire safety.

E. cinerea, silver dollar gum, 20-50' x 20-30', has silvery gray juvenile

TOP: *Eschscholzia californica* WITH *Myosotis sylvatica* 'ROSEA' RIGHT: *Eucalyptus leucoxylon*

leaves and long, narrow, gray-green mature leaves, reddish brown bark, and small, creamy white flowers. Tender, but usually regrows.

E. gunnii, cider gum, 30-75' x 20-45', has silvery blue juvenile leaves, blue-green mature leaves, reddish brown bark, and small, creamy white flowers. Quite hardy.

E. leucoxylon, 30-90' x 20-60', one of the hardiest showy-flowered eucalypts with clusters of large red or pink flowers.

E. nicholii, willowleaf peppermint, 30-50' x 15-40', elegant, smaller tree with pendulous branches and narrow, blue-green leaves.

E. sideroxylon, red ironbark, 30-90' x 30-60', variable tree with narrow blue-green leaves that turn bronzy in winter, dark brown, nearly black, furrowed trunk, and pendulous clusters of pink to crimson flowers in winter.

Euonymus (euonymus)

☀ ☀ ☀ ZONES VARY. DECIDUOUS OR EVERGREEN SHRUBS. SIZE VARIES.

💧💧 Adaptable and varied shrubs with a wide range of landscape uses. Evergreen types are excellent "backbone" plants. Best inland. Sun or shade, moderate to occasional water. Native to China, Korea, and Japan.

E. fortunei, 10-20', trailing or climbing vinelike, evergreen shrub with dark green leaves with toothed margins and stems that root where they touch the soil. The subspecies *radicans* makes a dense, 1' tall groundcover or, given support, will cover a wall or fence. Zones 2-17. 'Emerald Gaiety' is a good small filler.

E. japonicus, 8-10' x 6-8', upright evergreen shrub with glossy, dark green leaves. 'Microphyllus', boxleaf euonymus, 2' x 2', has small leaves and makes a good low hedge. Takes pruning well. 'Aureovariegatus', 8-10' x 6', has green leaves edged with creamy white. Zones 4-20.

TOP: *EUONYMUS JAPONICUS*
BOTTOM: *EUONYMUS JAPONICUS* 'MICROPHYLLUS' WITH NEPETA AND COLUMNS OF PITTOSPORUM

Euphorbia (euphorbia)

ZONES VARY. ANNUALS, PERENNIALS, AND SHRUBS. SIZE VARIES.

Most ornamental euphorbias are Mediterranean perennials prized for their bright green, yellow, or chartreuse bracts and interesting foliage colors and textures. Full sun to part shade, reasonable drainage, moderate to occasional water. Ignored by deer. Select carefully. Some euphorbias reseed readily in gardens, one (*E. esula*) is a wildland pest, and others require moist soils to thrive (e.g., *E. longifolia, E. palustris*).

E. amygdaloides, 3' x 1', perennial with dark green leaves, reddish underneath, and greenish yellow bracts in spring and summer. Sun, moderate water, or dry shade. 'Purpurea', 1' x 1', has purple leaves and stems and bright green bracts. Zones 2-24.

E. characias, 4' x 4', perennial with upright stems, blue-green leaves, and chartreuse flowers in late winter or early spring. Full sun, occasional water. The subspecies *wulfenii* has larger clusters of flowers. Zones 4-24.

E. dulcis 'Chameleon', 2' x 2', mounding perennial with maroon new leaves, maturing to dark green, and chartreuse bracts in summer. Full sun, occasional water. Self-sows. Zones 2-24.

E. myrsinites, creeping spurge, 6-12" x 12", perennial with trailing stems, bluish gray leaves, and greenish yellow bracts in late winter or early spring. Short-lived. Nice spilling over rocks. Part shade to full sun, occasional water. Zones 2-24.

E. 'Dean's Hybrid', 18"-2' x 18"-2', forms a dense mound of green leaves that turn blue-green in winter and chartreuse bracts in spring and again in fall. Zones N/A.

Euryops pectinatus (euryops)

 Zones 8, 9, 12-24. Evergreen shrub. 3'-5' x 3'-6'.

 Dependable producer of bright yellow, daisylike flowers over a long season. Silvery gray-green, deeply divided leaves. Full sun, occasional water. Ignored by deer. Native to South Africa. 'Viridis' has green leaves.

Euryops pectinatus 'Viridis'

Feijoa sellowiana (pineapple guava)

Zones 7-9, 12-24. Evergreen shrub or tree. 10-25' x 10-25'.

Slow-growing, easy-care shrub or multi-stemmed tree with glossy green leaves, silvery gray-green beneath, white flowers with prominent red stamens in spring, and grayish green fruit. Can be trained as espalier or pruned as a small tree. Full sun, good drainage, occasional to no water. Native to South America.

Mature *Feijoa sellowiana* pruned as multi-trunk tree

Festuca (fescue)

ZONES VARY. PERENNIAL GRASSES. SIZE VARIES.

Clump-forming grasses that make small, dense hummocks of narrow, green, blue-green, or grayish green leaves topped by erect to arching flower stalks, some tinged with pink or purple. Sun to part shade, good drainage, moderate water inland, occasional water near coast. Dig up and divide occasionally to renew. Rake out dead thatch to improve drainage.

F. amethystina, tufted fescue, 1-2' x 1', dense hummocks of narrow, almost hairlike, bluish green to blue-gray leaves and violet-tinted flower spikes. Sun or shade. Fairly drought tolerant in part shade. Native to Europe. Zones 2-10, 14-24.

F. californica, California fescue, 1-2' x 2-3', graceful, fountainlike, bluish green to blue-gray leaves and showy flower stalks rising 2' or more above the leaves. Part shade, occasional water. Native to California, Oregon, and Washington. Zones 4-9, 14-24. 'Blue Fountain' has bright blue-gray leaves and flower stalks to 4' tall. 'Serpentine Blue' is exceptionally blue-gray and seems more tolerant of hot locations.

F. idahoensis, Idaho fescue, 1-2' x 1-2', dense tufts of fine-textured, green to bluish green leaves and arching flower stalks to 3' tall, giving a fountainlike effect. Full to part sun; moderate to occasional water. Native to western North America, including the Bay Region. Zones 1-10, 14-24. 'Siskiyou Blue', once considered an especially gray form of *F. idahoensis*, is now believed to be a form of *F. ovina*, a European species.

F. occidentalis, western fescue, 1-2' x 1', dark green, tufted grass similar to *F. idahoensis* but more upright and adapted to shady conditions. Native from British Columbia to central California. Zones N/A.

Fraxinus (ash)

ZONES VARY. EVERGREEN AND DECIDUOUS TREES. SIZE VARIES.

Fast-growing, adaptable trees with large leaves divided into many leaflets. Good shade trees. Some

FESTUCA 'SISKIYOU BLUE'

BELOW: *FRAXINUS ANGUSTIFOLIA* WITH OLEANDERS

grow quite large. Most take heat and tolerate many kinds of soil.

F. angustifolia 'Raywood', Raywood ash, 25-35' x 25-35', fine-textured, compact, deciduous tree with lacy, lustrous, dark green leaves turning brilliant purplish red in fall. Good street tree. Full sun, moderate water. Zones 2-9, 12-24.

F. dipetala, California ash, 20-25' x 15-20', deciduous tree with narrow, green leaves and fragrant white flowers. Tolerates clay soils and seasonal flooding. Full sun, occasional water. Native to California and Baja California. Zones N/A.

F. uhdei, evergreen ash, 30-70' x 20-50', evergreen to partly deciduous, strongly upright to rounded tree with finely toothed, glossy, dark green leaves. Shallow-rooted. Fast-growing when young. Full sun, moderate water. Zones 9, 12-24.

F. velutina, Arizona ash, 30' x 30', deciduous, round-headed tree with narrow green leaves that turn yellow in fall. Native to California, the southwestern U.S., and Mexico. Full sun, moderate water. Zones 3-24.

ABOVE: *FREESIA* HYBRID
RIGHT: *FREMONTODENDRON CALIFORNICUM*

Freesia (freesia)

ZONES 8, 9, 12-24. PERENNIALS FROM CORMS. 6-12".

Narrow leaves in fans like little irises appear in late winter, followed by spikes of highly fragrant, tubular flowers on wiry stems in spring. Many hybrids with flowers ranging from white or yellow to lavender, purple, pink, red, bright yellow, or orange. Summer dormant. Full sun, no water. Naturalize rapidly where content. Native to South Africa.

Fremontodendron

(flannel bush)

ZONES 4-24. EVERGREEN SHRUBS OR TREES. 20' X 12-15'.

Fast-growing, short-lived, large-scale shrubs with leathery green leaves, gray felted beneath, and large, bright yellow flowers in spring followed by persistent,

bristly seed capsules. Leaves and fruit can irritate skin. Full sun, excellent drainage, no water. Ignored by deer. Native to California and Arizona.

F. californicum, common flannel bush, has roundish leaves and lemon yellow flowers in spring.

F. mexicanum, southern flannel bush, has lobed leaves and yellow-orange flowers that are larger and bloom over a longer period than *F. californicum*.

Named hybrids of the two species include 'California Glory', with long-lasting, deep yellow flowers; 'San Gabriel', with deeply incised, almost maplelike leaves; and 'Pacific Sunset', with deep orange-yellow flowers.

F. 'Ken Taylor', 4-6' x 12', is a mounding groundcover with golden yellow flowers with orange on the backs of the petals.

Garrya (silktassel)

ZONES VARY. EVERGREEN SHRUBS. SIZE VARIES.

Substantial, long-lived shrubs usually grown for their pendulous winter catkins but also attractive out of flower. Respond well to pruning as an informal hedge, small tree, or even large espalier. Afternoon shade inland, good drainage, occasional to no water.

GARRYA ELLIPTICA

G. elliptica, coast silktassel, 10-20' x 10-20', has wavy-edged, leathery, dark green leaves that are whitish and woolly beneath and long, hanging clusters of greenish yellow to greenish white flowers. Out of bloom looks something like a coast live oak. In bloom, it is unmistakable. Native to coastal California and Oregon. 'Evie' and 'James Roof' have especially dramatic flower displays. Zones 4-9, 14-24.

GAURA LINDHEIMERI 'SISKIYOU PINK'

G. fremontii, Fremont silktassel, 10' x 10', has glossy, smooth-edged, yellow green leaves and yellowish or purple catkins. Native to mountains of Washington, Oregon, California, and Arizona. Zones 3-10, 12, 14-17.

Gaura lindheimeri (gaura)

ZONES 2-24. PERENNIAL. 3-4' x 3-4'.

Airy-looking, easy plant with narrow green leaves on thin, arching stems and masses of small, fragile-looking, pink or white flowers. Blooms late spring to fall, spent flowers

dropping cleanly. Cut back to ground in winter. Self-sows and spreads underground, sometimes aggressively; best in confined planting areas. Full sun to part shade, good drainage, moderate to occasional water. Attractive to butterflies and bees. Native to southern U.S. and Mexico. 'Siskiyou Pink', 2-3' x 2-3', has green leaves mottled with maroon and dark pink flowers. 'Whirling Butterflies', 2-3' x 2-3', has pure white flowers from pink buds.

Gazania (gazania)

GAZANIA HYBRID

ZONES 8-24. PERENNIALS. SIZE VARIES.

Clumping or trailing perennials with green or gray-green leaves and colorful daisylike flowers spring to fall. Full sun, moderate to occasional water. Good seaside plants. Native to South Africa. Usually offered as named cultivars.

Clumping forms, 6-12" x 6-12", have dark green, usually lobed leaves with gray-woolly undersides and large flowers in yellow, orange, white, or rose-pink, sometimes multi-colored, often with darker centers. Trailing gazanias, 6-12" x 2-3', have silvery gray-green leaves and yellow, white, orange, or bronzy flowers. Clumpers are best as accents and fillers; tend not to fill in large areas. Trailing kinds are effective on banks or spilling over a wall.

Gilia (gilia)

GILIA TRICOLOR

ZONES 1-24. ANNUALS. SIZE VARIES.

Delicate-looking plants with finely divided, feathery leaves and colorful flowers in spring and summer. Full sun, good drainage, occasional water. Native to western North America, including California.

G. achilleifolia, blue gilia, 18-30" x 8-18", bushy plant with small clusters of deep blue to blue-violet flowers.

G. capitata, blue thimble flower, 8-30" x 8-12", has pale blue to blue-violet flowers in small, dense clusters resembling pincushions.

G. tricolor, bird's eyes, 12-18" x 8-12", has small, blue-violet flowers with striking pale blue pollen.

Ginkgo biloba (maidenhair tree)

ZONES 1-10, 12, 14-24. DECIDUOUS TREE. 50-80' x 25-50'.

Slow-growing, graceful tree noted for its brilliant yellow fall color, particularly stunning when leaves are left to carpet the ground like golden snow. Full sun, reasonable drainage, moderate water. Tolerates heat and drought. Native to China. 'Autumn Gold' is narrowly symmetrical when young, eventually spreading. 'Fairmount' is pyramidal. 'Saratoga' is upright, with a strong central leader. 'Jade Butterflies' is a smaller tree with particularly large, deeply lobed leaves and lacks the awkward juvenile character of the full-size ginkgo selections.

GINKGO BILOBA

Gladiolus (gladiolus)

ZONES 4-9, 12-24. PERENNIALS FROM CORMS. 1-2' x 1-2'.

GLADIOLUS CALLIANTHUS

Sword-shaped leaves and tubular flowers in many colors. Summer-flowering kinds require regular water. Spring-blooming, summer-dormant kinds such as those listed here are best for summer-dry climates. Full sun, good drainage, no water. Native to South Africa.

G. callianthus has widely flaring, white flowers with dark purple petal bases on tall stems.

G. tristis has widely flaring, creamy white to pale yellow fragrant flowers with darker yellow markings.

Glaucium (horned poppy)

ZONES VARY. PERENNIALS AND BIENNIALS. SIZE VARIES.

GLAUCIUM GRANDIFLORUM

Mounding plants with lobed or divided, grayish green leaves and summer flowers followed by long, slender seed capsules. Full sun, moderate water.

G. corniculatum, 12-18" x 12-18", biennial with red-orange flowers. Native to Europe and southwest Asia. Zones 2-24.

G. flavum, 1-3' x 18", perennial with blue-gray leaves, ruffled along the edges, and brilliant yellow or orange flowers. Native to the Mediterranean. Zones 8-24.

GREVILLEA LAVANDULACEA 'JADE PEARL'

G. grandiflorum, perennial forming compact rosettes of gray-green leaves and soft orange flowers with a darker orange spot at the base of each petal. Native to the Mediterranean. Zones N/A.

Grevillea (grevillea)

ZONES VARY. EVERGREEN SHRUBS AND TREES. SIZE VARIES.

Varied group of generally fine-textured plants ranging from small to medium-sized to large shrubs or trees with ferny, lobed, or needlelike leaves and spidery to brushlike flowers in fall, winter, or early spring. Attractive to hummingbirds. Full sun to part shade, good drainage, little to no water. Some are tender. Tolerate drought, heat, poor soils. Native to Australia. Many species and cultivars. Needle-leaved kinds ignored by deer.

G. lanigera, woolly grevillea, 3-6' x 6-10', variable shrub with hairy leaves and branchlets, giving the plant an overall grayish cast, and bright pink or reddish pink and cream flowers in spring. Zones 15-24.

G. lavandulacea is a variable shrub with needlelike leaves. 'Penola', 3-5' x 4', has gray-green leaves on arching branches and rose-red flowers in fall and winter. 'Jade Pearl', 4-6' x 8', has rose-red and creamy white flowers in winter and spring and forest-green leaves with a silvery cast. Zones 15-24.

G. robusta, silk oak, 50-60' x 30-35', fast-growing tree with ferny, dark green leaves, grayish white beneath, and large clusters of golden orange flowers in early spring. Thrives in heat. Zones 8, 9, 12-24.

G. rosmarinifolia, rosemary grevillea, 6' x 6', tough, hardy shrub with prickly, narrow green leaves, dark green on top and silvery beneath, and clusters of red and cream flowers in winter. 'Scarlet Sprite' grows about half as tall. Zones 8, 9, 12-24.

Hardenbergia (lilac vine)

ZONES VARY. EVERGREEN VINES. 10-12'.

Somewhat tender, twining vines with dark green leaves and showy clusters of small, lavender-purple, rose, or white flowers that resemble tiny sweet peas. Bloom late winter to early spring. Best near coast. Full sun to part shade, good drainage, moderate water. Native to Australia.

HARDENBERGIA VIOLACEA 'HAPPY WANDERER'

H. comptoniana has glossy, dark green leaves divided into three leaflets and violet-blue flowers in pendulous clusters. More tender than *H. violacea*. Zones 15-24.

H. violacea has undivided, leathery, dark green leaves with prominent veins and lilac, deep violet, rosy pink, or white flowers. Zones 8-24. 'Happy Wanderer' is especially vigorous, with pinkish purple flowers. 'Alba' has white flowers.

HELIANTHEMUM NUMMULARIUM 'WISLEY PINK'

Helianthemum nummularium (sunrose)

ZONES 2-9, 14-24. EVERGREEN SHRUB. 6-8" x 18"-3'.

Low-growing shrub with green or gray-green, softly downy leaves and single or double flowers in bright or pale shades of red, orange, yellow, pink, peach, or white. Each flower lasts just a day, but new buds open from late spring to early summer. Light shearing may promote rebloom. Full sun to part shade, excellent drainage, occasional water. Good coastal plant. Ignored by deer. Native to Turkey.

Many named cultivars. 'Stoplight' has gray-green leaves and brick-red flowers. 'Wisley Pink' has gray leaves and large pink flowers. 'Henfield Brilliant' has silvery gray leaves and coppery orange flowers.

Helictotrichon sempervirens (blue oat grass)

 ZONES 1-24. PERENNIAL GRASS. 2-3' X 2-3'.

 Handsome cool-season grass that forms a spiky mound of narrow, blue-gray leaves with tall stems bearing upright plumes of straw-colored flowers in late spring or early summer. Full sun, good drainage, occasional water near coast, moderate water inland. Rake out dead thatch to improve drainage. Native to the Mediterranean. 'Sapphire' has narrower, slightly bluer leaves.

HELICTOTRICHON SEMPERVIRENS WITH HELIOPSIS, ASCLEPIAS, AND ACHILLEA

Helleborus (hellebore)

 ZONES VARY. PERENNIALS. SIZE VARIES.

Varied group of shade-loving perennials grown for attractive foliage and flowers. Many of the most widely grown hellebores

HELLEBORUS X *STERNII* WITH PHORMIUM BEHIND

(e.g., *H. niger*, *H. orientalis*) prefer regular water. Those below are quite content with ...oderate to occasional water in shade. Ignored by deer. Native to southern Europe ...d Asia.

...argutifolius, Corsican hellebore, 2-3' x 2-3', erect or sprawling perennial with large, ...ue-green leaves divided into sharply toothed leaflets and clusters of pale green ...wers in winter and spring. Native to Corsica and Sardinia. Zones 3-9, 14-24.

...oetidus, bear's foot hellebore, 30" x 30", has dark green leaves divided into long, ...row leaflets and clusters of light green flowers with purplish red edges. Native to ...rope. Zones 2-9, 14-24.

...vidus, 30" x 3', has blue-green leaves, purple on the undersides, and clusters of pale ...n flowers with a pinkish purple tinge in winter and spring. Native to Majorca. ...es 6-9, 14-24.

...ternii, 2-3' x 2-3', has bluish ...n leaves with creamy white ...ng and greenish white flowers ...a pinkish tinge in winter and ...g. Zones 4-9, 14-24.

...eraloe parviflora

(...ucca)

...2, 3, 7-16, 18-24. PERENNIAL. ...4'.

...ounding clump of almost ...nt, grasslike leaves with ...ellow filaments on the ...and tall, arching spikes of ...ellow flowers in late summer. ...ve to hummingbirds. Full ...d drainage, occasional ...hrives in heat. Native to ...nd New Mexico.

...omeles arbutifolia

(...)

...5-9, 14-24. EVERGREEN SHRUB ...E. 10-20' x 10-15'.

...e, long-lived shrub with dark ...n, leathery leaves with serrated margins, clusters of white flowers in early summer, and masses of bright red-orange berries in fall and winter. Good habitat plant. Full sun to part shade, good drainage, little to no water. Native to California and Baja California. 'Davis Gold' has narrow leaves and orange berries.

ABOVE: *HESPERALOE PARVIFLORA* LEFT: *HETEROMELES ARBUTIFOLIA* BERRIES

Heterotheca villosa (goldenaster)

ZONES N/A. PERENNIAL. 1' x 1'.

Low-growing perennial with softly hairy, gray-green leaves and golden yellow, daisylike flowers in summer. Full sun to part shade, good drainage, moderate to occasional water. Native to much of western North America, including California. 'San Bruno Mountain' forms a low mat of trailing stems with narrow, dark green leaves and flowers in late spring to summer.

HETEROTHECA VILLOSA

Heuchera (coral bells, alum root)

ZONES VARY. PERENNIALS. SIZE VARIES.

Compact clumps of rounded or heart-shaped, evergreen leaves with scalloped edges and graceful stalks bearing tiny, bell-shaped flowers from early spring to summer. Especially effective massed, when the delicate flowers seem to hover like a mist above the leaves. Part shade, good drainage, moderate to occasional water. Attractive to

HEUCHERA MAXIMA

hummingbirds. Many cultivars, mostly selected or bred for foliage color, may require more water.

H. maxima, island alum root, 1-2' x 3-4', has dark green, heart-shaped leaves and white or pinkish white flowers in early spring. Native to the Channel Islands. Zones 15-24.

H. micrantha, 1' x 1-2', has bronzy green leaves and dainty, creamy white flowers on reddish 2' stalks. A little more cold tolerant than *H. maxima*. Native from California north to British Columbia. Zones 1-10, 14-24.

Holodiscus discolor (cream bush, ocean spray)

ZONES 1-9, 14-19. DECIDUOUS SHRUB. 3-10' x 4-8'.

Open, upright, wild-looking shrub that provides a lengthy seasonal display. Tiny, creamy white flowers in long, pendulous, branched clusters are showy from late spring into summer, turning brownish tan as they dry in fall. Green leaves take on reddish to burgundy fall color, and clusters of seeds persist on bare branches into winter. Attractive to birds and bees. Good habitat plant for low-maintenance areas. Full sun to full shade, moderate to occasional water. Native to western North America.

Hyssopus officinalis (hyssop)

ZONES 1-24. PERENNIAL. 2' x 1'.

Compact plant with narrow, glossy, aromatic, dark green leaves and spikes of dark blue flowers in summer. Full sun to part shade, good drainage, moderate water. Attractive to butterflies and bees. Native to the Mediterranean. Some varieties have pink, purple, or white flowers.

Ipheion uniflorum (spring starflower)

ZONES 2-24. PERENNIAL FROM BULB. 4-12" x 6-8".

Summer-dormant bulb with strap-shaped leaves with a mildly oniony fragrance and late winter to early spring display of pure white, lavender, or clear blue, star-shaped flowers. Sun to part shade, good drainage, no summer water. Effective massed in open woodland or grassy meadow planting. Naturalizes rapidly by bulb offsets and seed. Native to South America. 'Alberto Castillo' has glaucous, white-dusted foliage and pure white flowers. 'Froyle Mill' has flattish, fragrant flowers of a luminous violet blue. 'Rolf Fiedler' has bright blue flowers with contrasting yellow anthers in spring and early summer.

TOP: *HOLODISCUS DISCOLOR* MIDDLE: *HYSSOPUS OFFICINALIS* BOTTOM: *IPHEION UNIFLORUM*

141

Iris (iris)

ZONES VARY. PERENNIALS FROM BULBS AND RHIZOMES. SIZE VARIES.

Dormant in summer and sending up leaves and flowers in late winter or early spring, many irises are ideal plants for dry-summer climates. There are water-loving irises, however, so select with care.

PACIFIC COAST IRIS 'COPPER' WITH *EUPHORBIA DULCIS* 'CHAMELEON'

So-called Dutch irises, which are native to the Mediterranean, grow from small bulbs, sending up thin, floppy leaves in late winter and elegant flowers with narrow petals on straight, tall stems in early spring. Summer-dormant, they prefer no summer water. Zones 2-24. 'Wedgewood' has large, lavender blue flowers with yellow markings in early spring.

Bearded irises, which grow from rhizomes, are dwarf to medium to tall, with fans of broad, flat leaves and medium to large, often ruffled flowers in a wide range of colors in spring. Full sun in cool-summer areas, afternoon shade in hot interior locations. Some highly bred forms are fairly fussy about soil, drainage, and timing of water. Old-fashioned varieties bloom year after year with virtually no care. Zones 1-24.

Pacific Coast hybrid irises are especially well suited to the Bay Region, wherever excellent drainage and dry summer dormancy can be assured. These native irises share the traits of other plants in the genus, including grasslike leaves, upright flower stems, and flowers with three petals and three sepals in bright colors, often with intricate markings. Each flower lasts only a few days, but another soon replaces it during the three- to four-week flowering season. The foliage usually ranges from ankle height to just below knee height. Many will take full sun along the coast, but in hot inland gardens they need light shade. Some

PACIFIC COAST IRIS 'CANYON SNOW' WITH *ERIGERON*

require regular summer water (*I. missouriensis*), others accept an occasional sprinkling (*I. douglasiana*), and some require a dry summer dormancy (*I. fernaldii, I. hartwegii, I. macrosiphon, I. munzii, I. purdyi,* and *I. tenuissina*). Zones 4-9, 14-24.

Isopogon formosus (rose coneflower)

ZONES 15-24. EVERGREEN SHRUB. 4-6' X 3-4'.

Erect, narrow shrub with finely divided, bright green leaves resembling those of some grevilleas and heads of rosy lavender flowers in late winter or spring. Full sun to part shade, good drainage, occasional water. Good cut flower. Native to Australia.

Ixia (African corn lily)

ZONES 7-9, 12-24. PERENNIALS FROM CORMS. 12-18" X 12".

Summer-dormant perennials with clumps of narrow, green, grasslike leaves and short spikes of brilliantly colored flowers in late spring. Full sun, good drainage, no summer water. Native to South America.

Jacaranda mimosifolia (jacaranda)

ZONES 12, 13, 15-24. DECIDUOUS TREE. 25-40' X 15-30'.

Spectacular lavender-blue spring flowers in pendulous, foot-long clusters are the main attraction of this sometimes multi-trunked specimen tree. Flowers are followed by

TOP: *ISOPOGON FORMOSUS*
MIDDLE: *IXIA MACULATA*
BOTTOM: *JACARANDA MIMOSIFOLIA* WITH *HIBISCUS SYRIACUS*

woody seedpods that add interest to arrangements. Finely divided, ferny leaves may appear before or with flowers. Tender. Full sun, good drainage, moderate water, protection from wind. Needs summer heat to flower well. Native to South America.

JASMINUM POLYANTHUM

Jasminum polyanthum
(pink jasmine)

☀ ☀
◖ ◖

ZONES 5-9, 12-24. EVERGREEN VINE. 20'.

Fast-growing vine with shiny, dark green leaves and dense clusters of intensely fragrant, star-shaped, white flowers from pink buds in late winter and spring. Quickly blankets arbor, fence, or ground; can be espaliered. Cut back after flowering to control ranginess and promote next year's bloom. Full sun to part shade, moderate to occasional water. In hot locations, roots need shade. Native to China.

Jubaea chilensis
(Chilean wine palm)

ZONES 12-24. PALM. 50-60' x 25'.

☀ ☀
◖

Regal palm with stiff, feathery fronds, dull green above and gray-green beneath, and an exceptionally broad, interestingly textured, gray trunk. Small purple flowers and yellow fruit not showy. Fronds self-pruning. Long-lived but slow-growing, taking decades to achieve mature

JUBAEA CHILENSIS

size. Full sun to light shade, occasional water. Takes cold but not extreme heat. Native to Chile.

Juniperus (juniper)

ZONES VARY. EVERGREEN SHRUBS. SIZE VARIES.

Slow-growing, long-lived plants ranging from flat groundcovers to large shrubs to trees with green to gray-green or bluish green foliage consisting of short needles or overlapping scales. Excellent choice for unwatered slopes. Full sun to part shade, good drainage, no water.

JUNIPERUS SABINA 'BUFFALO'

Best choices for most landscapes are the low-growing kinds, as some of the larger junipers can build up dense masses of dead material, highly flammable and difficult to remove. Most plants offered are named cultivars.

J. communis, 12" x 6-8', is prostrate with gray to gray-green foliage and trailing branches upturned at the tips. Native to California. Zones 1-24.

KNIPHOFIA CITRINA

J. sabina, savin juniper, ranges from mat-forming groundcovers to spreading, sometimes upright shrubs with green, scalelike leaves. 'Buffalo', 1' x 8' is one of the lowest. Zones 1-24.

Kniphofia (red-hot poker)

ZONES VARY. PERENNIALS. SIZE VARIES.

Green to blue-green, lancelike leaves and showy, upright spikes of tightly packed and overlapping, oblong, pendulous flowers in many shades of red, orange, yellow, or cream. Full sun to part shade, moderate to occasional water. Attractive to hummingbirds. Ignored by deer. Native to South Africa. Most plants offered are cultivars.

K. citrina, 2' x 2', small but vigorous grower with dark bluish green leaves. Flowers at the top of the spike are tangerine; lower flowers age from greenish yellow to yellow to creamy green. Zones 2-9, 14-24.

K. uvaria, 2-3' x 2-3', has green leaves and coral-red buds opening to orange or yellow flowers. Zones 2-9, 14-24.

Koelreuteria paniculata
(goldenrain tree)

KOELREUTERIA PANICULATA

ZONES 2-24. DECIDUOUS TREE.
20-35' x 20-40'.

Showy small tree with dark green leaves
turning yellow-orange in fall and large
clusters of yellow summer flowers followed
by papery seed capsules that resemble small
lanterns. Deep rooted. Good patio,
specimen, or street tree. Full sun,
reasonable drainage, moderate water.
Native to Asia. 'Rose Lantern' has
distinctive rose-pink seed capsules.
'September' has yellowish green seed capsules that turn reddish brown.

BELOW: *LAGERSTROEMIA*
INDICA 'WATERMELON'

Lagerstroemia indica (crape myrtle)

ZONES 7-10, 12-14, 18-21. DECIDUOUS SHRUB OR TREE. 25' x 15-25'.

Shrubby tree with peeling orange and gray bark, shiny green leaves turning orange-

red in fall, and dense clusters of crinkled, crepelike flowers in white to pink to reddish purple in summer to fall. Flowers best with winter chill and summer heat. Full sun, good drainage, moderate to occasional water. Tolerates drought, thrives in heat; can mildew in coastal climates. Good small street tree or patio tree. Native to India, China, and Korea. Many named hybrids of different sizes and flower colors, some resistant to mildew.

Lantana (lantana)

ZONES 8-10, 12-24.
EVERGREEN SHRUBS. 2' x 3-5'.

Mounding or trailing shrubs with dark green leaves tinged with red in winter and prolific displays of lilac, yellow, or white flowers in summer. Full sun, good drainage, occasional water. Attractive to butterflies and bees. Ignored by deer. Most plants offered are cultivars of two South American natives, *L. camara* and *L. montevidensis*.

LEFT: *Lantana* 'New Gold' with rosemary
BELOW: *Laurus nobilis*

Laurus nobilis (sweet bay, Grecian laurel)

ZONES 5-9, 12-24.
EVERGREEN TREE OR SHRUB. 12-40'x 12-40'.

Multi-stemmed tree or shrub with smooth, gray bark, leathery, dark green, aromatic leaves, and small, creamy white to yellow spring flowers followed by blue-black berries. Full sun to part shade, good drainage, moderate to occasional water. Good specimen or informal screen. Native to the Mediterranean. 'Aurea' has golden yellow new leaves. 'Saratoga' has broader, dark green leaves and a more upright growth habit.

Lavandula (lavender)

 ZONES VARY. EVERGREEN SHRUBS. SIZE VARIES.

Mounding to upright small shrubs with aromatic, green to gray-green or silvery gray, needlelike leaves and spikes of lavender to purple flowers. Full sun, good drainage, occasional water. Wonderful massed or mixed in dryish borders. Cut back annually to renew; replace when plants become leggy or woody. Attractive to butterflies and bees. Native to the Mediterranean. Many named cultivars.

BELOW: RIVER OF LAVENDER ON HILLSIDE WITH ORNAMENTAL GRASSES

L. angustifolia, English lavender, 1'-2' x 2'-3', has gray-green or silvery gray leaves and lavender to purple flowers on tall stems well above the leaves in summer. Zones 2-24. 'Hidcote' has bright gray-green leaves and deep purple flowers. 'Munstead' has lavender-blue flowers. 'Sachet' has short spikes of large, bright violet flowers.

L. dentata, French lavender, 3-4' x 4-6', has green or gray-green leaves and purple flowers topped with colorful bracts from spring into summer. Zones 8, 9, 12-24.

BELOW LEFT TO RIGHT: *LAVANDULA STOECHAS* 'MADRID WHITE' *L. ANGUSTIFOLIA* 'SACHET' *L. X INTERMEDIA* 'HIDCOTE GIANT' *L. STOECHAS*

L. x *intermedia*, hedge lavender, variable hybrid usually offered as named cultivars. 'Grosso' is especially fragrant and has bright lavender flowers. Zones 4-24. 'Hidcote Giant' has large, blue-violet flowers on tall stems.

L. stoechas, Spanish lavender, 3' x 2-3', erect and dense with short clusters of

summer flowers with large bracts giving the flowerhead the look of a small purple butterfly. Probably the tidiest, most drought tolerant, and most durable lavender, especially for coastal areas. Zones 4-24. 'Otto Quast' has deep purple flowers with dark purple bracts. 'Madrid White' has white flowers. 'Papillon' has long, lavender-purple bracts.

L. 'Goodwin Creek Grey', 2-3' x 2-3', is upright and dense, with silvery gray leaves and deep lavender to violet flowers almost all summer. Zones 8, 9, 12-24.

LEFT: *L.* X *INTERMEDIA* 'PROVENCE'
BELOW: *L. STOECHAS* 'PAPILLON'

Lavatera (tree mallow)

ZONES VARY. EVERGREEN SHRUBS, ANNUAL. SIZE VARIES.

Easy, fast-growing, upright plants with lobed, green to gray-green leaves and large, long-blooming flowers. Full sun, good drainage, moderate to occasional water. Tolerate heat, wind, drought, and salt spray. Prune to promote flowering.

L. assurgentiflora, 6-12' x 6-12', erect, evergreen shrub with pinkish purple flowers with white centers in spring and summer. Native to the Channel Islands of southern California. Zones 14-24.

Lavatera maritima, 3-6' x 3-5', is an evergreen shrub with gray-green leaves and whitish pink summer flowers with dark rose veining, deep rose-purple at the base, and reflexed petals. Needs part shade in hot climates. Native to the Mediterrranean. Zones 6-9, 12-24.

L. thuringiaca, 6-8' x 4', evergreen shrub with purplish pink flowers. Native to the Mediterranean. Zones 2-9, 14-24. 'Barnsley' has light pink flowers with darker pink centers.

THIS PAGE, CLOCKWISE FROM TOP RIGHT: *LAVATERA ASSURGENTIFLORA*, *L. MARITIMA*, *L.* 'SHORTY', *L.* 'COTTON CANDY' OPPOSITE: *L. THURINGIACA* 'BARNSLEY' WITH *PENSTEMON* 'EVELYN'

Layia platyglossa (tidytips)

ZONES 1-10, 14-24. ANNUAL. 6-18" X 6-12".

Fast-growing annual with narrow, green to gray-green leaves and neatly white-tipped, yellow, daisylike flowers in spring and early summer. Full sun, good drainage, little to no water. Attractive to butterflies. Good seaside plant. Effective on sunny hillsides and in meadow plantings. This California native may carpet the ground with yellow in valley grasslands or coastal habitats.

LAYIA PLATYGLOSSA

Leonotis leonurus (lion's tail)

ZONES 8-24. EVERGREEN SHRUB. 4-6' X 4-6'.

Robust, fast-growing, upright shrub with narrow, toothed, dark green leaves, velvety on the undersides, and velvety, vivid orange flowers in tiered whorls along tall stalks in fall. Attractive to butterflies, birds, and bees. Full sun, excellent drainage, moderate to little water. Plants may be lost in cold, wet winters. Native to South Africa.

LEONOTIS LEONURUS

Lepechinia (pitcher sage)

ZONES 7-9, 14-24. EVERGREEN SHRUBS. SIZE VARIES.

Easy, fast-growing, evergreen shrubs with softly hairy or felty, aromatic, green or grayish green leaves and short spikes of white, pale pink, or lavender, tubular flowers in spring or summer. Full sun with afternoon shade, good drainage, little to no water. Attractive to hummingbirds. Ignored by deer.

LEPECHINIA FRAGRANS

L. calycina, 3-5' x 1-2', has bright green, lance-shaped leaves and lavender flowers. Native to California.

L. fragrans, 3-5' x 2-3', has green leaves and pinkish white flowers in spring and summer. Native to California.

L. hastata, 3-4' x 2', has large, felty, gray-green leaves and reddish purple to magenta flowers in summer. Spreads by underground rhizomes. Native to Mexico and Hawaii.

Leptospermum (tea tree)

ZONES 14-24. EVERGREEN SHRUBS OR TREES. SIZE VARIES.

Long-lived, easy-care, fine-textured shrubs and small trees with masses of small white, pink, or red flowers in spring. Full sun, good drainage, occasional water. Best near coast, but fine inland with moderate water and protection from hard frost. Ignored by deer.

L. laevigatum, Australian tea tree, 10-30' x 10-30', has narrow, grayish green, rounded leaves and small white flowers. Old specimens are picturesque, with shaggy, gray bark and twisted branches. Native to Australia. 'Reevesii', 4-5' x 4-5', has larger leaves.

L. rotundifolium, 6' x 9', variable shrub with arching branches, tiny rounded gray-green leaves, and white, pink, or purplish pink flowers. 'Manning's Choice' has deep lavender-pink flowers.

L. scoparium, New Zealand tea tree, 3-6' x 4-8', has gray-green, needlelike leaves and showier flowers than *L. laevigatum*. Flowers range from white to red to many shades of pink. Good in arrangements. Native to Australia and New Zealand. Many named cultivars. 'Ruby Glow', 'Gaiety Girl' and 'Pink Pearl' are double-flowered varieties.

TOP: *LEPTOSPERMUM SCOPARIUM* 'RUBY GLOW'
BOTTOM: *L. ROTUNDIFOLIUM* 'MANNING'S CHOICE'

Lessingia (California aster)

ZONES N/A. PERENNIALS, ANNUALS.
SIZE VARIES.

Variable group of prostrate or erect annuals, perennials, and subshrubs native to California, the southwestern U.S., and Mexico, usually with grayish green to woolly, gray-white leaves and white, yellow, or lavender, daisylike flowers, typically with yellow centers. Some are native to small areas and are endangered (e.g. *L. germanorum*, San Francisco lessingia, which occurs only on San Francisco dunes). The following is available in nurseries.

LESSINGIA FILAGINIFOLIA 'SILVER CARPET'

L. filaginifolia 'Silver Carpet', 6-12" x 2-3', mat-forming perennial with gray-green

LEUCADENDRON 'SAFARI SUNSET'

leaves and lavender-pink, daisylike flowers in late summer and fall. Full sun, good drainage, moderate to occasional water.

Leucadendron
(leucadendron)

ZONES 16, 17, 20-24. EVERGREEN TREES AND SHRUBS. SIZE VARIES.

Upright, narrow or slightly spreading shrubs and trees with tiny flowers in conelike heads and showy bracts in winter. Striking in arrangements. Full sun, good drainage, moderate water. Good seaside plants. Prefer acid soils, some humidity, good air circulation. Not easy in gardens. Tender. Native to South Africa.

Leucojum (snowflake)

☼ ZONES VARY. PERENNIALS FROM BULBS. 12-18" X 12-18".

💧 Carefree, fall- or winter-blooming bulbs with narrow, strap-shaped leaves and nodding, white, bell-shaped flowers tipped with green. Full sun with afternoon shade, occasional water during summer dormancy. Naturalize where content. *L. aestivum*, summer snowflake, flowers in early spring. Native to Europe. 'Gravetye Giant' has many large flowers on each stem. Zones 1-10, 14-24. *L. autumnale*, autumn snowflake, flowers in fall. Native to the Mediterranean. Zones N/A.

LEUCOJUM AESTIVUM
'GRAVETYE GIANT'

Leucophyllum frutescens (Texas ranger)

☼ ZONES 7-24. EVERGREEN SHRUB. 6-8' X 6-8'.

💧 Slow-growing, rounded shrub with softly felted, bluish gray leaves and small lavender-pink flowers in spring or summer. Full sun, excellent drainage, occasional water. Tolerates heat, wind, and alkaline soil. Best in hot, interior locations; grows well but flowers poorly near the coast. Native to southwestern North America and Mexico. 'Compacta' grows 5' tall and wide. 'White Cloud' has white flowers.

LEUCOPHYLLUM FRUTESCENS

Leucospermum (pincushion)

ZONES 15-17, 21-24. EVERGREEN SHRUBS.
4-8' x 6-8'.

ABOVE: *LEUCOSPERMUM*
REFLEXUM WITH ALOES
RIGHT: *L. CORDIFOLIUM*

Tender and temperamental, not easy to grow, but fabulous late-winter to spring flowers in clusters resembling pincushions, dramatic in fresh and dried arrangements. Best near coast. Sensitive to both heat and frost. Full sun, excellent drainage, moderate water. Native to South Africa. Various species and named hybrids have flowers ranging from yellow to pale or bright orange to red-orange.

Leymus (lyme grass, wild rye)

ZONES VARY. PERENNIAL GRASSES. SIZE VARIES.

Bold and dramatic cool-season grasses with blue-gray to blue-green leaves and a tendency to spread by underground rhizomes. This can be a plus where erosion control is needed over large areas, but elsewhere these rampant spreaders may need to be contained. Sun to part sun, occasional water.

L. cinereus, 3-4' x 3-4', ashy wild rye, large-scaled, bold grass with pale green to grayish blue leaves aging to tawny straw color in summer. Thick, bristly flowers spikes add vertical accent to the clump. Prefers hot, interior locations, where it does best with occasional water. Native to eastern mountains of California and southern Canada. Zones N/A.

L. condensatus 'Canyon Prince', 4' x 3', is a compact, silvery blue-leaved, smaller and less rampant cultivar of a vigorous grass that grows too large and spreads too aggressively for most landscapes. The species is native to southwestern California and Mexico. Zones 7-12, 14-24.

L. triticoides, creeping wild rye, 1-3' x 1-2', has narrow green leaves. 'Grey Dawn' grows a little wider and has gray-green leaves. Zones N/A.

Liatris (blazing star, gayfeather)

ZONES VARY. PERENNIALS. SIZE VARIES.

Erect stems topped by showy spikes of purple, rose-purple, or white flowers in late summer arise from clumps of slender, grasslike leaves. Full sun, good drainage, good air circulation, moderate to occasional water. Attractive to butterflies and bees. Good cut flowers. Can be invasive. Native to central and eastern North America.

L. aspera, 3-5' x 1-2', has pinkish purple flowers and blooms later than *L. spicata*. Zones N/A.

L. punctata, 2-3' x 1-2', has fine, blue-green, slightly hairy leaves heavily dotted with resin and violet flowers. Zones N/A.

L. spicata, 18"-3' x 1-2', the most commonly available blazing star, has lavender or lilac flowers. Zones 1-10, 14-24.

Ligustrum japonicum

(Japanese privet)

ZONES 4-24. EVERGREEN SHRUB. 10-12'x 8'.

Resilient, long-lived shrub with dark green, waxy leaves and showy clusters of small white flowers in late spring followed by blue-black berries. Easily trimmed as a hedge or small tree, but leaves too large for shearing to be attractive. Sun, afternoon shade in hot areas, occasional water. Reseeds readily. Native to Japan and Korea. 'Rotundifolium', 5' x 3', has smaller leaves; good for narrow places, partial shade. 'Texanum', 8-10' x 4-6', has dense, lush foliage.

ABOVE: *LEYMUS CONDENSATUS* 'CANYON PRINCE' WITH *ARTEMISIA PYCNOCEPHALA* 'DAVID'S CHOICE'
LEFT: *LIATRIS PUNCTATA*

LIGUSTRUM JAPONICUM

Limonium perezii
(sea lavender, statice)

  Zones 13, 15-17, 20-24. Perennial. 12-18" x 2-3'.

Tender perennial forming clumps of large, leathery, green, basal leaves and rounded clusters of tiny, papery, pale purple and white flowers on tall stalks in summer. Full sun to part shade, good drainage, occasional water. Best near coast. Flowers long-lasting fresh or dried. Native to the Mediterranean.

RIGHT: *Limonium perezii*
BELOW: *Linanthus grandiflorus* (WHITE) WITH *Echium vulgare* AND *Eschscholzia californica*

Linanthus grandiflorus (large-flowered linanthus)

Zones 1-9, 14-24. Annual. 2' x 1'.

Dainty annual with fine, lush green, ferny leaves and dense clusters of pink-tinged white flowers spring to fall. Full sun to part shade, occasional water. Native to coastal northern California.

Linum (flax)

ZONES VARY. PERENNIALS AND
ANNUALS. SIZE VARIES.

Graceful, upright or mounding
plants with narrow leaves on
branching stems and cheerful
display of yellow, blue, red,
pink, or white flowers in spring
and summer. Full sun, excellent
drainage, moderate to occasional water. May be lost to rot or fungus in wet winters.

LINUM GRANDIFLORUM

L. flavum, golden flax, 12-18" x 18", perennial, upright in full sun, floppy in shade, with
bright green leaves and rich golden-yellow flowers. Likes heat and dry soils. Native to
central and southern Europe. 'Compactum', 6-8" x
8", is mounding, with almost continuous flowers
from spring to fall. Zones 2-24.

LOPHOSTEMON CONFERTUS

L. grandiflorum, flowering flax, 18-30" x 1', annual
with gray-green leaves and rosy red or pink
flowers in summer. Self-sows but is easily pulled.
Native to North Africa and naturalized in North
America. 'Bright Eyes' has white flowers.
'Rubrum' has scarlet flowers. Zones 1-24.

L. lewisii, 2-3' x 1-2', perennial with gray-green
leaves and true blue flowers on tall stems above
the leaves. Quite drought tolerant. Native from
Alaska to southern California. Zones N/A.

L. narbonense, 2' x 18", perennial with narrow, blue-
green leaves and open clusters of sky-blue flowers
with white centers. Native to the Mediterranean.
Zones 3-24.

L. perenne, blue flax, 2' x 18", perennial with
branched clusters of blue flowers from late spring
through summer. Cut back after flowering to
maintain bushiness. Accepts part shade. Native to
Europe and Asia. Zones 2-24.

Lophostemon confertus (Brisbane box)

ZONES 15-17, 19-24. EVERGREEN TREE. 30-45' x 25'.

Fast-growing, tender tree with a straight trunk,
reddish brown, flaking bark, leathery, bright green
leaves, and feathery white flowers in summer
followed by woody seed capsules. Best along
coast. Native to Australia. Full sun, occasional to
little water.

Luma apiculata (Chilean myrtle)

ZONES 14-24. EVERGREEN SHRUB OR TREE. 6-15' x 6-20'.

Fast-growing shrub or tree with small, dark green, aromatic leaves and small, white or pale pink flowers in summer, followed by abundant blue-black berries. Bark is cinnamon-brown and peeling on older plants. Sun to part shade, good drainage, moderate to occasional water. Good hedge or screen, nice specimen. Ignored by deer. Native to Chile.

Lupinus (lupine)

ZONES VARY. ANNUALS, PERENNIALS, EVERGREEN SHRUBS. SIZE VARIES.

Distinctive leaves divided into many leaflets and dense spikes of fragrant flowers resembling sweet peas. Full sun, excellent drainage, little to no water. Attractive to butterflies and bees. Usually ignored by deer. Perennial lupines need more water.

L. albifrons, silver bush lupine, 3-5' x 3-5', evergreen shrub with silvery gray-green leaves and purple flowers in spring to midsummer. Native from southern Oregon to Baja California. Zones N/A.

L. arboreus, 5-8' x 5-8', evergreen shrub with clusters of yellow, lilac, or white flowers in spring. Native to coastal California. Invasive in some north coastal dunes. Zones 4, 5, 14-17, 22-24.

L. microcarpus var. *densiflorus*, 1-2' x 1-2', annual with white, yellow, pink, or lavender flowers in tall spikes in spring. Native from California to British Columbia. Zones 3-24. 'Ed Gedling' has bright yellow flowers.

L. nanus, sky lupine, 6"-2' x 8"-1', annual with blue spring flowers. Self-sows. Native from California to British Columbia. Zones 3-24.

Lychnis coronaria (rose campion)

ZONES 1-9, 14-24. PERENNIAL. 18-24" x 12-18".

Short-lived perennial with downy, whitish gray leaves and bright magenta flowers in summer. Self-sows freely but easily pulled in small areas. Sun or light shade, little water. Native to southeastern Europe. 'Alba' has white flowers.

Lyonothamnus floribundus (Catalina ironwood)

ZONES 14-17, 19-24. EVERGREEN TREE. SIZE 30-50' x 15-25'.

Fast-growing, single- or multi-trunked tree with reddish brown, scaly, shredding bark, dark green leaves with pale undersides, showy clusters of creamy white flowers in early summer, and brown seed capsules that persist for months. There are two subspecies, differing primarily in leaf structure, ssp. *floribundus* and ssp. *asplenifolius*. Only one seems to be commercially available.

L. f. ssp. *asplenifolius*, fernleaf Catalina ironwood, lovely, tough, drought-tolerant tree with deeply lobed and divided leaves and cinnamon-brown bark. Best near coast but not seaside. Sun or part shade, excellent drainage, occasional deep watering. Can be pruned in winter to shape. Native to the Channel Islands of California.

TOP: *MACFADYENA UNGUIS-CATI*
BOTTOM: *MADIA ELEGANS*

Macfadyena unguis-cati

(cat's claw)

ZONES 8-24. EVERGREEN OR DECIDUOUS VINE. 25-40'.

Rampant, fast-growing vine with glossy, light green leaves and large, intensely yellow, trumpet-shaped flowers in early spring followed by long, thin seedpods. Clings with tendrils to rough surfaces. As a groundcover, forms dense, impenetrable mat. Prune hard after bloom to keep in check. Full sun to part shade, moderate water. Tolerates drought, clay soil; likes heat. Not for small spaces. Potentially invasive. Native to Central America.

Madia elegans (madia, tarweed)

ZONES N/A. ANNUAL. 3' x 3'.

Rosette-forming plant with velvety, aromatic leaves, and showy, yellow, daisylike summer flowers, sometimes with a maroon inner ring or blotch. Full sun, occasional water. Tolerates clay soils. Good cut flower. Native to California and Oregon.

OPPOSITE: *LYONOTHAMNUS FLORIBUNDUS*

Mahonia (mahonia)

Tough, spiny shrubs with glossy, dark green to grayish green hollylike leaves, masses of small, waxy, bright yellow to yellow-orange flowers, followed by orange, red, or blue berries. Full sun to part shade, most soils, moderate to occasional water. Attractive to birds.

M. aquifolium, Oregon grape, 6' x 5', erect, bushy, evergreen shrub with dark green leaves, bronzy when new, turning red or purplish in fall, and early spring flowers. Native from coastal British Columbia to northern California. Zones 2-12, 14-24.

M. x *media*, upright stems with long, divided leaves held horizontally near the ends and upright clusters of scented, yellow flowers in late fall and winter. 'Charity' grows to 15' x 12'. 'Lionel Fortescue' is half that size.

M. nevinii, Nevin mahonia, 4-6'x 4-6', evergreen shrub, new leaves reddish pink, turning gray-green, silvery below, yellow spring flowers, and red berries. Tolerates alkaline and clay soils. Native to southern California. Zones 7-24.

M. pinnata, California holly grape, 4-5' x 4-5', evergreen shrub with glossy green leaves, reddish orange in new growth, yellow spring flowers, and blue berries. Tolerates drought. Native to California and southern Oregon. Zones 4-9, 14-24.

M. 'Golden Abundance', 6' x 5', has glossy green leaves, profuse clusters of yellow flowers in early spring, and purplish blue berries. Zones 2-12, 14-24.

ABOVE: *MAHONIA* 'GOLDEN ABUNDANCE' RIGHT, LEFT TO RIGHT: *M.* X *MEDIA*, MAHONIA WITH BLUE BERRIES, *M.* 'GOLDEN ABUNDANCE'

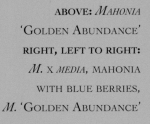

Malacothamnus (bush mallow, chaparral mallow)

ZONES N/A. EVERGREEN SHRUB. SIZE VARIES.

Tough and adaptable shrubs with softly hairy, gray-green, maplelike leaves and clusters of pink or white flowers in summer. Full sun to part shade, occasional water. Spread by underground stems, forming dense thickets, but not hard to contain. Good for erosion control. Attractive to birds and butterflies. Native to California and Baja California.

M. fasciculatus, 6-8' x 6', erect, with sharply lobed, gray-green leaves and large pink flowers. 'Casitas' has silvery pink flowers.

MALACOTHAMNUS FASCICULATUS

M. fremontii, 4-6' x 3-4', variable plant, usually compact and bushy with pale silvery pink flowers.

M. palmeri, 3-8' x 2-3', narrow, upright, fast grower with gray leaves and pink flowers. Tolerates clay soils.

Malvastrum lateritium (trailing mallow)

ZONES 8, 9, 14- 24. PERENNIAL. 8" x 5'.

Robust evergreen groundcover, rooting along its trailing stems, with broad, toothed, green leaves and saucer-shaped, salmon-pink flowers with distinct yellow centers in summer. Full sun, little to no water. Tolerates poor soil, heat, drought. Can overwhelm more delicate plants. Native to South America.

MALVASTRUM LATERITIUM

Matricaria recutita (chamomile)

ZONES 1-24. ANNUAL. 2' x 18".

Sprawling plant with finely divided, yellow-green leaves with a distinctive fragrance and white daisylike flowers with yellow centers in summer. Full sun, moderate to occasional water. Grows in most soils, as freely in the path as in the garden bed. Native to Europe and Asia; naturalized in North America.

MATRICARIA RECUTITA

Melaleuca (melaleuca, paperbark)

☀ ZONES VARY. EVERGREEN SHRUBS OR TREES. SIZE VARIES.

💧

🌿 Easy, tough, fast-growing, somewhat tender shrubs and trees with narrow, sometimes needlelike leaves, attractive, often spongy, peeling bark, and clusters of flowers with showy stamens resembling bottlebrushes followed by persistent woody seed capsules. Full sun, infrequent water. Tolerate heat, wind, salt spray, poor soil, drought. Some are invasive in parts of Australia and Florida, but do not seem so in the Bay Region. Native to Australia.

M. decussata, lilac melaleuca, 12-15' x 10-20', multi-trunked tree or shrub with narrow, bright green to bluish green leaves on pendulous branches and lavender flowers in late spring. Zones 9, 12-24.

M. incana, gray honey myrtle, 6-10' x 6-12', arching shrub with small, gray-green, slightly hairy leaves and small, creamy white spring flowers. Can be trained as small tree. Zones 8, 9, 12-24.

M. linariifolia, flaxleaf paperbark, 20-30' x 10-20', medium-sized tree with dark green leaves, white spongy bark, and white summer flowers. Zones 9, 13-24.

M. quinquenervia, paperbark, 20-40' x 15-25', upright tree with creamy white, peeling bark, narrow, pale green leaves, and creamy yellow or pinkish flowers in summer and fall. Zones 9, 12, 13, 15-17, 20-24.

M. styphelioides, prickly leaved paperbark, 25-40' x 15-25', tree with pendulous branches, small, prickly, light green leaves, and creamy white flowers in summer and fall. Zones 9, 13-24.

MELALEUCA QUINQUENERVIA WITH *MYOPORUM PARVIFOLIUM* GROUNDCOVER

Melianthus major (honey bush)

ZONES 8, 9, 12-24. EVERGREEN SHRUB. 6-12' x 8-10'.

Fast-growing, tropical-looking plant with sprawling habit and bold, grayish green leaves divided into deeply serrated leaflets. Tall spikes of reddish brown flowers in late winter and papery seed capsules in spring. Sun to part shade, moderate to occasional water. Ignored by deer. Native to South Africa.

MELIANTHUS MAJOR

Melica (melic)

ZONES N/A. PERENNIAL GRASSES. SIZE VARIES.

Cool-season, clumping grasses noted for their spikes of glistening, papery bracts. Full sun to part shade, good drainage, occasional to no water. Native to California.

M. californica, California melic, 1' x 1', tough plant with 2' tall flowering spikes and purple-tinted bracts. 'Temblor' forms tight clumps and has exceptionally fat flower spikes.

M. imperfecta, Coast Range melic, 18"-2' x 1', upright clumps with densely clustered, narrow, green leaves and slender, arching stems to 3' tall with wispy flowering spikes.

MELICA CALIFORNICA

M. torreyana, Torrey's melic, 1' x 1', neat and compact clumps of soft, narrow, green leaves and flowering stems to 2' tall. Prefers some shade.

Metrosideros excelsus
(New Zealand Christmas tree)

ZONES 16, 17, 23, 24. EVERGREEN TREE. 30' x 25-30'.

Low-branching, shrubby, somewhat tender tree with leathery leaves, deep green above and white-woolly beneath, and clusters of dark red or bright crimson flowers in spring and summer. Prefers coastal conditions, even seaside. Full sun, moderate water. 'Aurea' has pale yellow flowers.

METROSIDEROS EXCELSUS

Mimulus aurantiacus
(sticky monkeyflower)

☀ ☀   Zones 7-9, 14-24. Perennial. 3-4' x 3-4'.

◊ ◊

MIMULUS AURANTIACUS (YELLOW) WITH *PHACELIA CAMPANULARIA*

Shrubby perennial with sticky, narrow, dark green leaves and long-blooming, tubular, orange or yellow flowers in spring and summer. Full sun to part shade, good drainage, little to no water. Attractive to hummingbirds. Native to western North America. Many named cultivars, some more compact and many with larger flowers in colors ranging from white to yellow, coppery orange, red, or maroon. The subspecies *bifidus* has large, pale yellow to peach flowers; ssp. *longiflorus* has creamy white to yellow-orange flowers.

Miscanthus (miscanthus)

☀ ☀   Zones vary. Perennial grasses. Size varies.

◊

FALL COLORS OF *MISCANTHUS SINENSIS* 'ADAGIO' WITH BERBERIS

Clump-forming, warm-season grasses with gracefully arching leaves that turn yellowish, orange, or straw-colored in fall and ornamental plumes of flowers on tall stems. Full sun to light shade, moderate water. Self-sow freely with potential for invasiveness, especially in wet areas or irrigated landscapes. Cut back hard to renew.

M. sinensis, Japanese silver grass, variable grass usually offered as named cultivars. Native to China, Japan, Korea. Zones 2-24. 'Adagio', 2-3' x 2-3', rounded with narrow green leaves and pink flower plumes on 4-5' stems. 'Morning Light', 4-5' x 3-4', upright with narrow green leaves with creamy white margins, giving a silvery effect from a distance, and reddish pink flower plumes aging to cream. 'Sarabande', 4-5' x 4', upright with narrow, silvery green leaves with a central stripe. 'Yaku Jima', 3-4' x 4-5', widespreading with dark green leaves that turn reddish brown in fall. 'Zebrinus' 4' x 3', has bands of yellow on arching green leaves.

M. transmorrisonensis, evergreen miscanthus, 3-4' x 4-6', is a dramatic accent plant with narrow, green leaves spreading widely in all directions and flower plumes on stems to 6' tall. Somewhat less invasive than *M. sinensis*. Native to Taiwan. Zones 4-24.

MONARDELLA VILLOSA 'RUSSIAN RIVER'

Monardella (monardella)

ZONES 7-9, 14-24. PERENNIALS. SIZE VARIES.

Aromatic perennials with a sprawling habit, dark green to gray-green leaves, and red, pink, white, or purplish flowers in late spring and summer. Part shade, excellent drainage, little to no water. Attractive to hummingbirds and butterflies. Ignored by deer. Native to California and the western U.S.

M. macrantha, 6" x 12-18", mat-forming with shiny, dark green leaves, purplish stems, and brilliant red-orange flowers in tight, upward-facing clusters nestled among the leaves.

M. villosa, coyote mint, 1-2' x 12-18", semi-evergreen, with pungently scented, gray-green leaves and pale purple, rose, or white flowers.

Muhlenbergia (muhly)

ZONES VARY. PERENNIAL GRASSES. SIZE VARIES.

Medium to large, clump-forming, warm-season grasses with narrow leaves and silky plumes of flowers on tall stalks. Full sun to part shade, good drainage, little or no supplemental water along coast or in part shade; occasional deep watering in hot locations.

M. capillaris, pink muhly, 2-4'x 2-3', has dark green to olive green leaves and airy clouds of feathery pink to reddish purple flowers. Good seaside grass. Native to eastern U.S. Zones 4-24.

MUHLENBERGIA RIGENS

M. emersleyi, bull grass, 2' x 3-4', low-growing mound of glossy green to bluish green leaves with purplish flowers on tall stalks. Native to southwestern U.S. Zones 2-24.

M. lindheimeri, Lindheimer's muhly, 3-5'x 4-5', with narrow, blue-gray leaves and tall, slender, arching plumes of creamy yellow flowers. Native to Texas and Mexico. Zones 6-24.

M. rigens, deer grass, 3'x 3', dense clump of bright green leaves and tall, upright to arching stalks of creamy white to purplish flowers. Native to California, the southwestern U.S., and Mexico. Zones 4-24.

Muscari (grape hyacinth)

ZONES 1-24. PERENNIALS FROM BULBS. SIZE VARIES.

MUSCARI ARMENIACUM

Thin, floppy clumps of grasslike, fleshy leaves appearing after the first rains and spikes of small, fragrant, blue or white flowers in early spring. Full sun to part shade, good drainage, no summer water. Long-lived, summer-dormant, will naturalize where content. Native to the Mediterranean and Asia.

M. armeniacum, 8" tall stems, with bright blue flowers and floppy clumps of green leaves. 'Blue Spike' has flax-blue, double flowers. 'Early Giant' is larger and has darker blue flowers edged with white. 'Cantab' is smaller, with sky-blue flowers later in the season.

M. latifolium, 12" tall stems, bears only one leaf and a single flower spike with a two-toned effect, the lower flowers dark violet and the upper ones soft violet-blue.

Myoporum parvifolium

(myoporum)

ZONES 8, 9, 12-24. EVERGREEN SHRUB. 3-6" X 10'.

MYOPORUM PARVIFOLIUM

Fast-growing, mat-forming groundcover densely covered with narrow, mid-green leaves and tiny, white flowers in summer. Full sun, little water. Tender. Native to Australia. 'Prostratum' is the most commonly available. 'Putah Creek' is taller and not as widespreading. *M. laetum*, a tall, mounding shrub in the same genus, is invasive in coastal California.

Myrica californica (Pacific wax myrtle)

ZONES 4-9, 14-24. EVERGREEN SHRUB OR TREE. 10-30' x 10-30'.

Well-behaved, upright shrub or tree with shiny, dark green, aromatic leaves. Sun or part shade, most soils, moderate to occasional water. Good informal hedge or screen. Prefers coastal conditions, even seaside. Attractive to deer. Native from coastal California to Washington. 'Buxifolia' has shorter leaves.

MYRICA CALIFORNICA MAKES A TALL INFORMAL PRIVACY HEDGE

Myrsine africana

(African boxwood)

ZONES 8, 9, 14-24. EVERGREEN SHRUB. 3'-8' x 3'-6'.

Dense, rounded shrub with small, glossy, dark green leaves on upright stems. Clean, tidy shrub easily kept in shape by light pruning; can be sheared. Full sun or part shade, most soils, moderate to occasional water. Native to Africa, India, and China.

MYRSINE AFRICANA

. . . 171

Myrtus communis (myrtle)

ZONE 8-24. EVERGREEN SHRUB. 4-6' x 4-6'.

MYRTUS COMMUNIS
'VARIEGATA'

Fine-textured Mediterranean shrub with small, shiny, bright green, aromatic leaves and small, sweetly scented, creamy white flowers in spring. Full sun, excellent drainage, moderate to occasional water. Can be sheared or used as an informal hedge. Ignored by deer. 'Compacta' is smaller with smaller leaves. 'Variegata' has leaves with creamy white margins. 'Microphylla' has tiny leaves; good sheared boxwood substitute.

Nandina domestica (heavenly bamboo)

ZONES 4-24. EVERGREEN SHRUB. SIZE VARIES.

NANDINA DOMESTICA

Airy, upright shrubs resembling bamboo with narrow, medium-green leaflets that turn red, purple, or bronze in winter. Creamy white flowers in large, loose sprays and bright orange or red berries that persist for months. Sun to part shade, little water if given afternoon shade. Prune out older canes to open up to light below. Good informal hedge or specimen. Native to China and Japan.

'Compacta', 4-5' x 3', has narrower leaves. 'Harbour Dwarf', 2-3' and spreading, makes a good tall groundcover. 'Umpqua Chief', 5-6' x 3-4', has large leaflets and a good display of flowers and fruits. 'Woods Dwarf', 18" x 18", has crimson to scarlet fall color.

Narcissus (daffodil)

ZONES 1-24. PERENNIALS FROM BULBS. SIZE VARIES.

Cheerful, no-maintenance bulbs that naturalize in many soils and flower reliably, year after year, in late winter or early spring. Best in large drifts. Ignored by deer. Full sun, reasonable drainage, no water. Lift and replant only when the annual show begins to diminish, usually not for many years. Native to Europe and North Africa.

Nassella (needlegrass)

ZONES VARY. PERENNIAL GRASSES. SIZE VARIES.

Clump-forming, cool-season, summer-dormant grasses, green in fall and winter, golden in

summer, with feathery flowers. Full sun, good drainage; most need little to no water. Self-sow. Good for erosion control on banks. Cut back hard in fall to renew.

NARCISSUS 'SCARLET GEM'

N. cernua, nodding needlegrass, 1-2' x 1-2', forms dense, erect, fine-textured clumps of deep green leaves turning straw-colored in fall and purplish flowers on 2-3' spikes in spring. Native to California. Zones 7-9, 11, 14-24.

NASSELLA TENUISSIMA

N. lepida, foothill needlegrass, 1' x 1', similar to *N. cernua* but smaller. Spreads by self-sowing to form a rough turf. Native to California. Zones 7-9, 11, 14-24.

N. pulchra, purple needlegrass, 1-2' x 1-2', forms clumps of fine, flat leaf blades and purplish flowers. Native to California. Zones 5-9, 11, 14-24.

N. tenuissima, Mexican feather grass, 18"-2' x 2-3', graceful fountain of bright green, fine-textured, arching leaves and greenish to silvery flowers in early summer. Prefers moderate water. Can be invasive. Native to the southwestern U.S. and Mexico. Zones 2-24.

Nemophila (nemophila)

ZONES VARY. ANNUALS. 6-12" X 1'.

Delicate mounds of fernlike, light green leaves develop after winter rains and are covered with blue or white flowers in spring. Sun to part shade, good drainage. Let plants die down in the hot days of summer; they will reseed where content.

N. maculata, five-spot, has white flowers with purple spots on petal tips. Native to California. 'Violetta' has lavender flowers with a dark violet spot. Zones 1-9, 12-24.

N. menziesii, baby blue eyes, has sky-blue flowers with white centers. Native to California and southern Oregon. 'Penny Black' has dark purple flowers rimmed with white and white centers. Zones 1-24.

Nepeta (catmint)

ZONES 1-24. PERENNIALS. SIZE VARIES.

Low-growing, compact plants with soft, grayish green to blue-gray leaves and spikes of lavender flowers in late spring to summer. Sun, good drainage, moderate to occasional water. Attractive to butterflies, hummingbirds, and bees. Ignored by deer.

N. x *faassenii*, 1' x 2', has floppy spikes of lavender-blue flowers in late spring and scallop-edged, soft, gray-green leaves. 'Select Blue' has darker flowers. 'Snowflake' has pure white flowers.

N. racemosa, 6-12" x 2-3', has medium green to gray-green, finely hairy, roundish leaves and lavender flowers. Native to Turkey, the Caucasus, and Iran. 'Blue Ice' has pale blue flowers that fade to white. 'Blue Wonder' has dark blue flowers. 'Superba' is a smaller-leaved form with lavender-blue flowers over a long period.

174 . . .

N. 'Six Hills Giant', 3' x 3', forms a large mound of gray-green leaves and towering spikes of lavender-blue flowers over a long season.

Nerine (nerine)

ZONES 5, 6, 8, 9, 13-24. PERENNIALS FROM BULBS. SIZE VARIES.

Summer-dormant bulbs with spidery flowers, usually glowing pink, on naked stalks in fall, followed by strap-shaped leaves. Sun to light shade, good drainage, no summer water. Good cut flower. Native to South Africa. Some nerines (e.g., *N. filifolia*, *N. masoniorum*) are semi-evergreen and need summer water.

N. bowdenii has soft pink flowers marked with deeper pink on 2' stalks. 'Crispa' has wavy-edged petals.

N. sarniensis, Guernsey lily, has large, crimson, scarlet, pale pink, rose pink, or white flowers on 2' stalks.

Nerium oleander (oleander)

☀ ZONES 8-16, 18-24. EVERGREEN SHRUB. 3-20' x 3-12'.

Tough, attractive, long-lived shrub with narrow, dark green leaves and single or double, pink, white, red, salmon, or yellow flowers. Best inland. Revels in hot sun, tolerates drought but accepts water. Upright habit; can be trained as a single- or multi-trunked tree. Moderate to fast growth. Good hedge, windbreak, or specimen plant. Ignored by deer. Native to the Mediterranean. Many named cultivars.

'Sister Agnes', 20' x 12', vigorous grower with single, white flowers. 'Mrs. Roeding', 6' x 6', has smaller leaves and double, salmon pink flowers. 'Petite Pink' and 'Petite Salmon', 3-5' x 3-5', make good low hedges. 'Algiers', 10-12' x 6-10', has single, dark red flowers.

ABOVE: *NERIUM OLEANDER*

Nigella (love-in-a-mist)

ZONES 1-24. ANNUALS. SIZE VARIES.

Easy annuals with blue, lavender, pink, or purple flowers in spring, dying back to the ground in summer. Fine, threadlike leaves resembling those of fennel or dill; good for blending other plants in the garden or in arrangements. Long-lasting cut flowers. Self-sow, but easily pulled. Sun to part shade, good drainage, no water. Best for coastal gardens. Native to the Mediterranean.

LEFT: *NIGELLA DAMASCENA*
BELOW: *NIGELLA HISPANICA*

N. damascena, 12-18" x 12", has blue flowers and attractive papery seed pods.

N. hispanica, 2' tall, sparse, ferny foliage, unusual spidery seed pods, reddish maroon stamens, violet blue flowers in fall.

Nyssa sylvatica (sour gum)

ZONES 2-10, 14-21. DECIDUOUS TREE. 30-50' x 15-30'.

Pyramidal, upright tree, spreading and rounded in age, with pendulous lower branches and lustrous, dark green leaves that dependably turn yellow, orange, bright red, or scarlet in fall. Ornamental dark gray, red-tinged bark. Small greenish flowers inconspicuous; small bluish black fruits only when both male and female trees are present. Attractive year-round. Good shade tree. Nice specimen tree or in groves. Full sun to part shade, moderate to occasional deep watering. Native to eastern North America.

NYSSA SYLVATICA

Oenothera (evening primrose, sundrops)

ZONES VARY. PERENNIALS, BIENNIALS, ANNUALS. SIZE VARIES.

Large, showy, late spring to summer flowers in white, bright yellow, or pink. Some open during the day, most open in late afternoon. Good choice for harsh sites. Some species can be invasive (e.g., *O. speciosa*, *O. berlandieri*); some require regular water.

OENOTHERA HOOKERI WITH ACHILLEA AND ARTEMISIA

O. deltoides, desert primrose, 4-6" x 12", low-growing annual with gray-green leaves and oversized white flowers with yellow centers. Not easy; needs perfect drainage and no summer water. Native to California and the southwestern U.S. Zones N/A.

O. hookeri, 1' x 3', ground-hugging perennial with green leaves and tall spikes of large yellow flowers. Tolerates drought, flooding, wind, cold, but must have excellent drainage. Reseeds heavily. Native to western U.S. Zones 5-7, 14-24.

O. macrocarpa, Ozark sundrops, 6" x 2', perennial with narrow, lance-shaped leaves and large, pure yellow flowers in summer. Needs part shade in hot locations. 'Silver Blade' has silvery blue-green leaves. Native to southern U.S. Zones 1-24.

Olea europaea (olive)

ZONES 8-9, 11-24. EVERGREEN TREE OR SHRUB. SIZE VARIES.

Classic tree for hot, dry climates with richly textured bark and narrow, gray-green,

willowy leaves. Slow-growing, often multi-trunked. Full sun, occasional to infrequent water. Fruit attractive to and spread by birds; can be invasive in irrigated gardens and has been observed in riparian wildlands. 'Swan Hill' is a fruitless variety. 'Majestic Beauty' bears little fruit. 'Little Ollie', 6' x 12', is fine-textured and can be sheared as a low hedge.

Omphalodes (omphalodes)

ZONES VARY. PERENNIALS. SIZE VARIES.

Shade-loving plants with bright blue to deep blue flowers in spring. Part to full shade, good drainage, moderate to occasional water. Not for hot locations.

O. cappadocica, 6-12" x 18", forms slowly spreading, compact clumps of heart-shaped, satiny, bright green leaves and airy sprays of small, bright blue flowers with white centers in spring. Native to Turkey. Zones 3-9, 14-21. 'Starry Eyes' has deep blue flowers outlined in white.

O. verna, blue-eyed Mary, 3-6" x 3', forms a low mat with medium-green leaves and deep blue flowers with small, white centers on stalks above the foliage. Native to Europe. Zones 2-9, 14-21.

TOP: *OLEA EUROPAEA* 'MAJESTIC BEAUTY'
BOTTOM: *OMPHALODES CAPPADOCICA*

Origanum (oregano, marjoram)

ZONES VARY. PERENNIALS. SIZE VARIES.

Shrubby, mounding or mat-forming perennials with aromatic, usually woolly leaves and tiny pink to lavender flowers with showy bracts. Full sun, excellent drainage, occasional water. Attractive to butterflies and bees. Native to the Mediterranean.

O. amanum, 8" x 1', mound of bright green, hairy, heart-shaped leaves and pink-violet flowers with light green bracts aging to purple in late summer. Zones 2-24.

O. dictamnus, dittany of Crete, 8" x 2', trailing plant with slender, arching stems, roundish, woolly, gray-green leaves, and spikes of pink to purplish flowers with light green to chartreuse bracts summer to fall. Zones 8, 9, 12-24.

ORIGANUM ROTUNDIFOLIUM 'KENT BEAUTY'

O. rotundifolium, 6" x 1-2', nearly prostrate or cascading plant with green to grayish green, roundish leaves on sprawling stems and pink or lavender flowers with large, bright green bracts all summer. 'Kent Beauty', 4" x 12-18", has lavender-pink flowers and deep pink bracts. Zones 2-24.

Osmanthus (osmanthus)

☀ ☀
💧💧

ZONES VARY. EVERGREEN SHRUBS.
SIZE VARIES.

OSMANTHUS HETEROPHYLLUS

Neat, attractive shrubs with shiny, dark green to bright green leaves and tiny, fragrant white flowers. Sun along coast, afternoon shade inland, reasonable drainage, and moderate water. Tolerate some drought in shade. Native to Asia.

O. x *fortunei*, 6-15' x 6', slow-growing, upright, densely covered with hollylike leaves. Zones 4-10, 14-24. 'San Jose' grows more rapidly to 20' and is quite drought-tolerant along the coast.

O. fragrans, sweet olive, 6-10' x 6-8', has especially fragrant flowers in spring. Zones 8-9, 12-24. The subspecies *aurantiacus* has pale orange flowers in fall.

O. heterophyllus, hollyleaf osmanthus, 10-20' x 10-20', slow-growing with spiny-edged leaves. Excellent trimmed as informal hedge. Zones 4-10, 14-24. 'Variegatus', 8-10' x 8-10', has green leaves with white margins. 'Goshiki', 3-4' x 5', is a smaller variegated form.

Osteospermum (African daisy)

OSTEOSPERMUM FRUTICOSUM

ZONES 8, 9, 12-24. PERENNIALS. SIZE VARIES.

☀
💧💧

Mounding or trailing plants with prolific display of daisylike flowers in spring and fall, fewer in the heat of summer. Full sun, good drainage, moderate to occasional water. Cut back after flowering to renew. Native to South Africa. May be invasive.

O. fruticosum, trailing African daisy, 1-2' x 3-4', open habit, medium green, linear leaves, and lilac flowers fading to white. Good groundcover on slopes.

O. jucundum, 6"-2' x 2-3', forms clumps of lush green, linear leaves and large, white flowers with purple-pink undersides.

Pandorea pandorana (wonga-wonga vine)

☀
💧
🍃

ZONES 16-24. EVERGREEN VINE. 25-35'.

Vigorous, fast-growing climber with narrow, glossy green leaflets, tinted bronze when new, and creamy white, tubular or trumpet-shaped flowers in spring. Full sun, moderate water. Tender, but usually recovers. Native to Australia. 'Golden Showers' has golden yellow flowers.

PANDOREA PANDORANA

Papaver (poppy)

ZONES VARY. PERENNIALS, ANNUALS. SIZE VARIES.

Showy, ephemeral plants with gray-green to bluish green leaves and brightly colored flowers with papery, crepelike petals in spring or early summer. Full sun to part shade. Let them go dormant after flowering.

P. californicum, fire poppy, flame poppy, fire-following perennial of California chaparral with orange to brick red flowers. Zones N/A.

P. orientale, Oriental poppy, perennial with brief but glorious, mostly orange or red, early summer flowers. Many cultivars. Native to the Caucasus, Turkey, and Iran. Zones 1-11, 14-21.

P. rhoeas, Flanders field poppy, 3' x 1', annual with slender, branching stems and large, single or double flowers in white, pink, red, orange, lilac, or blue. Reseeds heavily. Native to Europe and Asia. Many named cultivars. Zones 1-24.

Parthenocissus (parthenocissus)

ZONES VARY. DECIDUOUS VINES. SIZE VARIES.

Vigorous, fast-growing, deciduous vines with lobed or divided, glossy, green leaves that turn orange or red in fall. Good for covering walls and fences. Full sun to part shade, little water. Native to China and Japan.

P. henryana, silvervein creeper, 10-15', not as vigorous as *P. tricuspidata*, with bluish green to bronzy green leaves with white veining, turning reddish purple in fall. Zones 4-9, 14-17.

P. tricuspidata, Boston ivy, 25-30', climbs without assistance on walls and structures, covering large areas with dense foliage, leaving a tracery of stems and a mixture of red and green leaves in fall. 'Green Showers' has larger green leaves that turn burgundy in fall. 'Veitchii' is a less rampant grower with smaller leaves. Zones 1-24.

PAPAVER RHOEAS IN FIELD OF WILDFLOWERS

PARTHENOCISSUS TRICUSPIDATA LEAVES IN FALL

Penstemon (beard tongue)

 ☀ ☀ ZONES VARY. PERENNIALS. SIZE VARIES.

◊ ◊ ◊ Herbaceous or woody-based perennials with narrow
green or gray-green leaves and tubular flowers in
many colors, usually on tall stalks. Best massed. Good
in arrangements. Full sun, good drainage, moderate to
no water. Cut back after flowering to renew.
Attractive to hummingbirds.

P. campanulatus, 2' x 2', prolific bloomer with lavender and white flowers in spring to
fall. No summer water. Native to Mexico. Zones N/A.

RIGHT: *PENSTEMON*
'STAPLEFORD GEM' BELOW:
P. X GLOXINIOIDES 'FIREBIRD'

P. centranthifolius, scarlet bugler, 2-3' x 1-2', has gray-green leaves and tall spikes of
bright red flowers in spring or early summer. Native to California and Baja California.
Zones 7-23.

P. clevelandii, 2-3' x 2', gray-leaved perennial with pink spring flowers. Native to southern California. Zones N/A.

P. x gloxinioides, border penstemon, 2-3' x 4', compact, bushy plants with narrow green leaves and large summer flowers on tall stems. 'Firebird' has mid-green leaves with reddish veins and scarlet flowers. 'Midnight', a hybrid between *P. x gloxinioides* and the Rocky mountain *P. strictus*, has deep purple flowers. Prefer moderate water, but will get by with less. Zones 6-9, 14-24.

P. heterophyllus, 1-2' x 2-3', with bluish green leaves and spikes of blue to reddish purple flowers in spring and early summer. Native to California. 'Blue Bedder' has bright blue flowers. Zones 7-24.

P. pinifolius, 30" x 2', has narrow, bright green leaves and red-orange flowers in summer. Native to New Mexico and Arizona. Zones 2-24.

P. spectabilis, royal beard tongue, 3-4' x 3-4', with green or grayish green leaves and purplish flowers in spring or early summer. Native to southern California and Baja California. Zones 7, 14-23.

PENSTEMON PINIFOLIUS (RED) AND P. STRICTUS

LEFT: *PENSTEMON X GLOXINIOIDES* CULTIVAR
RIGHT: *P. HETEROPHYLLUS* 'BLUE BEDDER'

Perityle incana (Guadalupe Island rock daisy)

PERITYLE INCANA

ZONES N/A. PERENNIAL. 3' x 3'.

Upright, shrubby perennial with silvery gray leaves and clusters of small, bright yellow flowers in spring. Full sun, excellent drainage, occasional water. Native to Guadalupe Island off the coast of Baja California.

Perovskia atriplicifolia

(Russian sage)

PEROVSKIA ATRIPLICIFOLIA

ZONES 2-24. PERENNIAL. 3-4' x 3-4'.

Upright, shrubby perennial with aromatic, velvety, gray-green leaves and widely branched, airy sprays of purplish blue flowers that rise above the leaves in late spring and summer. Full sun, good drainage, little water. Tolerant of heat and drought. Attractive to bees. Ignored by deer. May spread by underground rhizomes. Cut back hard in winter to renew. Native to western and central Asia. 'Blue Spires', a popular hybrid between *P. atriplicifolia* and *P. abrotanoides*, has dark purple flowers.

PHACELIA CAMPANULARIA

Phacelia (phacelia)

ZONES VARY. ANNUALS, PERENNIALS. SIZE VARIES.

Narrow, sticky, coarsely toothed green or grayish green leaves and tiny, bell-shaped, blue or purplish, sometimes white, flowers on one side of coiled stalks that are said to resemble scorpions' tails. Attractive to butterflies and bees. Full sun to part shade, good drainage, little to no water.

P. bolanderi, Bolander's phacelia, 6-18" x 3', perennial with gray-green leaves and pale blue to purplish flowers summer to fall. Thrives in dry shade, but flowers more in part sun. Native to northwestern California and southwestern Oregon. Zones N/A.

P. campanularia, California desert bluebells, 6-18" x 6-18", annual with coarsely toothed, gray-green leaves and bell-shaped deep blue flowers in spring. Zones 1-3, 7-24.

P. grandiflora, large-flowered phacelia, 2-3' x 2', upright annual with large lavender flowers in spring and early summer. Native to California. Zones N/A.

Philadelphus lewisii

(wild mock orange)

Zone 1-10, 14-24. Deciduous shrub. 4-10' x 6-12'.

Graceful, fountainlike shrub with soft green leaves and clusters of large, satiny, lightly fragrant, single white flowers in late spring. Part shade, moderate water. Tolerates some dryness, but loses leaves in drought. 'Goose Creek' has double white flowers.

Phlomis (phlomis)

 ZONES VARY. EVERGREEN SHRUBS AND PERENNIALS. SIZE VARIES.

 Velvety, woolly, or softly hairy, gray-green to yellow-green leaves and whorls of two-lipped, yellow or lilac-pink flowers on erect stems. Full sun, good drainage, occasional water. Ignored by deer. Native to the Mediterranean.

PHLOMIS FRUTICOSA WITH HYBRID VERBENA

P. fruticosa, Jerusalem sage, 4' x 6', variable evergreen shrub with woolly, soft green to gray-green leaves and bright yellow to yellow-orange flowers in late spring and early summer. Zones 3-24.

P. italica, 3-4' x 5-6', evergreen shrub with arching habit, gray-green, woolly leaves, and lilac-pink flowers in summer. Short-lived. Zones 5-24.

P. lanata, 2' x 3', evergreen shrub with small, roundish leaves, sage green above and whitish gray beneath, and yellow flowers held just above the leaves in summer. Zones 7-24.

Phoenix canariensis

(Canary Island date palm)

ZONES 9, 12-24. PALM. 60' X 50'.

Imposing and theatrical in landscapes large enough to accommodate its mature size. Bright green, arching fronds and small, yellow flowers in large, pendulous clusters. Slow-growing when young. Full sun, good drainage,

PHOENIX CANARIENSIS

moderate water. Older specimens quite drought tolerant. Native to the Canary Islands.

Phormium (New Zealand flax)

ZONES 7-9, 14-24. PERENNIALS. SIZE VARIES.

Architectural plants with sword-shaped leaves and tall, branched spikes of reddish to yellow, tubular flowers in late spring and summer. Grown for their foliage, they vary *PHORMIUM* 'GUARDSMAN' from miniature to gigantic, but even medium-sized plants eventually grow quite large.

Full sun to part shade, good drainage, moderate water in sun, occasional water in shade. Tolerate heat and salt spray, but leaves may burn in afternoon sun. Ignored by deer. Place larger plants where they can reach full height and spread; unattractive when leaves are cut back. Native to New Zealand.

P. cookianum, mountain flax, 4-5' x 8-10', broad, low clumps of gracefully arching, green leaves and yellow flowers. Hybrids of this plant usually stay smaller than those of *P. tenax*. 'Tricolor' has light green leaves with creamy yellow margins.

P. tenax, 9-12' x 9-12', upright with bronzy green leaves, arching near the top, and red or red-orange flowers. Many named cultivars, with leaf color ranging from gray-green to purplish to bronze, often with contrasting stripes. Old plants tend to revert to brownish green or gray, and some grow much larger than advertised. 'Jack Spratt' is a true dwarf, 1-2' x 1-2', with curling, reddish brown leaves. 'Tom Thumb' stays quite small, 2-3' x 2-3', with green, wavy-edged leaves with reddish margins. 'Tiny Tiger', 1-2' x 1-2', has gray-green leaves with creamy white margins. 'Pink Stripe', 5-6' x 5-6', has gray-green leaves with attractive pink margins.

Many named hybrids between the two species, some of which lose their attractive coloration as they age. 'Maori Maiden', 3-4' x 4-6', has salmon pink leaves with olive green margins. 'Surfer', 3-4' x 5-6', has reddish bronze leaves with a grayish green central stripe. 'Guardsman', 6-8' x 6-8', has bronzy maroon leaves edged with scarlet and creamy white.

Photinia (photinia)

ZONES VARY. EVERGREEN SHRUBS OR TREES. SIZE VARIES.

Fast-growing, tough, large shrubs often used for screening or windbreaks because of their broad, dense habit. New leaves coppery red, bright red, or burgundy; older leaves glossy, dark green or medium green and leathery. Broad, flat clusters of small, white flowers at branch tips in early spring and red or black berries in fall to early winter.

PHOTINIA X *FRASERI* WITH *CEANOTHUS*

Trim back and tip prune to shape; leaves are too large for shearing. Can be espaliered or trained as small trees. Full sun to part shade, moderate to occasional water.

P. x fraseri, Fraser's photinia, 10-15' x 10-15', large shrub with burgundy-red to bright bronzy red new growth. 'Red Robin' has bright red new leaves. Zones 4-24.

P. serratifolia, Chinese photinia, 15-30' x 15-20', tree or large shrub with rounded canopy; leaves have serrated margins; new growth coppery, more subtle than *P. x fraseri*; bright red berries. Native to China. Zones 4-16, 18-22.

Pinus (pine)

ZONES VARY.
EVERGREEN TREES.
SIZE VARIES.

Variable group of small to large, cone-bearing trees with long, slender needles. Full sun to part shade, good drainage, occasional deep watering during droughts or if rains fail in late fall.

P. attenuata, knobcone pine, 20-50' x 20-25', fast-growing tree, often multi-trunked, shrubby on poor soils, with yellow-green needles. Full sun, little water. Native to mountains of southern Oregon and California. Zones 2-10, 14-21.

P. canariensis, Canary Island pine, 50-80' x 20-25', fast-growing, with long needles, bluish when new, maturing to dark green. Native to the Canary Islands. Zones 8, 9, 12-24.

P. coulteri, Coulter pine, 30-80' x 20-40', moderate growth, with dark green needles and huge, heavy cones. Tolerates heat, wind, drought. Native to California and Baja California. Zones 3-10, 14-23.

P. edulis, piñon pine, 10-20' x 8-16', slow-growing, densely foliaged tree with dark green needles. Native to mountains of California deserts and southwestern states. Zones 1-11, 14-21.

TOP: *PINUS SABINIANA*
BOTTOM: *P. MUGO MUGO*

P. eldarica, Afghan pine, 30-80' x 15-20', drought-tolerant desert pine that also thrives along the coast. Native to Afghanistan and Pakistan. Zones 7-9, 11-24.

P. halepensis, Aleppo pine, 30-60' x 20-40', moderate growth, with light green needles and open, irregular habit. Tolerates heat, wind, seacoast conditions. Native to the Mediterranean. Zones 8, 9, 11-24.

P. mugo mugo, mugho pine, 4-8' x 8-15', shrubby, mounding, eventually widespreading pine with dark green needles. Native to mountains of Europe. Zones 1-11, 14-24.

P. sabiniana, foothill pine, digger pine, 40-80' x 30-50', has long, gray-green needles, a rounded crown, and large, dark brown cones. Native to foothills of California. Zones 3-10, 14-21.

Pistacia chinensis (Chinese pistache)

ZONE 4-16, 18-23. DECIDUOUS TREE. 30-60' x 30-60'.

PISTACIA CHINENSIS

Adaptable and attractive tree with reliable bright orange to scarlet fall color even in mild climates. Full sun, occasional deep watering. Thrives in heat and drought. Tolerates alkaline soils. Native to China. Reportedly invasive in riparian areas in some parts of California.

Pittosporum (pittosporum)

ZONES VARY. EVERGREEN SHRUBS OR TREES. SIZE VARIES.

Dependable and attractive shrubs and trees with glossy, leathery leaves and small, intensely fragrant, creamy white or yellowish flowers in spring. Full sun to part shade, moderate to occasional water. Good hedges or windbreaks. Can be pruned, although the natural shapes are pleasing.

P. crassifolium, 25' x 20', has grayish green, rounded leaves and maroon flowers. Prefers coastal conditions. Native to New Zealand. 'Variegatum' has creamy white leaf margins. 'Compactum', 3-4' x 3' is a dwarf variety. Zones 9, 14-17, 19-24.

P. eugenioides, 20-40' x 15-30', tall, shrubby tree with wavy-edged, mid-green to yellow-green leaves and yellow flowers. Good fast screen. Heavy fruiting. Native to New Zealand. Zones 9, 14-17, 19-22.

P. phillyreoides, willow pittosporum, 12-20' x 10-15', slow-growing and smaller than some other pittosporums, with narrow, dark green leaves and a weeping habit. Fragrant yellow flowers. Tolerates heat and dryness. Native to Australia. Zones 8, 9, 12-24.

P. tenuifolium, 15-25' x 10-15', similar to *P. eugenioides* but with smaller leaves, darker stems, and purplish flowers. Tolerates seacoast conditions. Native to New Zealand. Zones 9, 14-17, 19-24. 'Marjorie Channon', 8' x 8', has green leaves edged with creamy white.

P. tobira, tobira, 6-15' x 6-15', has whorls of dark green leaves and creamy white, fragrant flowers. Native to Japan. 'Variegata', 5-10' x 5-10', has gray-green leaves with creamy white margins. 'Wheeler's Dwarf', 2-3' x 4-5', makes a tidy, low, mounding groundcover. Zones 8-24.

P. undulatum, Victorian box, 15-30' x 15-30', dense, single or multi-trunked, dome-shaped tree with glossy green, wavy-edged leaves and fragrant, creamy white flowers. Heavy fruiting. Native to Australia. Zones 16, 17, 21-24.

ABOVE: *Pittosporum crassifolium* 'Variegatum' with *Phormium*
LEFT: *P. crassifolium*

PLATANUS X *ACERIFOLIA*

Platanus (sycamore)

ZONES VARY. DECIDUOUS TREES. SIZE VARIES.

P. x *acerifolia*, London plane, 40-80' x 30-40', fast-growing, statuesque tree for large landscapes. Large, coarse, medium green, maplelike leaves turn pale yellow in fall. Attractive, peeling bark and round seed clusters that hang on the tree through winter.

Traditional street tree, although large, shallow roots can disrupt paving. 'Columbia' is resistant to diseases that cause early leaf drop. Full sun, moderate water. Zones 2-24.

P. racemosa, California sycamore, 30-80' x 20-50', fast-growing, picturesque, often multi-trunked tree with attractively mottled bark. Full sun to part shade, moderate water. Native to California. Zones 4-24.

Plecostachys serpyllifolia (Hottentot tea)

ZONES 8, 9, 14-24. PERENNIAL. 1-2' x 3-4'.

Low, mounding, shrubby perennial with tiny, softly hairy, silvery gray leaves and small creamy pink flowers in summer. Full sun to part shade, good drainage, moderate to occasional water. Potentially invasive. Native to South Africa.

Polypodium (polypody)

ZONES VARY. FERNS. SIZE VARIES.

Large group of ferns of wide distribution, some native to coastal areas of western North America. *P. californicum,* California polypody, is dormant in summer, reappearing with winter rains. Zones N/A. *P. glycyrrhiza,* licorice fern, grows on wet, mossy trees and logs in coastal forests. Zones 4-6, 14-24. *P. scouleri,* coast polypody, is evergreen. Part sun to full shade, no summer water. Zones 4-6, 15-17, 24.

POLYPODIUM CALIFORNICUM IN FOREGROUND AND UPRIGHT FRONDS OF HYBRID *P. SCOULERI*

Polystichum munitum
(western sword fern)

ZONES 2-9, 14-24. FERN. 3-5' x 3-4'.

Long-lived, evergreen, woodland fern with upright to spreading, leathery, dark green fronds, attractive in the garden and in arrangements. Shade, humus-rich soil, moderate to occasional water. Cut back to renew. Native to western North America.

NEW SPRING GROWTH OF *POLYSTICHUM MUNITUM*

. . . 193

Protea (protea)

ZONES 16, 17, 21-24. EVERGREEN SHRUBS. SIZE VARIES.

PROTEA REPENS

Good-looking, substantial shrubs with leathery, green to gray-green leaves, but grown for their astonishing flowerheads consisting of tight clusters of tubular flowers surrounded by brilliantly colored bracts. Tender, short-lived, fussy plants, challenging even for experienced gardeners. Full sun, acid soil, perfect drainage, protection from wind, good air circulation, occasional water. Native to South Africa. Many species and named cultivars.

Prunus (laurel, cherry, flowering plum)

ZONES VARY. EVERGREEN OR DECIDUOUS SHRUBS AND TREES. SIZE VARIES.

Evergreen laurels make good large hedges, windbreaks, and screens with showy flowers and fruits attractive to birds. Deciduous plums are valued for their foliage and flowers. Most fruit heavily and self-sow freely. Good habitat plants, but can be invasive.

P. caroliniana, Carolina laurel, 20-30' x 15-20', fast-growing, upright, evergreen shrub with glossy, green leaves and small, fragrant, creamy white flowers in late winter or spring, followed by blue-black fruit. Best near coast, but not seaside. Full sun to part shade, little or no water. Good screen or informal hedge. Native to eastern and southeastern U.S. Zones 5-24. 'Compacta', 10-15' x 6-8', is denser and more compact.

PRUNUS ILICIFOLIA SSP. *LYONII*

P. cerasifera, cherry plum, 30' x 30', upright or rounded, deciduous tree with green, coppery, or red leaves and creamy white to pink or white flowers in early spring, usually before leaves appear. Full sun, good drainage, occasional water. Tolerates clay soils. Seeds spread by birds. Native to Asia. 'Atropurpurea', purpleleaf plum, has coppery red new leaves and white flowers. 'Krauter Vesuvius' is smaller with dark purple-black leaves, pale pink flowers, and almost no fruit. 'Pissardii' has dark red-purple leaves and pale pink flowers that fade to white. Zones 2-22.

P. ilicifolia, hollyleaf cherry, 10-25' x 10-25', evergreen shrub with spiny-edged, dark green leaves, short spikes of fragrant, creamy white flowers in spring, and dark reddish purple fruit. Part shade, good drainage, moderate to occasional water. Handsome small tree or clipped hedge. Native to California. The subspecies *lyonii*, native to the Channel Islands, has smooth-edged, dark green leaves and darker red or blue-black fruit. Zones 5-9, 12-24.

P. lusitanica, Portugal laurel, 15-25' x 15-25', large, evergreen, often multi-trunked shrub or tree with large, glossy, dark green leaves and fragrant, creamy white flowers in long, pendulous spikes in spring, followed by heavy crop of dark blue-purple fruit, readily spread by birds. Full sun to part shade, little or no water. Native to the Mediterranean. Zones 4-9, 14-24.

Punica granatum (pomegranate)

ZONES 5-24. SEMI-DECIDUOUS SHRUB OR TREE. SIZE VARIES.

Partly deciduous shrub with glossy, bright green or yellow-green leaves and trumpet-

shaped, single or double, red-orange, sometimes white or yellow flowers in summer, followed by round, red-orange fruit in fall if heat is sufficient. Larger varieties can be trained as a single-stem tree. Excellent specimen plant; also attractive as an informal hedge. Full sun to light shade, moderate to occasional water. Tolerant of alkaline soils and drought. Native to southern Asia.

'Chico', 3' x 3', has double, red-orange

PUNICA GRANATUM
'CHICO'

flowers and bears little fruit. 'Nana', 3' x 6', has red-orange flowers and small, red fruit. 'Legrellei', 8-10' x 8-10', has creamy white double flowers marked with red.

Quercus (oak)

ZONES VARY. EVERGREEN AND DECIDUOUS TREES AND SHRUBS. SIZE VARIES.

Few plants are more evocative of the natural California landscape than its own native oaks. Two Mediterranean natives, *Q. ilex*, holly oak, and *Q. suber*, cork oak, also do well in the Bay Region. Full sun to part shade, good drainage, occasional to no water.

Q. agrifolia, coast live oak, 20-70' x 25-80', dense, rounded, evergreen tree with dark gray bark and leathery, hollylike, dark green leaves. Seedlings come up in part shade, but mature trees thrive in full sun. Tolerates drought, heat, wind. Faster growing than popularly believed. Native to coastal California and Baja California. Zones 7-9, 14-24.

Q. chrysolepis, canyon live oak, 20-60' x 20-60', rounded, spreading, evergreen tree with pale gray, furrowed bark and leathery leaves, glossy green above and grayish with yellow-green hairs beneath. Slow-growing, long-lived, adaptable to varying conditions. Native to foothills of southwestern Oregon to California and Baja California. Zones 3-11, 14-24.

Q. douglasii, blue oak, 30-50' x 40-70', widespreading, deciduous tree with light gray bark and bluish green leaves; good fall color. Tolerates drought, heat, and occasional flooding. Native to dry foothills in central and southern California. Zones 3-11, 14-24.

OPPOSITE, TOP TO BOTTOM:
OAKS (*QUERCUS AGRIFOLIA*)
SHADE SEATING AREA WITH
HEUCHERA, BLUE FESCUE,
AND VINE MAPLE;
Q. AGRIFOLIA FLOWERS;
NEW LEAVES OF *Q. KELLOGGII*

Q. garryana, Garry oak, 40-90' x 30-60', slow-growing, deep-rooting, deciduous tree with glossy, dark green, lobed leaves that turn reddish brown in fall. Native from British Columbia to California. Zones 4-11, 14-23.

Q. kelloggii, California black oak, 30-80' x 30-80', has a broad, rounded crown, dark gray, deeply fissured bark, and pinkish new leaves that mature to dark glossy green, turning yellow or orange in fall. Part shade in hot climates, occasional water. Native to low mountains of southern Oregon to southern California. Zones 6, 7, 9, 14-21.

Q. lobata, valley oak, 70-80' x 70-80', deciduous tree with a massive trunk and wide-spreading branches at maturity. Deeply lobed leaves are dark green above, paler gray-green beneath. Tolerates heat. Best where roots can tap groundwater or creek bank storage. Too large at maturity for all but the grandest landscapes. Native to California's Central Valley and foothills away from coastal influence. Zones 3-9, 12-24.

Ranunculus (ranunculus, buttercup)

ZONES VARY. PERENNIALS. SIZE VARIES.

Summer-dormant perennials with finely divided leaves and colorful flowers in spring. Full sun, good drainage, no summer water. Grow as annuals if dry summer dormancy cannot be ensured.

RANUNCULUS ASIATICUS
'TANGERINE'

R. asiaticus, Persian ranunculus, 1-2' x 1-2', tuberous-rooted perennial with green leaves and brightly colored, double or semi-double flowers in early spring. Native to the eastern Mediterranean. Many named cultivars. Zones 1-24.

R. californicus, California buttercup, erect to almost prostrate perennial with waxy-looking, lemon-yellow flowers in spring. Native to coastal western North America to Baja California. Best near coast. Zones N/A.

Ratibida (coneflower)

RATIBIDA COLUMNIFERA

ZONES 1-24. PERENNIALS. SIZE VARIES.

Easy and fast-growing, erect plants with deeply divided, green to grayish green leaves and distinctive summer flowers consisting of rounded or cylindrical, conelike heads surrounded by drooping yellow petal-like ray flowers. Tolerate heat, poor soil. Full sun, good drainage, moderate water. Short-lived but reseed, sometimes aggressively. Long-lasting cut flowers. Attractive to birds and butterflies. Ignored by deer. Native to central and eastern North America.

R. columnifera, Mexican hat, 30" x 1', has tall, upright flowerheads surrounded by drooping yellow or mahogany red and yellow ray flowers.

R. pinnata, prairie or yellow coneflower, 3-4' x 1-2', has rounded, buttonlike flower-heads and dramatically drooping yellow ray flowers.

Rhamnus (rhamnus)

ZONES VARY. EVERGREEN OR DECIDUOUS SHRUBS OR TREES. SIZE VARIES.

Rugged, attractive shrubs for informal hedges and screens. The following evergreen shrubs thrive in sun or part shade with good drainage and occasional water. Good habitat plants. Attractive to deer.

R. alaternus, Italian buckthorn, 10-20' x 10-15', upright plant with shiny, dark green leaves. Attractive year-round. Accepts shearing and pruning; can be trained as a neat, multi-stemmed, small tree. Adaptable coastal or inland. Native to the Mediterranean. Zones 4-24. 'Variegata', 6-8' x 6-8', has lighter green leaves with creamy white margins.

R. californica, coffeeberry, 3-15' x 6-8', has shiny, dark green leaves, inconspicuous flowers, and berries that turn from green to red to black as they mature. Looks groomed without pruning. Native to California and southwestern Oregon. Zones 4-9, 14-24. 'Eve Case', 4-8' x 4-8', forms a dense mound with large berries. 'Mound San Bruno', 4-6' x 6-8', is densely covered with narrow, dark green leaves. 'Seaview Improved', 1-2' x 6-8', makes a good groundcover with small, dark green leaves and dense clusters of berries.

R. crocea, redberry, 2-3' x 3-6', has small, roundish, dark green leaves and bright red berries. Little to no water; some shade inland. Native to coast ranges of northern California to Baja California. The variety *ilicifolia* has toothed leaves. Zones 7, 14-24.

Rhaphiolepis (Indian hawthorn)

 ZONES 8-10, 12-24. EVERGREEN SHRUBS. SIZE VARIES.

Neat and attractive, easy-care shrubs widely used in western landscapes. Dark green, leathery leaves, sometimes bronzy in new growth, and long-lasting clusters of pink or white flowers from spring to fall, followed by dark blue fruits. Full sun to part shade, occasional water; afternoon shade in hot locations. Tolerate seaside conditions. Highly attractive to deer.

RIGHT: RHAPHIOLEPIS INDICA BERRIES **BELOW:** *R. INDICA* 'SPRINGTIME'

R. indica, Indian hawthorn, 4-5' x 5-6', has shiny, toothed leaves on bronzy stems and white flowers tinged with pink. Native to China. Most plants offered are cultivars. 'Ballerina', 2-3' x 3-4', has deep rosy pink flowers. 'Clara', 3-5' x 3-5', has reddish new leaves and white flowers. 'Enchantress', 3' x 5', has rose-pink flowers. 'Jack Evans', 4-5' x 4', has bright pink flowers. 'Springtime', 4-6' x 4-6', has deep pink flowers.

R. umbellata, yeddo hawthorn, 4-8' x 4-8', has dark green, roundish leaves and white flowers. Native to Japan and Korea. 'Minor', 3-4' x 3-4', is dense, compact, and slow-growing with small, dark green leaves with a burgundy tinge.

R. 'Majestic Beauty', 10-12' x 8-10', is larger in leaf, flower, and form. Can be trained as small tree. Light pink to white flowers.

Rhodanthemum hosmariense (Moroccan daisy)

 ZONES 14-24. PERENNIAL. 8-12" x 2'.

Neat mat of finely divided, silvery gray leaves and large, white, daisylike flowers with yellow centers almost year-round. Full sun, good drainage, occasional to no water. Native to Morocco.

RHODANTHEMUM HOSMARIENSE

Rhus (sumac)

ZONES VARY.
EVERGREEN AND
DECIDUOUS SHRUBS AND
TREES. SIZE VARIES.

Tough shrubs and trees, lovely in form and foliage. Full sun to part shade, good drainage, occasional water. Good bankcovers, windbreaks, screens, habitat plants.

R. glabra, smooth sumac, 10' x 10', upright, deciduous shrub or tree with

green leaves divided into long, narrow leaflets, turning scarlet in fall. Showy red fruits hang on bare branches into winter. Native to much of North America. Zones 1-10, 14-17.

ABOVE: *RHUS INTEGRIFOLIA*
LEFT: *R. OVATA*

R. integrifolia, lemonade berry, 3-10' x 3-10', evergreen shrub with leathery, toothed, rounded, dark green leaves and white to pinkish spring flowers followed by red fruit. Best along coast, where it takes wind in stride and needs little or no water; somewhat tender inland. Native to coastal southern California and Baja California. Zones 8, 9, 14-17, 19-24.

R. lancea, African sumac, 15-25' x 15-25', small-scale, sometimes multi-trunked evergreen tree, with narrow, dark green leaflets giving a graceful, weeping effect and reddish brown new bark aging to gray. Good street tree; roots do not raise paving. Self-sows readily. Native to South Africa. Zones 8, 9, 12-24.

R. laurina, laurel sumac, 6-15' x 6-15', fast-growing, rounded, evergreen shrub with reddish bark and light green leaves on pinkish stalks. Small, white flowers in spring and early summer. Tender; best near coast. Native to coastal southern California and Baja California. Zones 14-17, 19-24.

R. ovata, sugar bush, 8-12' x 8-12', densely branched, rounded, evergreen shrub with leathery, dark green leaves, often with reddish, wavy margins, and small white flowers. Excellent inland. Native to California, the southwestern U.S., and northwestern Mexico. Zones 9-12, 14-24.

Ribes (currant, gooseberry)

☀ ☀ ☀ ZONES VARY. EVERGREEN AND DECIDUOUS SHRUBS. SIZE VARIES.

◊ ◊ ◊ Ornamental currants and gooseberries are grown for their graceful habit, colorful fruits, ornamental foliage, and impressive displays of pendant flowers. Sun to part shade, moderate to occasional water. Good habitat plants. Flowers attractive to hummingbirds.

R. aureum, golden currant, 3-6' x 3-6', deciduous shrub for interior locations with light green leaves and clusters of bright yellow flowers in spring. Sun to part shade, moderate water. Native to inland areas of western North America. Zones 1-12, 14-23.

R. malvaceum, chaparral currant, 5' x 5', deciduous shrub with hairy, medium-green leaves and pink flowers in fall and winter. Native to mountains of coastal California. Zones 6-9, 14-24. 'Montara Rose' takes some sun; blooms in early winter.

R. sanguineum, red flowering currant, 5-12' x 5-12', deciduous shrub with maplelike, dark green leaves and drooping clusters of deep pink to red flowers in spring. The variety *glutinosum*, with pink flowers, is most often available. Drought-tolerant in coastal gardens with some shade. Native to coastal areas from central California to British Columbia. Zones 4-9, 14-24. 'White Icicle' and 'Inverness White' have white flowers. 'King Edward VIII' and 'Barrie Coate' have red flowers. 'Claremont' has pink flowers aging to red.

CLOCKWISE FROM TOP: *RIBES SPECIOSUM*, *R. AUREUM*, *R. SANGUINEUM*, *R. SANGUINEUM* 'CLAREMONT' WITH *ECHIUM WILDPRETII*, BERRIES OF *R. AUREUM*

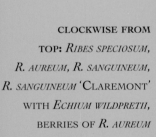

R. speciosum, fuchsia-flowered gooseberry, 4-8' x 6-10', partly deciduous shrub with stiffly arching, spiny stems, glossy, dark green leaves, and drooping red flowers with long stamens in winter to

spring. Native from coastal central California to Baja California. Zones 7-9, 14-24.

R. viburnifolium, evergreen currant, 3-6' x 4-12', has arching stems, roundish, leathery, dark green leaves, and light pink flowers midwinter to spring. Excellent groundcover for dry shade. Native to Catalina Island and Baja California. Zones 5, 7-9, 14-17, 19-24.

RIBES SANGUINEUM VAR. *GLUTINOSUM* **BELOW LEFT:** *R. SANGUINEUM* 'INVERNESS WHITE' **BELOW RIGHT:** *R. SANGUINEUM* 'CLAREMONT'

Romneya coulteri (matilija poppy)

ZONES 4-12, 14-24. PERENNIAL. 6-8' x 3-5'.

Magnificent, upright California native with bluish gray-green leaves on tall stems and huge, crinkled, pure white flowers with bright golden-yellow centers in early summer. Difficult to start, then spreads aggressively by underground rhizomes. Good bank holder. Dramatic but short-lived cut flowers. Full sun, good drainage, no water. Cut back hard after bloom. 'White Cloud' is especially vigorous.

ROMNEYA COULTERI

Rosa (rose)

ZONES VARY. DECIDUOUS AND EVERGREEN SHRUBS. SIZE VARIES.

Although roses in general have a reputation for needing lots of attention and water, there are roses that thrive with moderate to occasional deep watering, especially if heavily mulched and not fertilized in the heat of summer. Some old ramblers and climbers are quite drought tolerant, especially in moisture-retentive clay soils.

CLOCKWISE FROM BELOW:
RAMBLER *ROSA* 'APPLE BLOSSOM'
R. BANKSIAE 'ALBA PLENA'
R. BANKSIAE 'LUTEA'

R. banksiae, Lady Banks' rose, is a semi-deciduous, almost rampant climber to 20' with few thorns, shiny green leaves, and masses of yellow or white flowers in spring. Easily contained by regular pruning. Full sun to part shade, moderate water. Native to China. 'Alba Plena' has double white flowers. 'Lutea' has double yellow flowers. Zones 4-24.

R. californica, California wild rose, 3' x 6', thorny, spreading shrub

rose with arching stems that root where they touch the ground and whitish pink to rose-pink, single flowers with bright yellow stamens spring through midsummer. Part shade except along coast, moderate water. Native to California. Zones N/A.

R. rugosa, rugosa rose, 3-6' x 3-6', hardy, tough, repeat-flowering shrub rose with glossy green leaves and large, single to double fragrant flowers from spring to fall. Flowers don't last long but keep coming. Full sun, moderate to occasional water. Tolerates frost, wind, drought, and salt spray. Good bank cover or hedge, but thorns are prickly and plants sucker heavily from the base. Native to Asia. Zones 1-24.

R. wichuraiana, durable, dense, nearly evergreen rambler to 10-12' long, growing up and over fences and rooting where branches come in contact with soil. Clusters of large, fragrant, single white flowers with yellow stamens in summer. Good bankcover. Native to Japan, China, Korea. Zones 3-9, 12-24.

R. woodsii, 3-5' x 3-6', adaptable wild rose with small, light to dark pink fragrant flowers. Suckers freely and can form dense thickets, though not particularly thorny. Good habitat plant. Native to much of central and western North America. Zones N/A.

Rosmarinus officinalis
(rosemary)

ZONES 4-24. EVERGREEN SHRUB.
SIZE VARIES.

Variable shrub, prostrate to upright or spreading, with narrow, needlelike leaves and masses of tiny blue flowers in late winter and spring. Full sun, good drainage, little to no water. Good seaside plant. Attractive to butterflies and bees. Ignored by deer. Native to the Mediterranean.

Many named cultivars. 'Collingwood Ingram', 2-3' x 2-3', is a mounding shrub with bright blue flowers. 'Huntington Carpet', 1-2' x 4-8', creeps widely or cascades over walls. 'Ken Taylor, 2-3' x 4-5', has arching branches and dark blue flowers. 'Lockwood de Forrest', 2' x 4-6', is low and trailing with pale blue flowers. 'Majorca Pink', 2-3' x 2-4', has lilac-pink flowers. 'Tuscan Blue', 4-6' x 3-5', is an upright plant with light blue to deep violet-blue flowers. 'Irene', 12-18" x 2-3', is spreading or mounding with deep lavender-blue flowers. 'Prostratus', 2' x 4-8', mounding or cascading over walls, has pale lavender-blue flowers.

ABOVE: *ROSMARINUS OFFICINALIS* 'TUSCAN BLUE'
LEFT: *R. OFFICINALIS*

Rubus (bramble, rubus)

☀ ☀ ZONES VARY. DECIDUOUS AND EVERGREEN SHRUBS. SIZE VARIES.

💧 Low, scrambling or erect plants with clusters of white flowers resembling small roses. Excellent habitat plants. Good for dryish shade. Ignored by deer.

R. parviflorus, thimbleberry, 3-10' x 5-10', scrambling, somewhat spindly, deciduous shrub with fragrant, white flowers with crinkled petals in spring, small red fruits, and large green leaves that turn orange and red in fall. Part shade, good drainage, moderate to occasional water. Spreads by rhizomes, forming a thicket. Also self-sows; can be invasive. Native to western and central North America, including California, and northern Mexico. Zones N/A.

RUBUS PENTALOBUS

R. pentalobus, 6-12" x 6', vigorous, evergreen groundcover densely clothed with heavily textured, lobed, green leaves on spiny branches that keep out weeds. Part shade, good drainage, occasional water. White summer flowers followed by golden yellow fruit. Native to Taiwan. Zones 4-6, 14-17.

Rudbeckia (rudbeckia)

Zones 1-24. Perennials, biennials. Size varies.

Easy, cheerful plants with large yellow or orange, daisylike flowers with a darker central cone. Full sun, moderate to occasional water. Once established, rudbeckias require much less water than they usually are given. Most are native to eastern North America.

R. californica, California coneflower, 3-5' x 2-3', upright plant with deep green leaves and bright yellow flowers with green central cones in summer and fall. Good long-stemmed cut flower. Native to California.

R. fulgida, 3' x 2', spreading widely by rhizomes, upright plant with large, dark green leaves and yellow flowers with black to brown central cones in summer. 'Goldsturm' is more compact with larger flowers.

R. hirta, black-eyed Susan, 3-4' x 1-2', biennial or short-lived perennial with upright habit, coarsely hairy stems and leaves, and large, yellow-orange summer flowers with black central cones.

Ruta graveolens (rue)

ZONES 2-24. PERENNIAL. 2-3' x 2-3'.

Shrubby perennial with aromatic, blue-green to gray-green, divided leaves and small, greenish yellow flowers in mid- to late summer. Full sun, good drainage, moderate to occasional water. Cut back in winter or early spring. Ignored by deer. Native to the Mediterranean. 'Jackman's Blue' is compact with gray-blue leaves.

RUDBECKIA HIRTA 'INDIAN SUMMER'

RUTA GRAVEOLENS WITH COMFREY

Salvia (sage)

☀ ◑ ZONES VARY. EVERGREEN OR DECIDUOUS SHRUBS, PERENNIALS, ANNUALS.
SIZE VARIES.

Dozens of species and cultivars of sage are offered in the nursery trade, but some require regular water. The following evergreen shrubs and shrubby perennials are drought-tolerant, requiring only occasional water in summer. Most prefer full sun and good to excellent drainage. Attractive to hummingbirds, butterflies, and bees. Ignored by deer.

SALVIA SONOMENSIS

S. apiana, white sage, 4-5' x 4', evergreen shrub, coarsely branched, with fragrant, woolly, whitish gray-green leaves and white flowers tinged with lavender in spring. Native to southern California and Baja California. Zones 7, 9, 11, 13-24.

S. candelabrum, 3-4' x 3', has gray-green leaves on long, thin, branching stems and large, violet and white summer flowers. Native to Spain. Zones N/A.

S. chamaedryoides, germander sage, 2' x 3-4', perennial with small, silvery gray leaves and bright blue flowers in early summer and again in fall. Native to Mexico. Zones 8, 9, 12, 14-24.

S. clevelandii, Cleveland sage, 3-5' x 3-5', rounded evergreen shrub with ashy gray-green, fragrant leaves and stunning lavender to blue-violet flowers in early summer. Native to southern California. Zones 8, 9, 12-24.

BELOW: *SALVIA APIANA*
OPPOSITE TOP: *S. OFFICINALIS*
WITH *ORIGANUM VULGARE*
'AUREUM' BOTTOM, LEFT TO
RIGHT: *S. CHAMAEDRYOIDES, S.
SEMIATRATA, S. SEMIATRATA*
(RED) AND *S. CANDELABRUM*
(WHITE)

S. greggii, autumn sage, 1-4' x 1-3', variable shrub with small, glossy green, mostly evergreen leaves and masses of tiny flowers, from white to pink to true red to intense violet-purple, in summer to fall. Native to southwestern Texas and northern Mexico. Zones 8-24.

S. leucophylla, purple sage, 3-5' x 3-5', evergreen shrub with wrinkled, silvery gray leaves and pale purple to pinkish purple flowers in spring. Native to southern California. 'Pt. Sal', 3-6' x 5-8', makes a big, sprawling groundcover, excellent near coast. Zones 8, 9, 14-17, 19-24.

S. officinalis, garden sage, 1-3' x 12-18", has aromatic gray-green leaves and spikes of lavender-blue, violet, pink, or white flowers in spring and summer. Native to the Mediterranean. Zones 2-24.

S. semiatrata, bicolor sage, 3-6' x 2-3', upright shrub with yellowish green leaves and lavender and violet flowers in late summer. Tender, needs excellent drainage, afternoon shade in hot climates, moderate water. Zones 16, 17, 21-24.

S. sonomensis, creeping sage, 8-12" x 3-4', shrubby perennial with green to gray-green leaves and spikes of lavender-blue flowers on leafless stems in late spring to early summer. Cascades nicely over walls. Good for dryish shade. Native to California. Zones 7, 9, 14-24.

Sambucus mexicana (Mexican or blue elderberry)

 Zones 2-24. Deciduous shrub or tree. 10-30' x 10-20'.

Fast-growing, wild-looking shrub or tree with shiny green, divided leaves and flattish clusters of creamy white flowers in spring, followed by blue-black berries with a whitish bloom. Full sun to light shade, occasional to no water. Cut back to the ground in winter to control. Good screen, windbreak, or large, informal hedge. Excellent habitat plant. Native from California north to British Columbia. Other elderberries prefer regular water.

Santolina (santolina)

  Zones vary. Evergreen shrubs. 2-3' x 2-3'.

Low, mounding shrubs with aromatic, green or grayish green foliage and small bright yellow to creamy yellow, button-shaped flowers in summer. Full sun, occasional water. Fast-growing and adaptable, but short-lived; thrive in most soils with little water; tolerate both heat and cold. Cut back in spring and trim after flowering to maintain form. Native to the Mediterranean.

ABOVE: NATIVE GARDEN
WITH *SAMBUCUS MEXICANA*
PRUNED AS SMALL TREE

S. chamaecyparissus, lavender cotton, has whitish gray leaves and bright yellow flowers. Zones 2-24. 'Compacta' is lower growing.

S. rosmarinifolia, has narrow, green leaves that resemble rosemary and bright yellow flowers. Zones 3-9, 14-24. _____ 's more compact.

Santolina rosmarinifolia

_____ weet box)

_____ ERGREEN SHRUBS.

_____ est and most _____ nts for dry shade. _____ k green leaves _____ r the plant and maintain a neat, formal appearance without pruning. Tiny, _____ nt flowers in late winter and early spring are followed by small, blue-black _____. Part to full shade, good drainage, moderate to occasional water. Native to _____ the Himalayas. Ignored by deer.

_____ *humilis*, 18" x 3-8', mounding groundcover that spreads by underground runners. Blue-black fruit. Zones 3-9, 14-24.

S. ruscifolia, 4-6' x 3-7', upright shrub with dark red fruit. Zones 4-9, 14-24.

Low hedge of *Sarcococca hookerana humilis* in shade of live oak

Schinus molle (California pepper tree)

ZONES 8-9, 12-24. EVERGREEN TREE. 25-40' x 25-40'.

SCHINUS MOLLE AT
MISSION SAN LUIS REY

Large, fast-growing, adaptable tree, sometimes multi-trunked, often wider than tall with a rounded canopy. Needs room to spread. Bright green, lacy leaves on gracefully weeping branchlets. Mature trees have fantastically gnarled and twisted trunks. Clusters of tiny white flowers followed by decorative pink berries in fall and winter. Full sun, little to no water. Native to Peru, but planted around California missions as early as the 1830s. Invasive in riparian areas in some parts of southern California.

Scilla peruviana (Peruvian scilla)

ZONES 14-17, 19-24. PERENNIAL FROM BULB.
10-12" TALL.

Easy summer-dormant bulb with long-lasting, dome-shaped clusters of densely packed bluish purple, sometimes white, flowers. Full sun, good drainage, no summer water.

Good for naturalizing.
Native to the
Mediterranean. Some
other species of *Scilla*
require summer water.

Sedum (stonecrop)

Zones vary. Succulent
perennials. Size varies.

A huge group of plants,
highly variable in size,
shape, color, and cultural
tolerances. Some are
tender. Many prefer
afternoon shade. All need
good to excellent
drainage, moderate to
occasional water. Native
to many parts of the
world.

S. rubrotinctum, pork and
beans, 6-8" x 10", with
bulbous, red-tinted green
leaves and yellow spring
flowers. Light shade, little
to moderate water.
Protect from frost and
heat. Native to Mexico.
Zones 8, 9, 12, 14-24.

S. spathulifolium, 4" x 12",
with rosettes of blue-
green to gray-green leaves
tinged reddish purple and

yellow, star-shaped flowers in spring and summer.
Drought-tolerant. Native from California north to
British Columbia. 'Purpureum' has deep purple
leaves with a silvery white bloom. 'Cape Blanco',
'Campbell Lake', and 'False Klamath Cove' are all
good gray forms. Zones 2-9, 14-24.

S. spurium, 3-6" x 2-3', trailing stems with dark
green, sometimes bronzy, leaves and pink flowers
in summer. Native to the Caucasus. 'Dragon's
Blood' has purplish bronze leaves and dark red
flowers. 'Tricolor' has green leaves edged with
creamy white. Zones 1-10, 14-24.

TOP TO BOTTOM: *Scilla
peruviana*, *Sedum
spurium* 'Tricolor',
S. spathulifolium

. . . 213

Sempervivum (houseleek)

SEMPERVIVUM TECTORUM

ZONES 2-24. SUCCULENT PERENNIALS. SIZE VARIES.

Rosette-forming succulents with green to gray-green leaves tinged pink, purple, red, orange, or brown and clusters of tiny, star-shaped, pink, red, yellow, or creamy white summer flowers. Rosettes die after flowering, but offsets quickly form dense colonies. Sun to part shade, excellent drainage, moderate to occasional water. Afternoon shade in hot locations. Native to Europe, northern Africa, and eastern Asia. Many species and cultivars.

S. arachnoideum, cobweb houseleek, 3" tall, large group of plants with gray-green foliage with web-like hairs and bright red flowers.

S. calcareum, 3-6" tall, rosettes of tapering, green to blue-green leaves with brownish maroon tips and pinkish white to creamy white flowers.

S. tectorum, hens and chicks, 4-12" tall, with offsets forming tight clumps to 2' across. Gray-green leaves with red-brown tips and pink to red flowers on upright stalks. Frost hardy but not tolerant of high heat.

Senecio cineraria (dusty miller)

ZONES 4-24. PERENNIAL. 2-3' x 2-3'.

SENECIO CINERARIA 'SILVER DUST'

Shrubby perennial with woolly, whitish gray, lobed leaves and clusters of small, creamy white or yellow flowers almost year-round. Full sun to part shade, good drainage, occasional water. Cut back occasionally to renew. Ignored by deer. Native to the Mediterranean.

Senna (cassia)

ZONES VARY. EVERGREEN SHRUBS. SIZE VARIES.

Fast-growing, somewhat weedy, low-maintenance shrubs valued for their showy yellow, pink, or white flowers in winter and spring. Noted for ability to thrive in hot, dry, windy conditions. Full sun, good drainage, occasional water. Formerly in the genus *Cassia* and still often offered under that name. Potentially invasive.

S. alata, candlestick plant, 6-10' x 8-12', has showy yellow flowers in erect spikes in summer. Native to South America. Zones N/A.

S. nemophila, desert cassia, 6' x 6', has grayish green, narrow leaves and lightly scented, buttercup-yellow flowers. Native to Australia. Zones 12-24.

Sequoia sempervirens (coast redwood)

ZONE 4-9, 14-24. EVERGREEN TREE. 60-100' x 25-30'.

Fast-growing, pyramidal tree with columnar trunk, thick, reddish, fibrous bark, and short, flat, pointed leaves with a feathery appearance, green above and gray-green to blue-green beneath. Ancient trees are several hundred feet tall, and newly planted trees will grow fast to a substantial height and spread. Allow plenty of room for widespreading lower branches and roots. Not for hot, interior locations. Full sun to part shade along coast, moderate to occasional water. Leave fallen leaf litter as mulch

for extensive, shallow roots. Native to coastal central California and Oregon in areas with dependable summer fog.

Many named cultivars with slightly differing colors and habits. 'Aptos Blue' and 'Santa Cruz' have drooping branches with grayish green leaves. 'Soquel' is a fine-textured tree with grayish green leaves and a thick trunk. 'Monty' has a denser branching habit with soft, weeping, blue-green leaves.

Sesleria (moor grass)

ZONES N/A. PERENNIAL GRASSES. 6-12" x 1-2'.

Tough, long-lived, cool-season clumping grasses with stiff, narrow, bright green to grayish or bluish green leaves. Flowers on slender stems in fall. Full sun to part shade, moderate water. Good small-scale groundcover or edging along pathways. Most effective massed. Native to Europe.

S. autumnalis, autumn moor grass, 6-12" x 1-2', upright habit, bright green to yellow-green leaves with whitish flowers held well above the foliage in late summer.

S. caerulea, blue moor grass, 6-12" x 6-12", has broad, two-toned leaves, dark blue-green above, silvery beneath, and small flowers rising barely above the foliage.

Sidalcea malviflora
(checkerbloom, checker mallow)

ZONES 2-9, 14-24. PERENNIAL. 2' x 1-2'.

Upright or sprawling perennial with large, pink or purplish pink flowers in early spring. Summer-dormant without water; cut back and let it go dry. Sun to part shade, good drainage, no summer water. Native to vernally damp spots in California and Oregon.

ABOVE: *SESLERIA AUTUMNALIS* WITH LAVENDER AND EUPHORBIA LEFT: *SIDALCEA MALVIFLORA*

Sideritis (sideritis)

ZONES N/A. PERENNIAL. 12-18" x 18".

SIDERITIS CYPRIA

Clump-forming perennials with woolly, silvery white leaves and whorled spikes of pale yellow or yellow-green flowers in summer. Full sun, heat, excellent drainage, moderate to occasional water. Native to the Mediterranean.

Sisyrinchium bellum (blue-eyed grass)

ZONES 2-9, 14-24. PERENNIAL. 6-12" x 6-18".

Diminutive plant with green or bluish green, irislike leaves and star-shaped, upward-facing, lavender or blue spring flowers that close at night and on cloudy days. Self-sows freely. Best planted in large drifts. Full sun to

SISYRINCHIUM BELLUM
WITH ERIGERON

light shade, occasional water. Native to coastal California and Oregon. 'Greyhound Rock' has pale blue flowers and grayish green leaves. 'Rocky Point' has short, broad leaves and purple flowers. 'Figueroa' has green leaves with creamy white margins and blue flowers. *S. californicum*, yellow-eyed grass, is a similar plant with yellow flowers for wet areas.

Solanum (solanum)

ZONES VARY. EVERGREEN TO SEMI-DECIDUOUS VINES AND SHRUBS. SIZE VARIES.

Medium to fast-growing

SOLANUM JASMINOIDES

vines or vining shrubs with clusters of star-shaped flowers. Excellent for fences, trellises, and arbors. Full sun to part shade, moderate to occasional water. Cut back hard to control and renew. Native to South America. Ignored by deer.

S. crispum, blue potato vine, 10-12', has green leaves and fragrant, lilac-blue flowers with yellow centers in summer. Needs help to climb. 'Glasnevin' has darker blue flowers. Zones 8, 9, 12-24.

S. jasminoides, potato vine, 20-30', fast-growing, twining vine with purple-tinged green leaves and lightly scented, white flowers with yellow centers almost year-round. Zones 8, 9, 12-24.

S. rantonnetii, blue potato bush, 8-12' x 6-10', sprawling shrub with bright green leaves and royal purple flowers with golden yellow centers almost year-round. Can be pruned to upright tree form or spread out along a fence like a vine. 'Royal Robe' is more compact with darker purple flowers. Zones 12, 13, 15-24.

S. umbelliferum, 1-3' x 3-4', mound of silvery gray-green leaves and pale to dark lavender-blue flowers with yellow centers. Tolerates clay soils, little water. Native to coastal California. Zones N/A.

S. xantii, 2-3' x 2-3', evergreen shrub with green leaves and purple flowers. Full sun, little to no water. Native to California. Zones 7-9, 11, 14-24.

Solidago (goldenrod)

ZONES VARY. PERENNIALS. SIZE VARIES.

Low-maintenance, long-lived, summer- and fall-flowering perennials with narrow, green leaves and small, bright yellow flowers, usually in dense, compact clusters at the ends of tall stems. Full sun to part shade, any soil, moderate to occasional water. Attractive to butterflies and bees. Native to many parts of North America.

S. caesia, blue-stemmed goldenrod, 3' x 2', has dark green leaves and compact clusters of yellow fall flowers in leaf axils along graceful, arching, purplish stems. Part shade. Native to eastern North America. Zones N/A.

SOLIDAGO CANADENSIS

S. californica, California goldenrod, 1-4' x 1-2', has felted, gray-green leaves and yellow flowers on short spikes in late summer to fall. Part shade, little to no water. Easy. Native to California. Zones N/A.

S. canadensis, Canada goldenrod, 3-5' x 3', variable plant with grayish green leaves and yellow flowers on tall, arching stems; good back-of-border plant. Native to North America. Zones N/A.

S. rugosa, rough-stemmed goldenrod, 1-4' x 3-5', similar to Canada goldenrod but with even more arching flower stems. 'Fireworks', 3' x 3', forms a roundish, compact shower of yellow. Zones 1-11, 14-23.

Sparaxis tricolor (harlequin flower)

☀ ZONES 9, 12-24. PERENNIAL FROM CORM. 1' x 1'.

◊ Basal fans of summer-dormant, sword-shaped leaves and loose spikes of widely flaring, funnel-shaped flowers on wiry stems in spring. Long-lasting cut flowers are combinations of pink, purple, red, white, or yellow. Full sun, good drainage, no summer water. Native to South Africa.

SPARAXIS TRICOLOR

Sphaeralcea (globe mallow)

☀ ZONES VARY. PERENNIAL. 2-4' x 2'.

◊ Upright to sprawling plants with shallowly lobed, softly hairy, green to gray-green leaves and salmon to red-orange or pink flowers in late summer. Full sun, good drainage, little water. *S. incana* is native to the southwestern U.S. *S. munroana* is native to the western U.S., including California.

SPHAERALCEA INCANA

Sporobolus (sacaton)

☀ ZONES VARY. PERENNIAL GRASSES. SIZE VARIES.

◊◊ Warm-season bunchgrasses with arching, feathery plumes of flowers. Full sun, moderate to occasional water. Tolerate some drought, saline and alkaline soils, and periodic flooding. Native

to central and southern North America, including California, and Mexico.

S. airoides, alkali sacaton, 2-3' x 2-3', has bluish or gray-green leaves turning yellow in fall and feathery flower plumes, pinkish fading to silvery pale straw, on erect to arching, 4-5' stems. Zones 1-24.

S. heterolepsis, prairie dropseed, 4' x 3', handsome, fine-textured, arching mound of narrow, emerald green leaves turning golden yellow in fall, and airy panicles of flowers in summer. Zones N/A.

Stachys byzantina (lamb's ears)

ZONES 1-24. PERENNIAL. 6-12" x 3'.

Low, widespreading perennial grown primarily for its rosettes of softly woolly, silvery gray leaves. Full to part sun, good drainage, moderate to occasional water. Leaves brown in hot sun and turn mushy with heavy rains in winter; plants often recover but may need periodic replacement. Spikes of small, pink to purplish summer flowers are attractive to bees. Lovely filler and edging plant. Native to the Caucasus and Iran. Many cultivars. 'Silver Carpet' is a non-flowering variety that spreads more slowly.

STACHYS BYZANTINA 'SILVER CARPET' WITH *ROSA* 'THE FAIRY' AND HARDY GERANIUMS

OPPOSITE PAGE BOTTOM, LEFT TO RIGHT: *SPOROBOLUS HETEROLEPSIS*, *S. AIROIDES*

Stipa (feather grass)

☀ ZONES VARY. PERENNIAL GRASSES. SIZE VARIES.

💧💧 Dramatic, clumping, cool-season grasses with narrow, arching, grayish green leaves and shimmering golden flowerheads rising high above the leaves in summer. Full sun, moderate to occasional water. Potentially invasive.

S. arundinacea, pheasant's tail grass, 2' x 2', has arching green leaves with coppery tints turning coppery yellow in fall, and feathery flowers in summer rising slightly above leaves. Native to New Zealand. Zones 14-24.

ABOVE: *STIPA ARUNDINACEA* WITH STACHYS AND PHORMIUM

RIGHT: *S. GIGANTEA*

S. gigantea, giant feather grass, 2-3' x 2-4', arching leaves with open, airy plumes of flowers on 6' stems. Full sun to light shade, moderate to occasional water. Native to the Mediterranean. Zones 4-9, 14-24.

Stylomecon heterophylla (wind poppy)

ZONES N/A. ANNUAL. 1-2' x 1'.

Nodding buds opening in spring or early summer to fragrant, salmon-orange or tangerine, crepelike poppy flowers with darker colors at petal bases and yellow to orange stamens. Full sun to light shade, excellent drainage, occasional water. Attractive to bees. Native to California. 'White Satin' has large, pure white flowers with yellow stamens.

Styphnolobium japonicum

(Japanese pagoda tree)

ZONES 2-24. DECIDUOUS TREE. 50-70' x 50-70'.

Fine-textured, deciduous tree with dark green leaves divided into many small leaflets and faintly fragrant, creamy white to pale yellow pea flowers in long, pendulous clusters in summer. Full sun to part shade, good drainage, moderate to occasional water. Needs some summer heat to flower well. Native to China.

Styrax officinalis var. *redivivus*

(snowdrop bush)

ZONES N/A. DECIDUOUS SHRUB. 6-15' x 6-10'.

Woodland shrub with drooping, white, sweetly fragrant, bell-shaped flowers with prominent yellow stamens in spring, bright green to grayish green leaves turning yellow to orange in fall, and attractive round seed capsules. Unlike most other kinds of styrax, this California native takes some drought. Shade to part sun, good drainage, moderate water.

LEFT: *STYLOMECON HETEROPHYLLA* WITH GILIA BELOW: *STYPHNOLOBIUM JAPONICUM* BOTTOM LEFT: *STYRAX OFFICINALIS* VAR. *REDIVIVUS* FLOWERS

Symphoricarpos albus (snowberry)

ZONES 1-11, 14-21. DECIDUOUS SHRUB.
3-5' x 3-5'.

Mounding thicket of arching stems airily covered
with small, roundish or lobed, mid-green leaves
and pink, bell-shaped flowers in spring followed
by striking white berries that remain on the plant
into winter. Part shade, occasional to little water.
Attractive to birds and butterflies. Good habitat
plant for dry woodland gardens. Native to much
of North America, including California.

*SYMPHORICARPOS
ALBUS* BERRIES

TAGETES LEMMONII

Tagetes lemmonii

(Mexican bush
marigold)

ZONES 8-10, 12-
24. PERENNIAL.
3-6' x 4-6'.

Sprawling,
shrubby, short-
lived perennial
with finely
divided, aromatic
leaves and
golden-yellow
flowers
periodically all
year. Full sun to
part shade,
occasional water.
Plants are more
compact in poor
soils. Attractive
to butterflies.
Ignored by deer.
Damaged by
frost but usually
survives. Tip
prune to control
legginess. Native
to southwestern
U.S. and
Mexico.

Tanacetum (tansy)

☀ ZONES VARY. PERENNIALS. SIZE VARIES.

◊◊◊ Easy, sun-loving perennials with small, yellow flowers. Self-sow readily; potentially invasive with water.

T. densum ssp. *amanii*, 6-8" x 18", mat-forming plant with silvery gray-green leaves and dotted with small, yellow flowers in late spring. Good small-scale groundcover. Full sun, good drainage, moderate to occasional water. Native to Turkey. Zones 3-24.

T. vulgare, 3' x 2', has bright green leaves and yellow flowers in summer. Weedy and rambunctious, but easily pulled. Sun or part shade, little to no water. The variety *crispum*, fern-leaf tansy, is more ornamental than the species. Native to Europe. Zones 1-24.

TANACETUM VULGARE
VAR. *CRISPUM*

TECOMARIA CAPENSIS 'AUREA'

Tecomaria capensis (Cape honeysuckle)

ZONES 12, 13, 20-24. EVERGREEN VINE. 15-30'.

Fine-textured, shrubby vine with shiny, dark green leaves and clusters of brilliant orange to red-orange, trumpet-shaped flowers in fall to spring. Pruned hard in early years, it can be trained to a neat shrub of almost any size. Dies back during hard frosts, but recovers quickly. Full sun to part shade, good drainage, occasional water. Attractive to hummingbirds. Tolerates wind, salt air. Native to South Africa. 'Aurea' has yellow flowers.

BELOW: SHEARED *TEUCRIUM FRUTICANS* WITH *CALAMAGROSTIS* X *ACUTIFLORA* 'KARL FOERSTER' BOTTOM: TAPESTRY OF THYMES

Teucrium (germander)

ZONES VARY. PERENNIALS. SIZE VARIES.

Shrubby, upright perennials with small, green or gray-green leaves and summer flowers in terminal spikes. Full sun, excellent drainage, occasional water. Attractive to butterflies and bees. Ignored by deer. Native to the Mediterranean.

T. fruticans, bush germander, 4-6' x 4-6', has small, silvery gray-green leaves and lavender-blue flowers. Accepts shearing. Zones 4-24. 'Azureum' has darker blue flowers. 'Compactum', 3' x 3', is dense and more compact.

T. x *lucidrys*, 1' x 2', upright plant with dark green, toothed leaves and reddish purple flowers. Good low hedge or edging. Cut back annually to maintain form. Zones 2-24. 'Compactum', 6" x 2-3', has smaller leaves and flowers.

Thymus (thyme)

ZONES 1-24. PERENNIALS. SIZE VARIES.

Ground-hugging mats to mounding, sprawling, or upright perennials with aromatic, green to gray-green leaves and masses of tiny flowers in spring or summer. Shear occasionally to neaten and promote flowering. Full sun to part shade, good drainage, moderate to occasional water. Attractive to bees. Ignored by deer. Native to the Mediterranean.

T. x *citriodorus*, lemon thyme, 1' x 2', erect or sprawling, medium green leaves with a lemony fragrance and pale lilac flowers in summer. Part shade. 'Lime' has lime-green leaves.

T. pseudolanuginosus, woolly thyme, 2-3" x 3', flat mat of woolly, gray-green leaves and pink flowers in summer. Best in small areas or between rocks or stepping stones.

T. serpyllum, creeping thyme, 3" x 3', has roundish, dark green leaves and lavender to purple flowers in summer. Moderate water. Many named cultivars with varying leaf and flower colors.

Tibouchina urvilleana

(princess flower)

ZONES 16, 17, 21-24. EVERGREEN SHRUB. 5-15' x 3-10'.

Tender, fast-growing, upright and open shrub with large, royal purple flowers in early winter to late spring and velvety, green to gray-green leaves edged with red; new growth covered with bronzy red hairs. Prefers roots in shade, top in sun. Best along coast. Good drainage, moderate water. Prune lightly for best form. Native to Brazil.

TIBOUCHINA URVILLEANA WITH WHITE SHASTA DAISIES

Trachycarpus fortunei (windmill palm)

ZONES 4-24. PALM. 30' x 10'.

Hardy palm with dark green, fan-shaped fronds and thick trunk covered with matted fibers. Good along coast. Full sun to part shade, good drainage, moderate water. Native to China.

TRICHOSTEMA LANATUM

Trichostema lanatum
(woolly blue curls)

ZONES 14-24. EVERGREEN SHRUB. 2-5' x 4-6'.

Dramatic but touchy and usually short-lived California native with narrow, aromatic, dark green leaves with white-woolly undersides and clusters of blue to purplish flowers on tall stalks in spring. Full sun, excellent drainage, no summer water. Plant on mounds or slopes in fast-draining soil. Pruning may promote bloom through summer.

Triteleia (triteleia, brodiaea)

ZONES VARY. PERENNIALS FROM CORMS. 1-2' TALL.

Easy, summer-dormant perennials with a few grasslike leaves and dense or open clusters of cup-shaped flowers with flared petals in spring or early summer. Full sun to part shade, no summer water. Content in heavy clay soils if kept dry in summer. Excellent mixed with grasses, which support the floppy stems. Protect from rodents.

TRITELEIA IXIOIDES

T. bridgesii, Bridges' triteleia, robust and easy in gardens, with clusters of pink to rich blue-purple flowers that open sequentially, giving a long show from late spring to early summer. Prefers filtered sun. Native to California. Zones N/A.

T. hyacinthina, white brodiaea, has showy white flowers in spring. Native from central California to southwestern British Columbia. Zones 2-9, 14-24.

T. ixioides, golden brodiaea, has yellow flowers with bronzy stripes on each narrow petal. Native to central western California and southwestern Oregon. Zones 3-9, 14-24.

T. laxa, Ithuriel's spear, has broad, grasslike leaves and pale lavender to deep blue-violet flowers on slender stems. Multiplies rapidly; easiest triteleia for gardens. Native to northern California and southwestern Oregon. 'Queen Fabiola' has cornflower blue flowers. Zones 5-9, 14-24.

Tulbaghia (society garlic)

ZONES 13-24. PERENNIALS FROM RHIZOMES. 1-2' x 1-2'.

Narrow, evergreen, grasslike or strap-shaped leaves and clusters of trumpet-shaped pink or lavender flowers in spring to fall. Full sun, good drainage, moderate water. Tender, but usually recover. Ignored by deer. Native to South Africa.

T. simmleri, has broad, dull green to grayish green leaves with a garlicky odor when crushed and spikes of pale pink to purplish pink, sweetly fragrant flowers in late winter or early spring. 'Alba' has white flowers.

T. violacea, society garlic, has narrow, bluish green leaves and clusters of pale lavender to pinkish lavender flowers in spring and summer. Good border or edging plant. 'Silver Lace' has bluish green leaves with creamy white margins.

TULBAGHIA VIOLACEA

Tulipa (tulip)

☀
○ ZONES 1-24. PERENNIALS FROM BULBS. 8-12" TALL.

Although summer-dormant and adapted to dry-summer climates, most tulips do best where winters are long and cold, gradually or quickly declining in mild-winter areas. The species tulips described below are exquisitely simple compared to most hybrids and are some of the best choices where winters are mild. They multiply and naturalize well with full sun, excellent drainage, no summer water. Native to the Mediterranean.

T. bakeri has pale lilac, cup-shaped flowers with yellow petal bases in early spring. Leaves curl slightly backward, remaining close to the ground. 'Lilac Wonder' has larger and more widely open, rosy purple flowers with lemon-yellow petal bases.

RIGHT: *TULIPA CLUSIANA* 'TUBERGEN'S GEM'
BELOW: *T. CLUSIANA* VAR. *CHRYSANTHA*

T. clusiana has slender, upright, bicolored

flowers, red on the outside and white inside, in early to midspring. The variety *chrysantha* is yellow on the inside and rosy carmine on the outside and more star-shaped when fully open.

T. greigii has large, red-orange, midspring flowers with tapering petals and green leaves mottled with purplish brown. Many cultivars with white, pink, orange, red, or multicolored flowers.

T. saxatilis has broad, arching leaves and large, pale lilac, early spring flowers with yellow petal bases, initially cup-shaped, opening nearly flat.

CLOCKWISE FROM LEFT:
TULIPA GREIGII, T. GREIGII, T. CLUSIANA 'LADY JANE'

ULMUS PARVIFOLIA

Ulmus parvifolia
(Chinese elm)

ZONES 3-24.
SEMI-EVERGREEN TREE.
40-60' x 60'.

Open, widespreading, often low-branching tree with leathery, dark green, toothed leaves, weeping branchlets, and beautifully mottled bark. Full sun, moderate water. Native to China, Korea, Japan. 'Brea' has larger leaves and more upright habit. 'True Green' has small, deep green leaves retained year-round.

Verbascum (mullein)

ZONES VARY. PERENNIALS, BIENNIALS. SIZE VARIES.

Short-lived plants with rosettes of often hairy or felted, green or gray-green leaves and upright spikes of flowers in late spring or summer. Full sun, good to excellent drainage, moderate to occasional water. Tolerate alkaline soils. Remove spent flowers to encourage rebloom. Self-sow readily. Many named cultivars.

V. bombyciferum, 4-5' x 2', biennial with velvety gray-green leaves and tall spikes of yellow flowers. Native to Turkey. Zones 2-11, 14-24.

V. chaixii, 3' x 2', perennial with large, dark green leaves and tall spikes of pale yellow flowers with red centers. Native to Europe. 'Album' has grayish green leaves and white flowers with purple centers. Zones 2-11, 14-24.

V. phoeniceum, purple mullein, 2-4' x 2', perennial with dark green, deeply veined and crinkled leaves, hairy beneath, and spikes of purple, pink, or white flowers. Native to Europe. Zones 1-10, 14-24.

V. 'Arctic Summer', 3-5' x 2-3', perennial with sulphur yellow flowers on tall, stiff stems and white-woolly leaves. Zones 2-11, 14-24.

Verbena (verbena)

ZONES VARY. PERENNIALS. SIZE VARIES.

Fast-growing, groundcovering perennials for hot locations. Deep green to gray-green, finely divided leaves and clusters of small but showy flowers in summer. Full sun to part shade, good drainage, moderate to occasional water, protection from winter wet. Some species and hybrids need regular water (e.g., 'Homestead Purple'); some are tender. Ignored by deer.

V. bipinnatifida, 8-18" x 18"-2', has green leaves and purplish blue flowers. Native to western U.S. and Mexico. Zones 1-24.

V. bonariensis, 3-6' x 18"-3', an unusual giant in the family, has dark green leaves and purple flowers at the tips of tall, airy, branching stems. Self-sows; potentially invasive in irrigated gardens and riparian areas. Zones 8-24. Native to South America; naturalized in California.

V. lilacina, Cedros Island verbena, 1' x 3', with light green, deeply divided leaves and lilac flowers spring to fall. Excellent for hot, dry sites. Native to Baja California. Zones 12-24.

LEFT: *VERBASCUM BOMBYCIFERUM* WITH LAVENDER AND ROSE
BELOW: *VERBENA BONARIENSIS* WITH *NASSELLA TENUISSIMA*

Vitex agnus-castus

(chaste tree)

VITEX AGNUS-CASTUS

ZONE 4-24. DECIDUOUS SHRUB. 10-15' x 10-15'.

Handsome and adaptable, upright, usually multi-trunked shrub with aromatic, divided, gray-green leaves and spikes of fragrant, lavender-blue flowers in summer to fall. Blooms on new growth; cut back in winter to shape. Full sun or light shade, moderate to occasional water. Tolerates heat, clay soil. Ignored by deer. Native to the Mediterranean and central Asia. 'Latifolia' has broader leaves. 'Silver Spire' and 'Alba' have white flowers. 'Rosea' has pink flowers.

Vitis californica (California wild grape)

ZONES 4-24. DECIDUOUS VINE. 20-30'.

Large-leaved vine that climbs by tendrils, covering trees and shrubs as well as arbors and trellises. Gray-green new leaves turn bright green in summer, then yellow and red in fall. Full sun, moderate to occasional water. Drought deciduous in hot locations without water. Native to coastal California and Oregon. 'Roger's Red' turns brilliant red in fall. 'Russian River' has burgundy fall color. 'Walker Ridge', to 10' tall, has smaller leaves and bright red and yellow fall color.

VITIS CALIFORNICA
'ROGER'S RED' LEAVES
IN FALL

Washingtonia (fan palm)

ZONES 8, 9, 10, 11-24. PALMS. SIZE VARIES.

Tall, single-trunked, moderate to fast-growing palms with large, deeply folded palmate or fan-shaped fronds. Creamy white and yellow flowers hang in pendulous clusters from the crown in late spring or early summer, followed by black fruit. Roots are shallow and fibrous. Full sun, good drainage, tolerate drought but benefit from periodic deep watering. Fairly salt-tolerant. Effective grouped in parks or on large estates and stately in rows along urban boulevards. The two species below hybridize readily, and many variations occur.

W. filifera, California fan palm, 60' x 20', has a thicker trunk than *W. robusta* and does not grow as tall. Fronds of leaves are glistening dark green to grayish green with threadlike fibers along the margins and form a loose, open crown. Dead leaves remain

LEFT AND BELOW:
WASHINGTONIA FILIFERA

attached to the trunk, and if not removed will form a dry, brown "skirt" from the green-leaved crown to the ground. Native to California, Arizona, and Baja California.

W. robusta, Mexican fan palm, 70-100' x 10-15', taller than California fan palm and has a much narrower trunk. Fronds are smaller and leaf blades are bright green and lack the thready margins. Native to Mexico.

Watsonia (watsonia)

ZONES 4-9, 12-24. PERENNIALS FROM CORMS. SIZE VARIES.

Deciduous or evergreen perennials with fans of sword-shaped leaves and tubular, lilylike flowers on tall stalks. Full sun, reasonable drainage. Summer-dormant kinds need no summer water; evergreen kinds are content with moderate water. Spread by underground corms. Native to South Africa. Many hybrids. Ignored by deer.

W. aletroides, 8-12", has coral pink to scarlet flowers in mid- to late spring.

WATSONIA BEATRICIS HYBRID

W. beatricis, 2-3', is evergreen with erect flower spikes to 5' and orange, peach, or coral red summer flowers.

W. coccinea, 12", has bright red to orange or pink flowers on 18" stalks in early spring.

W. humilis, 6", dwarf with deep pink flowers on 12" stems in late spring.

Westringia fruticosa
(coast rosemary)

ZONES 8, 9, 14-24. EVERGREEN SHRUB. 3-6' X 5-10'.

Dense, widespreading, fine-textured shrub with green to gray-green, needlelike leaves and small, white or lavender flowers midwinter through spring. Full sun,

WESTRINGIA FRUTICOSA 'SMOKEY'

good drainage, occasional water. Tolerates wind and salt. Ignored by deer. Native to Australia. 'Smokey' has grayish green leaves with creamy white margins and white flowers with a tinge of violet. 'Wynyabbie Gem' has lavender blue flowers.

Wisteria (wisteria)

☀ ◑ ZONES VARY. DECIDUOUS VINES. 30'.

◐

Vigorous, adaptable, long-lived, and fast-growing once established, these woody vines offer breathtaking spring displays of flowers in pendulous clusters. Leaves are divided into many narrow leaflets, lending a graceful effect, and flowers are followed by long, velvety seedpods. Can be trained as large shrubs or weeping trees. Full sun to part shade, good drainage, occasional water. Native to China and Japan.

W. floribunda, Japanese wisteria, has long clusters of fragrant, violet or blue-violet flowers that open gradually over a long season. Many named cultivars with white, pink, purple, or lavender flowers. 'Longissima' has especially long clusters of light purple flowers. 'Longissima Alba' is similar but with white flowers. 'Rosea' has pinkish lavender flowers. Zones 2-24.

W. sinensis, Chinese wisteria, has long clusters of fragrant, purple flowers that open all at once in a theatrical display before leaves appear in spring. 'Alba' has particularly fragrant, white flowers. 'Black Dragon' has double, dark purple flowers. 'Plena' has double, lilac flowers. Zones 3-24.

WISTERIA SINENSIS WITH CUTLEAF LILAC

Xylosma congestum (xylosma)

ZONES 8-24. EVERGREEN SHRUB OR TREE.
8-15' x 8-10'.

Useful and adaptable shrub with shiny, yellowish green leaves, bronzy when new. Good informal hedge. Responds well to pruning, though shearing is unattractive. Can be trained as a small tree with gracefully drooping branches. Full sun, good drainage, occasional water. Native to China. 'Compacta' grows slowly to about half as large.

Yucca (yucca)

ZONES VARY. EVERGREEN SHRUBS AND PERENNIALS. SIZE VARIES.

Rosettes of sword-shaped leaves and clusters of creamy white flowers on tall stalks in early spring. Some form trunks. Clumps may expand outward by offsets. Full sun, excellent drainage, occasional deep watering. Native to many parts of North America.

Y. aloifolia, dagger plant, has gray-green leaves with smooth edges and white summer flowers flushed with purple on a 2' spike. Eventually develops a branched trunk 10-15' tall. 'Marginata' has yellow-edged leaves. Zones N/A.

Y. baccata, banana yucca, 3-4' x 4-5', slow-growing, spiky rosette of gray-green leaves with fibers along the margins. Stemless for a number of years, rosettes eventually form a short trunk. Native to California, the southwestern U.S., and Mexico. Zones 1-3, 7, 9-14, 18-24.

Y. rostrata, beaked yucca, has gray-green leaves with minutely toothed margins and white fall

XYLOSMA CONGESTUM

flowers on a tall spike. Eventually develops a trunk to 15'. Native to southern U.S. and northern Mexico. Zones N/A.

Y. schidigera, Mojave yucca, 3-12' x 4-5', rosettes of yellow-green to blue-green, sharp-tipped leaves on short trunks and creamy white flowers with a purple tinge. Native to California, the southwestern U.S., and Mexico. Zones 7-16, 18-24.

Y. whipplei, our lord's candle, 2-4' x 2-4', large rosette of narrow, bluish gray leaves with needlelike tips. After some years, a bold spike emerges from the rootstock bearing masses of creamy white flowers. Like agaves, but unlike most other yuccas, rosettes die after flowering and offsets may not be produced. Native to southern California and Baja California. Zones 2-24.

OPPOSITE TOP: *YUCCA WHIPPLEI* LEFT: *Y. ALOIFOLIA* 'MARGINATA' RIGHT: *Y. ROSTRATA*

PLANTS AT A GLANCE

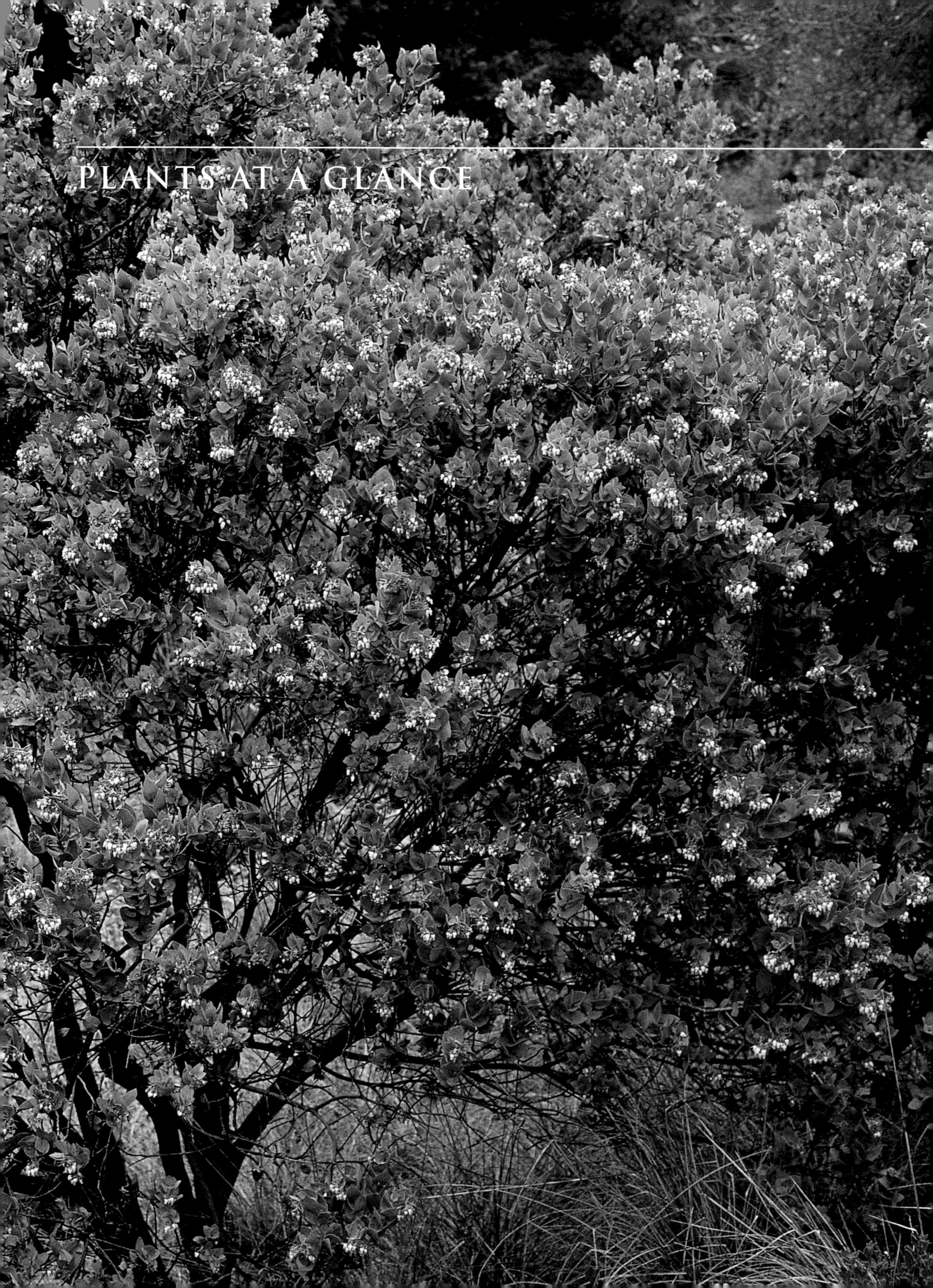

TREES

Plant Name		Deciduous	Evergreen	Exposure		
				Sun	Part Shade	Shade
Acacia	acacia	•	•	•		
Aesculus	buckeye	•		•	•	
Albizia	silk tree	•		•		
Arbutus	arbutus		•	•	•	
Brachychiton	bottle tree		•	•	•	
Calocedrus	incense-cedar		•	•	•	
Casuarina	she-oak		•	•		
Cedrus	cedar		•	•		
Celtis	hackberry	•		•	•	
Cercis	redbud	•		•	•	
Cercocarpus	mountain mahogany		•	•		
Chilopsis	desert willow	•		•		
x Chitalpa	chitalpa	•		•		
Cotinus	smoke tree	•		•	•	
Crataegus	hawthorn	•		•		
Cupressus	cypress		•	•		
Eriobotrya	loquat		•	•	•	
Eucalyptus	eucalyptus		•	•		
Feijoa	pineapple guava		•	•		
Fraxinus	ash	•	•	•		
Ginkgo	maidenhair tree	•		•		
Grevillea	grevillea		•	•	•	
Heteromeles	toyon		•	•	•	
Jacaranda	jacaranda	•		•		
Koelreuteria	goldenrain tree	•		•		
Lagerstroemia	crape myrtle	•		•		
Laurus	sweet bay		•	•	•	
Leptospermum	tea tree		•	•		

	WATER NEEDS			CLIMATE		Fast Growing	CA Native
Moderate	Occasional	Infrequent	None	Coastal	Inland		
	•	•		•		•	
•				•			
	•	•			•		
•				•			
	•					•	
•	•					•	
		•	•				•
•	•						•
	•					•	
	•	•	•	•		•	
•	•					•	
	•	•		•		•	
•	•			•		•	•
•	•						
•	•						
	•	•				•	
	•	•	•		•		
	•	•	•				
•	•						
•							•
	•	•					
•	•	•				•	
•	•	•				•	
	•	•		•			
•	•		•				•
•	•						
	•	•	•	•	•		•
	•	•				•	
		•					
	•	•	•	•	•	•	•

SHRUBS (cont'd.)

PLANT NAME		BLOOM TIME		EXPOSURE		
		Winter/ Spring	Summer/ Fall	Sun	Part Shade	Shade
Ribes	currant	•/•		•	•	•
Rosa	rose	/•	•/	•	•	
Rosmarinus	rosemary	/•		•		
Rubus	bramble	/•	•/		•	•
Salvia	sage	/•	•/•	•		
Sambucus	elderberry	/•		•	•	
Santolina	santolina		•/	•		
Sarcococca	sweet box	•/•			•	•
Senna	cassia	•/•		•		
Solanum	solanum	/•	•/•	•	•	
Styrax	snowdrop bush	/•			•	•
Symphoricarpos	snowberry	/•			•	
Tibouchina	princess flower	•/•		•	•	
Trichostema	woolly blue curls	/•		•		
Vitex	chaste tree		•/	•	•	
Westringia	coast rosemary	/•		•		
Xylosma	xylosma			•		

GRASSES AND GRASSLIKE PLANTS

PLANT NAME		BLOOM TIME		EXPOSURE		
		Winter/ Spring	Summer/ Fall	Sun	Part Shade	Shade
Andropogon	big bluestem		•/•	•	•	
Aristida	purple three-awn		•/	•		
Bouteloua	blue grama		•/	•		
Calamagrostis	reed grass	/•	•/	•	•	
Carex	sedge			•	•	•
Chondropetalum	Cape rush			•	•	
Deschampsia	hair grass	•/	•/•		•	

WATER NEEDS				CLIMATE		Fast Growing	CA Native
Moderate	Occasional	Infrequent	None	Coastal	Inland		
•	•	•	•				•
•	•	•				•	•
		•	•				
•	•	•					•
	•					•	•
	•	•	•			•	•
	•	•	•				
•	•						
	•	•	•				
•	•	•				•	•
•							•
	•	•	•				•
•				•		•	
					•		•
•	•						
	•	•					
	•	•				•	

WATER NEEDS				CLIMATE		Evergreen	CA Native
Moderate	Occasional	Infrequent	None	Coastal	Inland		
•	•						
	•	•	•				•
		•					•
•	•			•			
•	•					•	•
•	•					•	
•				•		•	•

GRASSES (cont'd.)

PLANT NAME		BLOOM TIME		EXPOSURE		
		Winter/ Spring	Summer/ Fall	Sun	Part Shade	Shade
Elymus	wild rye	/•		•	•	
Festuca	fescue		•/	•	•	
Helictotrichon	oat grass		•/	•		
Leymus	lyme grass		•/	•	•	
Melica	melic		•/	•	•	
Miscanthus	miscanthus		•/	•	•	
Muhlenbergia	muhly	/•	•/	•	•	
Nassella	needlegrass	/•	•/	•		
Sesleria	moor grass		/•	•	•	
Sporobolus	sacaton		•/	•		
Stipa	feather grass		•/	•		

PERENNIALS

PLANT NAME		BLOOM TIME		EXPOSURE		
		Winter/ Spring	Summer/ Fall	Sun	Part Shade	Shade
Acanthus	bear's breech	/•	•/		•	•
Achillea	yarrow		•/•	•		
Aeonium	aeonium	/•	•/	•	•	
Aethionema	stonecress	/•	•/	•		
Agapanthus	lily-of-the-Nile		•/	•	•	
Agastache	agastache		•/•	•	•	
Agave	agave	/•		•	•	
Allium	wild onion	/•	•/	•	•	
Aloe	aloe	•/•		•	•	
Alstroemeria	Peruvian lily		•/	•	•	
Amaryllis	belladonna lily		/•	•	•	
Anagallis	blue pimpernel	/•	•/	•		
Anchusa	bugloss		•/	•	•	

MISCANTHUS SINENSIS 'MORNING LIGHT' IN FALL COLOR

WATER NEEDS				CLIMATE		Evergreen	CA Native
Moderate	Occasional	Infrequent	None	Coastal	Inland		
	•	•					•
•	•					•	•
•	•					•	
	•					•	•
	•	•	•				•
•							
	•	•	•				•
•	•	•	•				•
•						•	
•	•						•
•	•					•	

WATER NEEDS				CLIMATE		Summer Dormant	CA Native
Moderate	Occasional	Infrequent	None	Coastal	Inland		
	•	•	•			•	
	•	•					
	•	•		•			
	•	•		•			
	•	•					
•	•						
	•	•		•			•
			•			•	•
	•			•			
•	•						
			•			•	
	•						
•							

PERENNIALS (cont'd.)

PLANT NAME		BLOOM TIME		EXPOSURE		
		Winter/ Spring	Summer/ Fall	Sun	Part Shade	Shade
Anemone	windflower	/•		•	•	
Anigozanthos	kangaroo paw	/•	•/	•		
Arctotis	African daisy	/•	•/	•		
Armeria	thrift	/•	•/	•		
Artemisia	artemisia			•		
Asclepias	milkweed	/•	•/	•		
Aster	aster		•/•	•	•	
Asteriscus	beach daisy	/•	•/•	•	•	
Babiana	baboon flower	/•		•	•	
Baileya	desert marigold	/•	•/•	•		
Ballota	false dittany		•/	•		
Bergenia	bergenia	•/•			•	•
Beschorneria	Mexican lily		•/	•	•	
Brachyscome	cutleaf daisy	/•	•/	•	•	
Brodiaea	brodiaea	/•		•	•	
Bulbinella	bulbinella	/•		•	•	
Calamintha	calamint		•/•	•	•	
Callirhoe	poppy mallow		•/•	•	•	
Calochortus	calochortus	/•		•	•	
Calylophus	sundrops	/•	•/	•	•	
Cerastium	snow-in-summer	/•	•/	•	•	
Clivia	clivia	/•			•	•
Colchicum	autumn crocus	/•	/•	•	•	
Coreopsis	coreopsis		•/	•	•	
Cosmos	cosmos		•/•	•		
Crassula	crassula	/•	•/•	•	•	
Crocosmia	crocosmia		•/	•	•	
Crocus	crocus	/•	/•	•	•	
Cyclamen	cyclamen	•/	/•		•	•
Cynoglossum	hound's tongue		•/		•	•

| WATER NEEDS | | | | CLIMATE | | Summer Dormant | CA Native |
Moderate	Occasional	Infrequent	None	Coastal	Inland		
			•			•	
	•			•			
•				•			
	•	•		•			•
	•	•	•	•	•		•
•	•			•			•
•	•			•			•
•		•		•			
			•			•	
		•	•	•			•
•	•						
•	•			•			
•	•						
•	•						
			•			•	•
			•			•	
•	•						
	•						
			•			•	•
•	•						
	•						
•	•			•			
			•			•	
	•	•		•			
•	•						
	•	•		•			
		•	•				
			•			•	
			•			•	
•	•	•	•				•

PERENNIALS (cont'd.)

PLANT NAME		BLOOM TIME		EXPOSURE		
		Winter/ Spring	Summer/ Fall	Sun	Part Shade	Shade
Dianthus	pink	/•	•/	•	•	
Dichelostemma	dichelostemma	/•		•		
Dietes	fortnight lily	/•	•/	•	•	
Dudleya	dudleya	/•	•/		•	
Dymondia	silver carpet		•/	•	•	
Echeveria	echeveria	/•	•/		•	
Echinacea	coneflower		•/	•		
Echium	echium	/•		•		
Engelmannia	Engelmann's daisy		•/•	•		
Epilobium	California fuchsia		•/•	•	•	
Epimedium	epimedium	/•	•/			•
Erigeron	fleabane	/•	•/•	•		
Eriogonum	buckwheat	/•	•/•	•		
Eriophyllum	woolly sunflower	/•	•/	•		
Erysimum	wallflower	/•	•/	•	•	
Eschscholzia	California poppy	/•		•		
Euphorbia	euphorbia	•/•	•/	•	•	
Freesia	freesia	/•		•		
Gaura	gaura	/•	•/•	•	•	
Gazania	gazania	/•	•/•	•		
Gladiolus	gladiolus	/•		•		
Glaucium	horned poppy		•/	•		
Helleborus	hellebore	•/•			•	•
Hesperaloe	red yucca		•/•	•		
Heterotheca	goldenaster		•/	•		
Heuchera	coral bells	/•	•/		•	•
Hyssopus	hyssop		•/	•	•	
Ipheion	starflower	•/•		•	•	
Iris	iris	/•		•	•	
Ixia	African corn lily	/•		•		

Moderate	Occasional	Infrequent	None	Coastal	Inland	Summer Dormant	CA Native
•							
			•			•	•
•	•	•	•				
		•	•	•			•
•	•			•			
•	•	•		•			
•							
		•	•	•			
•	•						
	•	•	•				•
•	•	•					•
		•					•
		•	•				•
		•	•				•
•	•			•			•
			•			•	•
•	•	•	•				
			•			•	
•	•						
•	•						
			•			•	
•							
•	•	•	•				
	•				•		
•	•						•
•	•						•
•							
			•			•	
	•	•	•			•	•
			•			•	

PLANT NAME		BLOOM TIME		EXPOSURE		
		Winter/ Spring	Summer/ Fall	Sun	Part Shade	Shade
Kniphofia	red-hot poker		•/•	•	•	
Lessingia	California aster		•/•	•		
Leucojum	snowflake	•/	/•		•	
Liatris	blazing star		•/	•		
Limonium	sea lavender		•/	•	•	
Linum	flax	/•	•/	•		
Lychnis	rose campion		•/	•	•	
Malvastrum	trailing mallow		•/	•		
Mimulus	monkeyflower	/•	•/	•	•	
Monardella	monardella	/•	•/		•	
Muscari	grape hyacinth	/•		•	•	
Narcissus	daffodil	/•		•		
Nepeta	catmint		•/	•		
Nerine	nerine		/•	•	•	
Oenothera	evening primrose	/•	•/	•		
Omphalodes	omphalodes	/•			•	•
Origanum	oregano		•/	•		
Osteospermum	African daisy	/•	/•	•		
Papaver	poppy	/•		•	•	
Penstemon	beard tongue	/•	•/	•	•	
Perityle	Guadalupe rock daisy	/•		•		
Perovskia	Russian sage		•/	•		
Phacelia	phacelia		•/	•	•	
Phormium	New Zealand flax		•/	•	•	
Plecostachys	Hottentot tea		•/	•		
Ranunculus	buttercup	/•		•		
Ratibida	coneflower		•/	•		
Rhodanthemum	Moroccan daisy	/•	•/•	•		
Romneya	matilija poppy		•/	•		
Rudbeckia	rudbeckia		•/•	•		

	WATER NEEDS			CLIMATE		Summer Dormant	CA Native
Moderate	Occasional	Infrequent	None	Coastal	Inland		
•	•						
•	•			•			•
	•					•	
•	•						
	•			•			
•	•						•
		•	•				
		•	•				
		•	•				•
		•	•				•
			•			•	
			•			•	
•	•						
			•			•	
		•	•				•
•	•			•			
	•						
•	•						
			•			•	•
•	•	•	•				•
	•						
	•	•					
		•	•				•
•	•						
•	•						
		•	•			•	•
•							
	•	•	•				
		•	•				•
•	•						•

PERENNIALS (cont'd.)

PLANT NAME		BLOOM TIME		EXPOSURE		
		Winter/ Spring	Summer/ Fall	Sun	Part Shade	Shade
Ruta	rue		•/	•		
Salvia	sage	/•	•/•	•		
Scilla	scilla	/•		•		
Sedum	stonecrop	/•	•/	•	•	
Sempervivum	houseleek		•/	•	•	
Senecio	dusty miller	/•	•/•	•	•	
Sidalcea	checkerbloom	/•		•	•	
Sideritis	sideritis		•/	•		
Sisyrinchium	blue-eyed grass	/•		•	•	
Solidago	goldenrod		•/•	•	•	
Sparaxis	harlequin flower	/•		•		
Sphaeralcea	globe mallow		•/	•		
Stachys	lamb's ears		•/	•	•	
Tagetes	bush marigold	/•	•/•	•	•	
Tanacetum	tansy	/•	•/	•		
Teucrium	germander		•/	•		
Thymus	thyme		•/	•	•	
Triteleia	triteleia	/•		•	•	
Tulbaghia	tulbaghia	/•	•/•	•		
Tulipa	tulip	/•		•		
Verbascum	mullein		•/	•		
Verbena	verbena		•/	•	•	
Watsonia	watsonia	/•	•/	•		
Yucca	yucca	/•		•		

WATER NEEDS				CLIMATE		Summer Dormant	CA Native
Moderate	Occasional	Infrequent	None	Coastal	Inland		
•	•						
	•						•
			•			•	
•	•			•			•
•	•						
	•						
			•			•	
•	•						
	•	•					•
•	•						•
			•			•	
	•	•					•
•	•						
	•						
•	•	•	•				
	•						
•	•						
			•			•	•
•				•			
			•			•	
•	•						
•	•						
	•	•	•				
	•	•					•

ANNUALS AND BIENNIALS

PLANT NAME		BLOOM TIME		EXPOSURE		
		Winter/ Spring	Summer/ Fall	Sun	Part Shade	Shade
Anagallis	blue pimpernel	/•	•/	•		
Anchusa	bugloss		•/	•	•	
Arctotis	African daisy	/•	•/	•		
Brachyscome	Swan River daisy	/•	•/	•	•	
Clarkia	clarkia	/•		•	•	
Collinsia	Chinese houses	/•		•	•	
Coreopsis	coreopsis		•/	•	•	
Cosmos	cosmos		•/•	•		
Cynoglossum	hound's tongue		•/		•	•
Dianthus	pink	/•	•/	•	•	
Dimorphotheca	African daisy	/•		•		
Gilia	gilia	/•	•/	•		
Glaucium	horned poppy		•/	•		
Layia	tidytips	/•		•		
Linanthus	linanthus	/•	•/	•	•	
Linum	flax	/•	•/	•		
Lupinus	lupine	/•		•		
Madia	madia		•/	•		
Matricaria	chamomile		•/	•		
Nemophila	nemophila	/•		•	•	
Nigella	love-in-a-mist	/•		•	•	
Oenothera	evening primrose	/•	•/	•		
Phacelia	phacelia	/•		•	•	
Rudbeckia	rudbeckia		•/•	•		
Stylomecon	wind poppy	/•		•		
Verbascum	mullein		•/	•		

Water Needs				Climate		Summer Dormant	CA Native
Moderate	Occasional	Infrequent	None	Coastal	Inland		
	•						
•							
•				•			
•	•						
			•			•	•
			•			•	•
	•	•					
•	•						
•		•	•			•	•
•							
	•	•	•				
	•	•	•				•
•							
			•			•	•
	•						•
•	•						•
		•	•				•
	•						•
•	•						•
			•			•	
			•	•		•	
		•	•				•
		•	•				•
•	•						•
	•						•
•	•						

FERNS

PLANT NAME		EXPOSURE		
		Sun	Part Shade	Shade
Dryopteris	California wood fern			•
Polypodium	polypody		•	•
Polystichum	western sword fern			•

VINES

PLANT NAME		Deciduous	Evergreen	EXPOSURE		
				Sun	Part Shade	Shade
Bougainvillea	bougainvillea		•	•		
Campsis	trumpet vine	•	•	•	•	
Clytostoma	violet trumpet vine		•	•	•	
Distictis	blood-red trumpet vine		•	•	•	
Euonymus	euonymus		•	•	•	•
Hardenbergia	lilac vine		•	•	•	
Jasminum	jasmine		•	•	•	
Macfadyena	cat's claw	•	•	•	•	
Pandorea	wonga-wonga vine		•	•		
Parthenocissus	parthenocissus	•			•	•
Solanum	solanum		•	•	•	
Tecomaria	Cape honeysuckle		•	•	•	
Vitis	wild grape	•		•		
Wisteria	wisteria	•		•	•	

WATER NEEDS				CLIMATE		Summer Dormant	CA Native
Moderate	Occasional	Infrequent	None	Coastal	Inland		
			•	•		•	•
			•			•	•
•	•						•

WATER NEEDS				CLIMATE		Fast Growing	CA Native
Moderate	Occasional	Infrequent	None	Coastal	Inland		
•	•			•		•	
•	•					•	
	•			•		•	
•	•			•		•	
•	•						
•				•			
•	•					•	
•	•				•	•	
•				•		•	
	•	•				•	
•	•	•				•	
	•	•		•			
•	•					•	•
	•					•	

PALMS

PLANT NAME		EXPOSURE		
		Sun	Part Shade	Shade
Brahea	brahea	•		
Chamaerops	Mediterranean fan palm	•		
Jubaea	Chilean wine palm	•	•	
Phoenix	Canary Island date palm	•		
Trachycarpus	windmill palm	•	•	
Washingtonia	fan palm	•		

	WATER NEEDS			CLIMATE		CA Native
Moderate	Occasional	Infrequent	None	Coastal	Inland	
•	•					
•						
	•			•		
•	•			•		
•						
	•					•

PLANTS FOR HOT SITES

Hot sites in full sun are one of the greatest challenges for the low-water gardener. Most plants require more water in hot sun than with afternoon shade, and many plants simply won't make it. Sometimes the best solution is to plant trees first and wait for some shade. The following are good choices for hot locations. Some may need at least some supplemental water.

Trees

Acacia baileyana, Bailey acacia
Albizia julibrissin, silk tree
Brachychiton populneus, bottle tree
Casuarina cunninghamiana, river she-oak
Casuarina stricta, mountain she-oak
Cedrus atlantica, Atlas cedar
Cedrus deodara, deodar cedar
Celtis australis, European hackberry
Celtis sinensis, Chinese hackberry
Cercocarpus betuloides, birchleaf mountain
    mahogany
Chilopsis linearis, desert willow
x *Chitalpa tashkentensis*, chitalpa
Crataegus phaenopyrum, Washington thorn
Cupressus arizonica, Arizona cypress
Cupressus sempervirens, Italian cypress
Fraxinus dipetala, California ash
Fraxinus 'Raywood', Raywood ash
Fraxinus velutina, Arizona ash
Ginkgo biloba, maidenhair tree
Grevillea robusta, silk oak
Jacaranda mimosifolia, jacaranda
Lagerstroemia indica, crape myrtle
Melaleuca linariifolia, flaxleaf paperbark
Melaleuca styphelioides, prickly leaved
    paperbark
Olea europaea 'Swan Hill', fruitless olive
Pinus brutia, Calabrian pine
Pinus coulteri, Coulter pine
Pinus halepensis, Aleppo pine
Pistacia chinensis, Chinese pistache
Styphnolobium japonicum, Japanese
    pagoda tree
Quercus agrifolia, coast live oak

Quercus douglasii, blue oak
Quercus lobata, valley oak
Schinus molle, California pepper tree

Shrubs

Acacia redolens, prostrate acacia
Agave filifera, threadleaf agave
Agave shawii, Shaw's agave
Artemisia californica, California sagebrush
Artemisia caucasica, silver spreader
Atriplex canescens, four-wing saltbush
Atriplex lentiformis, big saltbush
Baccharis pilularis, coyote brush
Cercocarpus betuloides, birchleaf mountain
    mahogany
Cistus salviifolius, sageleaf rockrose
Cistus x *skanbergii*, rockrose
Cotoneaster dammeri, bearberry
    cotoneaster
Dasylirion wheeleri, desert spoon

FREMONTODENDRON CALIFORNICUM IN NATIVE MEADOW GARDEN

OPPOSITE: DASYLIRION, BARREL CACTUS, AEONIUM, AND ECHIUM

Coreopsis species, coreopsis
Erigeron karvinskianus, Santa Barbara daisy
Eriogonum species, wild buckwheat
Hesperaloe parviflora, red yucca
Malvastrum lateritium, trailing mallow
Muhlenbergia rigens, deer grass
Nepeta x faassenii, catmint
Oenothera hookeri, evening primrose
Perovskia atriplicifolia, Russian sage
Romneya coulteri, matilija poppy
Teucrium x lucidrys, germander
Teucrium fruticans, bush germander
Verbena bonariensis, verbena

Vines

Bougainvillea, bougainvillea
Macfadyena unguis-cati, cat's claw
Tecomaria capensis, Cape honeysuckle

Dodonaea viscosa, hop bush
Elaeagnus pungens, silverberry
Encelia farinosa, encelia
Feijoa sellowiana, pineapple guava
Fremontodendron californicum, fremontia
Grevillea rosmarinifolia, rosemary grevillea
Juniperus sabina, juniper
Lavatera thuringiaca, tree mallow
Lavatera trimestris, tree mallow
Leucophyllum frutescens, Texas ranger
Lupinus albifrons, silver bush lupine
Nerium oleander, oleander
Rosmarinus officinalis, rosemary
Salvia apiana, white sage
Salvia clevelandii, Cleveland sage
Salvia greggii, autumn sage
Santolina chamaecyparissus, lavender cotton
Santolina rosmarinifolia, santolina
Senna artemisioides, feathery cassia
Senna nemophila, desert cassia
Vitex agnus-castus, chaste tree

TOP: PEROVSKIA ATRIPLICIFOLIA ABOVE: ROMNEYA COULTERI BELOW RIGHT: NEPETA X FAASSENII

Perennials, Annuals, Grasses

Achillea millefolium, common yarrow
Agapanthus mollis, lily-of-the-Nile
Allium species, wild onion
Amaryllis belladonna, belladonna lily
Baileya multiradiata, desert marigold
Bouteloua gracilis, blue grama

PLANTS FOR DRYISH SHADE

Dry shade is often considered a challenge for gardeners, but a north-facing slope or wooded lot is the perfect place for many plants. Some may flower less, or assume a taller, more open habit, but most will need less supplemental water. Shade is a plus for the low-water gardener.

Shrubs

Arbutus unedo, strawberry tree
Arctostaphylos uva-ursi, bearberry
Correa species, Australian fuchsia
Cotoneaster species, cotoneaster
Euonymus fortunei, winter creeper
Euphorbia amygdaloides, euphorbia
Garrya elliptica, silktassel
Garrya fremontii, Fremont silktassel
Heteromeles arbutifolia, toyon
Holodiscus discolor, cream bush
Juniperus species, juniper
Mahonia aquifolium, Oregon grape
Mahonia pinnata, California holly grape
Myrsine africana, African boxwood
Myrtus communis, myrtle
Nandina domestica, heavenly bamboo
Pittosporum tobira, tobira
Rhamnus alaternus, Italian buckthorn
Rhamnus crocea, redberry

Ribes sanguineum, red-flowering currant
Ribes viburnifolium, evergreen currant
Rubus parviflorus, rubus
Rubus pentalobus, thimbleberry
Sarcococca hookerana humilis, sweet box
Symphoricarpos albus, snowberry

Perennials, Grasses, Ferns, Vines

Acanthus mollis, bear's breech
Clivia miniata, clivia
Dryopteris arguta, California wood fern
Festuca occidentalis, western fescue
Helleborus argutifolius, Corsican hellebore
Helleborus foetidus, bear's foot hellebore
Heuchera maxima, island alum root
Heuchera micrantha, coral bells
Iris Pacific Coast hybrids
Parthenocissus tricuspidata, Boston ivy

ABOVE: HELLEBORE GROUNDCOVER IN BACKYARD HABITAT GARDEN

PLANTS FOR CLAY SOILS

Clay soils are common in the Bay Region. These "heavy" soils have both advantages and disadvantages for the gardener. They hold water longer, but they drain more slowly, which is good for some plants and death to others. They also warm up more slowly than lighter soils, but they provide more nutrients. You can take steps to improve drainage, or you can choose plants that thrive in clay soils. Some clay-tolerant plants are listed below.

Trees

Arbutus 'Marina', arbutus
Callistemon viminalis, weeping bottlebrush
Casuarina species, she-oak
Celtis species, hackberry
Cercis occidentalis, western redbud
Crataegus phaenopyrum, Washington thorn
Cupressus species, cypress
Fraxinus dipetala, California ash
Ginkgo biloba, maidenhair tree
Koelreuteria bipinnata, goldenrain tree

Melaleuca styphelioides, prickly leaved
    paperbark
Sequoia sempervirens, coast redwood

Shrubs

Arbutus unedo, strawberry tree
Callistemon citrinus, lemon bottlebrush
Chaenomeles cultivars, flowering quince
Correa alba, C. pulchella, Australian fuchsia
Cotinus coggygria, smoke tree

ARBUTUS UNEDO

Dendromecon harfordii, *D. rigida*, bush poppy
Escallonia cultivars, escallonia
Feijoa sellowiana, pineapple guava
Heteromeles arbutifolia, toyon
Holodiscus discolor, cream bush
Mahonia aquifolium, *M. nevinii*, mahonia
Nerium oleander, oleander
Osmanthus heterophyllus, hollyleaf
    osmanthus
Punica granatum, pomegranate
Rhamnus alaternus, Italian buckthorn
Rosa rugosa, *R. wichuraiana*, rose
Sambucus mexicana, Mexican elderberry
Symphoricarpos albus, snowberry
Vitex agnus-castus, chaste tree

Perennials

Acanthus mollis, bear's breech
Achillea clavennae, *A. tomentosa*, yarrow
Agapanthus cultivars, lily-of-the-Nile
Allium species, wild onion
Asclepias speciosa, *A. tuberosa*, milkweed
Bergenia cordifolia, *B. crassifolia*, bergenia
Brodiaea species, brodiaea
Callirhoe involucrata, poppy mallow
Carex species, sedge
Chondropetalum tectorum, Cape rush
Coreopsis species, coreopsis
Crocosmia cultivars, crocosmia
Dietes bicolor, *D. iridioides*, fortnight lily
Echinacea purpurea, purple coneflower
Erigeron glaucus, *E. karvinskianus*, erigeron

Eschscholzia californica, California
    poppy
Heuchera maxima, *H. micrantha*, coral
    bells
Kniphofia uvaria, red-hot poker
Leucojum species, snowflake
Mimulus aurantiacus, monkeyflower
Narcissus species, daffodil
Nepeta x *faassenii*, *N. racemosa*, catmint
Perovskia atriplicifolia, Russian sage
Phlomis species, phlomis
Phormium cultivars, New Zealand flax
Ruta graveolens, rue
Salvia species, sage
Sidalcea malviflora, checkerbloom
Sisyrinchium bellum, blue-eyed grass
Solidago species, goldenrod
Sphaeralcea munroana, globe mallow
Teucrium fruticans, *T.* x *lucidrys*,
    germander
Verbena bonariensis, verbena

CLOCKWISE FROM TOP:
KNIPHOFIA UVARIA
'SUNNINGDALE YELLOW',
CROCOSMIA 'SOLFATARE',
HEUCHERA MICRANTHA 'PALACE
PURPLE'

Grasses

Andropogon gerardii, big bluestem
Deschampsia species, hair grass
Leymus species, wild rye
Muhlenbergia species, muhly

Vines

Parthenocissus tricuspidata, Boston ivy
Vitis californica, California wild grape

Ferns

Dryopteris arguta, California wood fern

TOP: *Clarkia* 'Aurora' (PINK)
AND *C.* 'Charmine' (RED)
BOTTOM: *Muhlenbergia*
rigens

Annuals

Clarkia species, clarkia
Cosmos cultivars, cosmos
Madia elegans, madia

GROUNDCOVERS

Groundcovers don't have to be flat on the ground. Sometimes they are mounding and mid-height.

Mid-Height

Abelia x *grandiflora* 'Edward Goucher', glossy abelia
Acacia redolens, prostrate acacia
Arctostaphylos 'Pacific Mist', manzanita
Baccharis pilularis 'Twin Peaks', coyote brush
Ceanothus griseus var. *horizontalis* 'Carmel Creeper', wild lilac
Cistus salviifolius 'Prostratus', sageleaf rockrose
Coprosma x *kirkii*, coprosma
Correa reflexa, correa
Cotoneaster horizontalis, rock cotoneaster
Cotoneaster microphyllus, rockspray cotoneaster
Euonymus fortunei, winter creeper
Grevillea x *gaudichaudii*, grevillea
Nepeta 'Six Hills Giant', catmint
Ribes viburnifolium, evergreen currant
Rosmarinus officinalis 'Ken Taylor', rosemary
Rosa wichuraiana, rose
Santolina chamaecyparissus, lavender cotton
Sarcococca hookerana humilis, sweet box

Cotoneaster dammeri, bearberry cotoneaster
Dymondia margaretae, silver carpet
Juniperus chinensis 'Parsonii', juniper
Juniperus communis, juniper
Juniperus sabina 'Buffalo', juniper
Myoporum parvifolium, myoporum
Nepeta x *faassenii*, catmint
Nepeta racemosa, catmint
Rosmarinus officinalis 'Huntington Carpet', rosemary
Rubus pentalobus, rubus
Teucrium x *lucidrys*, germander

TOP: *Cotoneaster horizontalis*
BOTTOM: *Teucrium* x *lucidrys*

Low

Low, flat or mounding groundcovers are valuable plants for carpeting the ground or slowing erosion on slopes. Some of the best for the Bay Region are the following.

Arctostaphylos uva-ursi, bearberry
Arctostaphylos hookeri 'Monterey Carpet', Monterey manzanita
Arctostaphylos edmundsii 'Carmel Sur', Little Sur manzanita
Arctostaphylos 'Emerald Carpet', manzanita

TREES FOR SMALL SPACES

Many urban and suburban gardens do not have space for large trees. Those listed are small trees or shrubs that can be trained as single- or multi-trunked "standards" or small trees.

Acacia boormanii, snowy river wattle
Acacia cultriformis, knife acacia
Acacia pravissima, ovens wattle
Arbutus unedo, strawberry tree
Arctostaphylos manzanita, common
    manzanita
Callistemon viminalis, weeping bottlebrush
Cercis occidentalis, western redbud
x *Chitalpa tashkentensis*, chitalpa
CRATAEGUS PHAENOPYRUM   *Cotinus coggygria*, smoke tree

Crataegus phaenopyrum, Washington thorn
Dodonaea viscosa, hop bush
Eriobotrya deflexa, bronze loquat
Feijoa sellowiana, pineapple guava
Garrya elliptica, coast silktassel
Heteromeles arbutifolia, toyon
Koelreuteria paniculata, goldenrain tree
Lagerstroemia indica, crape myrtle
Laurus nobilis, Grecian laurel
Luma apiculata, Chilean myrtle

Melaleuca decussata, lilac
    melaleuca
Melaleuca incana, gray honey
    myrtle
Melaleuca nesophila, pink
    melaleuca
Myrica californica, Pacific wax
    myrtle
Nerium oleander, oleander
Olea europaea 'Swan Hill',
    fruitless olive
Osmanthus heterophyllus, hollyleaf
    osmanthus
Pittosporum phillyreoides, willow
    pittosporum
Pittosporum tobira, tobira
Rhaphiolepis 'Majestic Beauty',
    Indian hawthorn
Rhus lancea, African sumac
Xylosma congestum, xylosma

Mid-Sized Trees

The following trees and shrubs are
medium-sized and can be accommodated
in many landscapes.

Acacia baileyana, Bailey acacia
Acacia pendula, weeping acacia
Acacia x *stenophylla*, shoestring acacia
Albizia julibrissin, silk tree
Arbutus 'Marina', arbutus
Brachychiton populneus, bottle tree
Celtis australis, European hackberry
Celtis sinensis, Chinese hackberry
Eriobotrya japonica, loquat
Eucalyptus nicholii, willowleaf peppermint
Fraxinus angustifolia 'Raywood', Raywood
    ash
Fraxinus dipetala, California ash
Fraxinus velutina, Arizona ash
Lophostemon confertus, Brisbane box
Melaleuca linariifolia, flaxleaf paperbark
Melaleuca styphelioides, prickly leaved
    paperbark
Metrosideros excelsus, New Zealand
    Christmas tree

Nyssa sylvatica, sour gum
Pistacia chinensis, Chinese pistache
Pittosporum eugenioides, pittosporum
Pittosporum undulatum, pittosporum
Prunus cerasifera, purpleleaf plum
Prunus lusitanica, Portugal laurel
Styphnolobium japonicum, Japanese
    pagoda tree

COTINUS COGGYGRIA
'ROYAL PURPLE'

FEIJOA SELLOWIANA

TREES FOR LARGE LANDSCAPES

The following trees are magnificent specimens, but ultimately grow too large for all but public parks or open spaces, commercial landscapes, and the grandest private gardens. Plant them where you can.

Calocedrus decurrens, incense-cedar
Cedrus atlantica, Atlas cedar
Cedrus deodara, deodar cedar
Cupressus sempervirens, Italian cypress
Eucalyptus leucoxylon, white ironbark
Eucalyptus sideroxylon, red ironbark
Ginkgo biloba, maidenhair tree
Pinus canariensis, Canary Island pine
Pinus coulteri, Coulter pine
Pinus eldarica, Afghan pine
Platanus x acerifolia, sycamore
Quercus agrifolia, coast live oak
Quercus garryana, Garry oak

Quercus lobata, valley oak
Schinus molle, California pepper tree
Sequoia sempervirens, coast redwood
Ulmus parvifolia, Chinese elm
Washingtonia filifera, California fan palm
Washingtonia robusta, Mexican fan palm

ABOVE: *PLATANUS X ACERIFOLIA* (SYCAMORE) WITH *CUPRESSUS SEMPERVIRENS* (ITALIAN CYPRESS) AND *PRUNUS CERASIFERA* 'ATROPURPUREA' (PURPLE-LEAF PLUM)
OPPOSITE: *QUERCUS AGRIFOLIA*

HEDGES, SCREENS, AND WINDBREAKS

Sometimes what a landscape needs most is a hedge or screen to provide privacy or protection from wind. The following trees and shrubs are some good choices.

Trees

Brachychiton populneus, bottle tree
Calocedrus decurrens, incense-cedar
Casuarina species, she-oak
Cupressus arizonica, Arizona cypress
Eucalyptus gunnii, cider gum
Melaleuca nesophylla, pink melaleuca
Olea europaea 'Swan Hill', fruitless olive
Pinus canariensis, Canary Island pine
Pinus coulteri, Coulter pine
Quercus agrifolia, coast live oak
Schinus molle, California pepper tree
Sequoia sempervirens, coast redwood

Pittosporum tobira, tobira
Pittosporum eugenioides, pittosporum
Pittosporum undulatum, pittosporum
Prunus caroliniana, Carolina laurel
Prunus ilicifolia, hollyleaf cherry
Rhamnus alaternus, Italian buckthorn
Rhamnus californica, coffeeberry
Rhaphiolepis indica, Indian hawthorn
Rhaphiolepis umbellata, yeddo hawthorn
Westringia fruticosa, coast rosemary
Xylosma congestum, xylosma

Shrubs

Abelia x *grandiflora*, glossy abelia
Arbutus unedo, strawberry tree
Arctostaphylos densiflora 'Howard McMinn', manzanita
Callistemon citrinus, lemon bottlebrush
Dodonaea viscosa, hop bush
Elaeagnus pungens, silverberry
Escallonia cultivars, escallonia
Feijoa sellowiana, pineapple guava
Garrya elliptica, silktassel
Grevillea rosmarinifolia, rosemary grevillea
Heteromeles arbutifolia, toyon
Leptospermum scoparium, New Zealand tea tree
Ligustrum japonicum, Japanese privet
Melaleuca decussata, lilac melaleuca
Melaleuca incana, gray honey myrtle
Myrica californica, Pacific wax myrtle
Myrsine africana, African boxwood
Myrtus communis, myrtle
Nerium oleander, oleander
Osmanthus heterophyllus, hollyleaf osmanthus
Photinia x *fraseri*, Fraser's photinia
Photinia serratifolia, Chinese photinia

ATTRACTING BIRDS AND BUTTERFLIES

The following are some plants that may bring butterflies and birds to your garden. Host plants for butterfly larvae provide food for caterpillars, but they often are not the same plants as those on which adult butterflies feed. Hummingbirds may check out many flowering plants for potential nectar, but will reliably return to their favorites. Birds of many kinds are attracted to plants for nesting and cover as well as food.

Plant Type	Birds	Hummingbirds	Butterflies	Butterfly Larvae
Trees				
Acacia	•			
Aesculus	•	•	•	•
Albizia	•	•		
Arbutus	•			
Celtis	•			
Cercis		•		
Chilopsis	•	•		
Crataegus	•			•
Eriobotrya	•			
Eucalyptus		•		
Melaleuca		•		
Pinus	•			•
Platanus				•
Prunus				•
Quercus	•			•
Schinus	•			
Shrubs				
Abelia		•	•	
Arbutus	•	•		
Arctostaphylos	•	•	•	
Atriplex	•			
Banksia	•	•		
Berberis	•			
Buddleja		•	•	
Callistemon	•	•		
Caryopteris			•	
Ceanothus		•	•	•
Chaenomeles	•	•		
Choisya			•	
Correa		•		
Cotoneaster	•		•	
Echinacea		•	•	
Elaeagnus	•			

TOP TO BOTTOM, LEFT TO RIGHT: *Acacia cultriformis, Aesculus californica, Albizia julibrissin, Arctostaphylos densiflora* 'Howard McMinn', *Banksia ericifolia, Callistemon viminalis* 'Little John', *Caryopteris x clandonensis* 'Dark Knight', *Ceanothus* 'Julia Phelps', *Correa pulchella, Crataegus phaenopyrum*

Plant Type	Birds	Hummingbirds	Butterflies	Butterfly Larvae
Escallonia			•	
Feijoa	•	•		
Garrya	•			
Grevillea	•	•		
Heteromeles	•	•	•	
Holodiscus	•	•		•
Lantana		•	•	
Lavandula		•	•	
Lavatera		•		•
Leonotis	•	•	•	
Leucophyllum		•		
Ligustrum	•			
Myrica	•			
Philadelphus			•	
Photinia	•			
Prunus	•			•
Rhamnus	•		•	•
Rhus	•		•	
Ribes	•	•	•	
Rosa				•
Rosmarinus	•	•	•	
Sambucus	•	•	•	
Senna				•
Symphoricarpos	•		•	
Trichostema		•		
Vitex		•		

Perennials, Annuals

Plant Type	Birds	Hummingbirds	Butterflies	Butterfly Larvae
Achillea			•	•
Agapanthus			•	
Agastache		•	•	
Allium			•	
Aloe		•	•	
Armeria			•	
Asclepias		•	•	•
Aster			•	•
Baileya			•	
Beschorneria		•		
Calylophus			•	
Carex				•
Clarkia		•	•	
Coreopsis	•		•	
Cosmos	•		•	
Crocosmia		•		
Dianthus			•	

TOP TO BOTTOM, LEFT TO RIGHT: *Lantana* 'Samantha', *Lavandula stoechas* 'Papillon', *Lavatera trimestris*, *Philadelphus lewisii*, *Senna alata*, *Achillea* 'Summerwine', *Agapanthus* 'Storm Cloud', *Agastache foeniculum*, *Asclepias tuberosa*, *Clarkia amoena*, *Coreopsis verticillata* 'Moonbeam', *Crocosmia masoniorum*

Plant Type	Birds	Hummingbirds	Butterflies	Butterfly Larvae
Dichelostemma		•		
Echinacea	•		•	
Echium		•	•	
Epilobium		•	•	
Erigeron			•	
Eriogonum			•	•
Erysimum			•	
Gaura			•	
Gladiolus			•	
Heuchera		•		
Iris		•		
Kniphofia		•	•	
Liatris			•	
Lupinus		•		•
Mimulus		•		•
Nepeta			•	
Origanum			•	
Penstemon		•	•	•
Ranunculus			•	
Rudbeckia			•	
Ruta				•
Salvia		•	•	
Sedum		•	•	
Sidalcea				•
Solidago	•		•	
Tagetes			•	
Verbena			•	

Vines

Plant Type	Birds	Hummingbirds	Butterflies	Butterfly Larvae
Campsis		•		
Tecomaria		•		
Wisteria				•

TOP TO BOTTOM, LEFT TO RIGHT: *ECHIUM* 'BLUE BEDDER', *EPILOBIUM CANUM* 'SILVER SELECT', *ERIGERON GLAUCUS*, *GLADIOLUS* 'HOMOGLAD', *HEUCHERA* 'WENDY', *IRIS* 'BEAUX ARTS', *KNIPHOFIA* 'CHRISTMAS CHEER', *LUPINUS LATIFOLIUS*, *MIMULUS AURANTIACUS*, *NEPETA* X *FAASSENII*, *RANUNCULUS ASIATICUS*, *VERBENA* 'TRINIDAD'

OPPOSITE: *ALOE ARBORESCENS* WITH PUYA

Chapter Four

THE LANDSCAPE OVER TIME

Landscapes are living systems, and they change over time—not just from one season to another, but from one year or one decade to the next. And why, indeed, would we not want them to change? Watching the landscape grow and change, helping to shape the change, is among the most satisfying rewards of gardening.

Billions of dollars are devoted to the largely futile effort to halt change in the landscape, to keep things just as they are. Trees are topped and shrubs are sheared to keep them at a predetermined size. Chemicals are applied to force plants to behave the way we think they should. The ground is raked and blown to keep leaves and other organic matter from accumulating. It seems an odd pursuit, gardening.

If nature is allowed to have its way, the five-gallon tree you plant today will soon be shading out those sun-loving perennials. Shrubs will overtop grasses, grasses will crowd out annuals, and low-growing groundcovers will scramble over everything in their path. Weeds will attempt to take over wherever the soil is disturbed. Leaves, twigs, flowers, and fruits will carpet the ground.

Below ground, if all is well, a complementary adventure is taking place. Tree roots spread far more widely than most of us imagine, taking nourishment and water from wherever they can be found. Roots of shrubs, perennials, and grasses reach down and out, seeking their own sources of food and moisture. The soil itself is alive with earthworms, bacteria, fungi, insects, and other organisms. What is our role as gardeners? To aid the natural processes that rejuvenate the soil, supporting the plants that grow in it, or to fight the outcomes from above?

Our responsibilities, and our options, likely will vary with the age of the landscape. A newly installed landscape may benefit from interventions that differ from those required by a mature landscape. We should expect and plan for fewer, not more, resources and less activity on our part over time. If we've designed our landscapes with their long-term independence in mind, we should have less to do as plants mature and soils improve. If plants require more care and more water as they age, we've chosen the wrong plants for the location.

SOME BASICS

There is no single right way to install and maintain a new landscape. Some experts swear by soil preparation, noting that amending the soil with plenty of organic matter makes the difference between plants that thrive and those that merely survive or don't make it at all. Others observe that amending the soil, or even disturbing it more than necessary, degrades soil quality, discourages plant roots from spreading beyond the amended area, and shifts nutrients from unavailable organic forms to readily available forms that favor the growth of weeds.

For many years, the rule of thumb for planting holes was twice as wide as the

OPPOSITE: A NATURALISTIC

GARDEN

rootball and one and a half times as deep, with the rootball set on a cone of compacted backfill. Conventional wisdom currently suggests making planting holes no deeper than the rootball and up to three to five times as wide, setting the rootball directly on undisturbed soil. Some experts, however, advise digging holes just large enough to hold the rootball.

Fertilizers once were routinely added to holes at planting time, and yearly fertilizing schedules were provided. Today many professionals recommend against fertilizing plants adapted to the soils in which they're grown, especially natives. Inorganic fertilizers can burn plant leaves and disturb or destroy beneficial soil organisms.

What is the gardener to do? Not surprisingly, the answers depend on the quality of the soil and what you plan to grow. Natives planted in soil to which they are adapted don't need amendments or fertilizers. Planted in soil that has been disturbed or degraded by urban development, even plants native to the local area may need some extra help, at least at the outset. Is your planting site an old one, with soil undisturbed for decades, or are you installing a landscape where new construction or compaction has compromised soil quality?

A basic understanding of the physical and biological properties of soil and the characteristics of roots is helpful in making decisions about what to do in a particular situation.

It Starts with Soil

Some characteristics of soil are relatively fixed, and the gardener must work around or with them. Other characteristics are highly dependent on how the soil is managed. Both fixed and variable characteristics of soil affect plant growth.

Relatively fixed characteristics include soil texture, or the proportions of different mineral particles of varying size. Sand particles are the largest, and clay particles are the smallest, with silt in between the two. Sandy soils have a coarse texture, drain quickly, and tend to be low in nutrients. Clayey soils are fine-textured, drain slowly, and usually are more fertile than sandy soils. Silty soils are intermediate in texture, drainage, and fertility. Soils that have characteristics of all three are called loams.

Also relatively fixed are the depth and arrangement of topsoil and subsoil and the distance to bedrock or the water table. Natural soils may be shallow or deep, and bedrock or water may be quite near the surface in some locations. Typically there is a gradual transition between topsoil and subsoil, although abrupt transitions do occur, for example, following landslides or erosion. Soil texture and the arrangement and depth of topsoil and subsoil affect infiltration of water, drainage and water-holding capacity, and the physical space available for plant roots.

More dynamic or changeable soil qualities include organic content and biodiversity, or the number and mix of living

WATER PENETRATION IN (LEFT TO RIGHT) SAND, SILT, AND CLAY

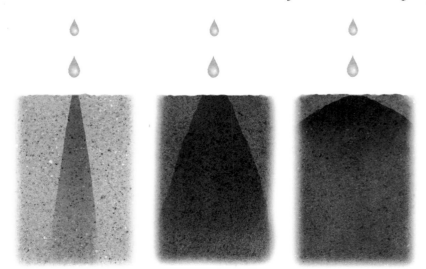

organisms in the soil. Also affected by soil management is soil structure, or the number, size, and arrangement of pore spaces between soil particles. Soil structure, biodiversity, and organic content influence how air, water, and dissolved nutrients move through the soil.

Natural soil is a combination of inorganic mineral particles, decomposing organic matter, and a wide variety of soil organisms. Soil organisms play numerous roles in the production of healthy, fertile soil. Larger organisms, such as worms and insects, aerate the soil and digest organic residues, breaking them into finer particles and distributing them throughout the soil. Microorganisms, such as bacteria, fungi, and algae, further break down this organic material, processing and releasing plant nutrients. Some microorganisms produce substances that bind soil mineral particles together. The continuous formation of mineral aggregates by the activity of soil organisms improves infiltration, water-holding capacity, and aeration of the soil. Recycling of organic matter and distribution of nutrients increase soil productivity.

There is another kind of soil—"urban" soil, which is soil that has been significantly altered during grading and construction or damaged by use and compaction. Depth and arrangement of soil layers are routinely altered during construction, and soil structure and biological diversity are easily damaged when soil is disturbed or compacted. Many gardeners today are faced with a site where natural soils have been removed, graded, compacted, imported, mixed, and replaced in ways designed to support buildings and roads but not necessarily conducive to gardening. Especially vulnerable under such conditions are deep-rooted trees and plants that require good drainage, but all plants may suffer when soil structure, organic content, and biodiversity are damaged or destroyed.

Plant Roots

The ability of plants to absorb water and nutrients from the soil is directly related to their capacity to develop an adequate root system. Roots need physical space in which to grow, and they need soil with pore spaces large enough for diffusion of oxygen and removal of carbon dioxide and other gases. Roots grow where air, water, and nutrients are available in the right amounts; too much or too little of any of these can result in decline or death of the plant.

PLANT ROOTS VARY IN DEPTH AND SPREAD

The volume of a plant's root system usually is as large as that of the stems and leaves, and in some plants, or in some soils, the root system is much larger than the aboveground portions of the plant. Much of the root system is contained within the dripline, but, especially in mature trees, roots often extend well beyond.

The two main types of roots are tap roots and fibrous roots. Tap root systems consist of a large primary root with many branches, while fibrous root systems have a mass of roots of about equal size.

ROOTS OF MATURE
TREES OFTEN EXTEND
WELL BEYOND THE
CANOPY

Although each plant is genetically programmed to develop a particular kind of root system, soil conditions have a marked influence on the extent and nature of plant roots. The depth, spread, and degree of root branching are influenced by factors such as soil texture, structure, depth, fertility, and moisture levels.

Roots anchor the plant in the soil, seek out and take up water, store energy, produce chemicals that help regulate plant growth, and participate in a complex web of nutrient exchange. As roots absorb nutrients for the plant, they exude sugars, organic acids, and other substances that feed and stimulate the activity of many soil organisms.

Mycorrhizal fungi are one example of the many interactions between plant roots and soil organisms. These fungi live on or in the fine roots of most plants and benefit plants in various ways. By extending the reach and surface area of plant roots, they greatly enhance the ability of roots to absorb water and nutrients. Some also increase the stability of soil aggregates or help to break down minerals. The relationship is mutually beneficial, as the fungi receive nourishment from plant roots. Plant growth is enhanced by the presence of mycorrhizal fungi, particularly in dry or infertile soils.

Gardens as Ecosystems

Natural ecosystems rely for their health and productivity on nutrient cycling, one of many cycles that support life on earth. The nutrient cycle works with the water cycle and the energy of the sun to create conditions for plant growth. The nutrient cycle is biologically complex but conceptually simple. Nutrients move through plants, animals, and soil organisms in a continuous cycle that sustains them all through recycling and reuse of organic matter. Some nutrients escape into the air, some are washed away by water and erosion, some are leached down past the roots of plants, but in a healthy, functioning ecosystem, sufficient amounts remain available to sustain life.

In biological systems, nutrients are cycled through food chains. Organic matter from plants and animals is broken down by soil organisms, releasing nutrients that can be used by other animals and plants. When we interrupt this cycle by removing plant residues, sending them off to landfills, we deplete the soil and deprive plants, animals, and soil organisms of the nutrients they need to thrive. When we inject into this cycle chemical fertilizers, pesticides, and herbicides, we destroy or decrease the activity of

BELOW: NUTRIENTS MOVE THROUGH PLANTS, ANIMALS, AND SOIL ORGANISMS IN A CONTINUOUS CYCLE

ORGANIC MATTER FROM PLANTS AND ANIMALS IS BROKEN DOWN BY SOIL ORGANISMS

WATER AND AIR PENETRATE SOIL

PLANTS ABSORB WATER AND NUTRIENTS

ROCKS DISINTEGRATE, RELEASING MINERALS INTO SOIL

beneficial organisms that make nutrients available to plants. When we discourage wildlife, we eliminate from the ecosystem a critical component of the cycle of life. An artificial system such as this is not self-sustaining and requires continuous intervention from the gardener.

THE NEW LANDSCAPE

Planting

Plants will grow better and live longer if they are properly installed in the ground. In summer-dry climates with mild winters, the best time to plant usually is fall, when the soil is still warm but daytime temperatures are cooling off and the rainy season is not far away. The second best time to plant is late winter or early spring, when the soil is warming up and is dry enough to dig but there is still some chance of spring rains. It is possible to plant at other times of year, but winter-wet soils are easily compacted and summer plantings will require a lot of water.

First, check the drainage in the spot you wish to plant. Dig a hole about 18" deep and fill it with water. If the soil is dry, let it drain and fill the hole again. If the second filling drains away in an hour or less, drainage is good. If it takes an hour or two to drain, drainage is fair. If the hole retains water for several hours to a day, you may need to select a plant that appreciates such conditions or choose another location. Drainage can be improved to some extent by digging a deep pit beneath the planting hole with a post-hole digger and filling the pit with drain rock. Subsurface drains also can be installed to drain water away from the plant.

When you're ready to plant, dig a hole no deeper than the rootball and at least twice as wide. If the soil is loose, and the plant is likely to sink when it's watered in, you may want to dig a slightly shallower hole. The goal is to keep the base of the stem or trunk just above soil level without exposing the roots.

Next, make the hole deeper and wider at the outer edges to provide extra space for roots to spread. Roughen up the sides with a pick or shovel. A slick, even surface may discourage roots from spreading into adjacent soil.

Gently remove the plant from its container. Roughen up the edges of the rootball with your hands and carefully pry loose and separate any encircling roots. Avoid cutting or damaging roots, especially larger ones. Place the rootball in the hole and spread any exposed roots down and outward into the loosened soil.

If your soil is of reasonably good quality, simply return dug soil to the hole. If your soil is compacted, you may want to amend backfill soil by mixing in well composted organic matter. This will increase moisture retention of sandy soils and improve drainage of clayey soils. In subsequent years, you can add organic matter to the surface of the soil or mix it into the top inch or two, avoiding disturbance of the soil at deeper levels.

Fertilizer is not needed unless the soil is deficient in particular nutrients necessary for plant growth. Fast-acting chemical fertilizers encourage annual weeds and can promote weak or too rapid growth at the expense of strong root systems. Dry-adapted plants, especially natives, compete most effectively with weeds in the comparatively austere conditions in which they grow naturally.

Form a low berm of soil around the base of the plant, outside the perimeter of the rootball. This berm should be removed when the plant matures and roots spread into surrounding soil. Watering basins around mature plants can impede the flow of water to the broader root zone and concentrate moisture around the crown of the plant.

PLACE STAKES OUTSIDE ROOTBALL AND LAP TIES LOOSELY TO ALLOW SOME TRUNK MOVEMENT

If your site is windy or if you are planting from large nursery containers, you may want to stake trees for the first two or three years. Stakes should be placed well outside the rootball and perpendicular to prevailing winds. Lap soft material such as rubber or cloth loosely around the trunk to avoid abrasion of the bark and allow some trunk movement. Remove the ties and stakes when the roots have become established and the tree is able to stand on its own. Unstaked trees tend to develop stronger trunks.

Mulch the area around the plant with compost, wood chips, or other organic material, keeping mulch away from the trunk or stem. Water thoroughly after planting, applying as much water as the soil will absorb.

Watering

Newly planted landscapes will need supplemental watering for at least the first dry season, even if plants are adapted to summer drought. Watering regularly for two dry seasons will help plants develop strong stems and extensive root systems. By the third year, plants should be thriving with moderate to no supplemental water except during periods of extended hot weather.

Incorrect watering is the source of many plant problems, including susceptibility to pests and diseases, yellowing of leaves, stunting of roots, and general failure to thrive. Unfortunately, there are no rules that apply to all soils, sites, or plants.

NATURAL GARDENING

Have you ever observed an outstanding mountain meadow and wondered who did the design and who does the maintenance? Natural gardening is an attempt to understand how natural processes shape these gems of Mother Nature.

In nature the right plant is in the right place because ultimately the wrong plant would not survive. In gardens we sometimes go to great lengths to keep that wrong plant alive. Most gardeners know enough to place shade plants in shade and sun-loving plants in sun, but usually the situation is more complex.

Something magical begins to happen, and the design begins to feel right, when drought-tolerant plants are grouped together, water-loving plants are grouped by water, and tall plants are not shading short ones. Natural gardeners tend to look at design not as something artificial that is transferred from paper to the garden, but instead as something that arises out of the ground and fits the land like a glove.

In the wild, there are annuals, perennials, and bulbs; plants that bloom early and those that bloom late; deciduous and evergreen plants; herbaceous and shrubby ones. Maintenance comes from nature itself, such as grazing by animals or insects, burning, or scouring by rain or snow. Insects scavenge through foliage, while mushrooms amend the soil. Fallen leaves and decomposing twigs and brush alternate with fallen petals as root food and habitat for many beneficial creatures.

A NATURAL GARDEN
LIGHTLY MAINTAINED

In a cultivated garden situation, when a plant type is missing from the design and nature would have it there, weeds tend to move in, creating a constant problem. In natural gardening, native or ornamental plants that proliferate quickly are introduced gradually to replace the less desirable ones. In the absence of fire and grazing elk, the gardener must play their roles, while enlisting the aid of birds, insects, worms, frogs, lizards, and salamanders.

In natural gardening, dead-heading and clean-up become a fine art of balance, involving timing and restraint. A staggered maintenance schedule helps. Islands of perennials, such as bunchgrasses, yarrows, or ferns, can be left unclipped for a few years. Tall plants are pruned with the seasons in mind, and hedgerows are cleaned out only half at a time. Pathways are mulched with materials at hand, layered as if thatched, and leaf litter and twigs are left or discreetly placed wherever possible.

Natural gardening is not necessarily the same as native gardening; it is a large umbrella under which many beautiful and easy kinds of gardens can be found. Common sense and sensitivity to one's natural surroundings can make any garden more enjoyable and easier to maintain. When done well, the garden begins to have a life of its own.

Don Mahoney, horticulture manager
Strybing Arboretum, San Francisco, California

Successful gardeners learn to read the signs of moisture stress, which can result from too much or too little water. Soil type, type of plant, topography, and weather all play a role.

Soil type. Plants in clay soils need water less often than those growing sandy soils, and sandy soils hold less water with each application. Avoid frequent, shallow waterings. Apply water slowly and deeply, avoiding runoff. Allow the soil dry out at least partially between waterings, but don't let it dry out completely except for plants that require a dry summer dormancy. It's easier to maintain soil moisture than to wet completely dry soil.

Plant type. Plants differ in the amount of water they need to thrive. Most plants adapted to dry summers have leaf or root characteristics that reduce transpiration or increase their ability to draw on available moisture in the soil. Deep-rooted shrubs and trees benefit from more water applied less often than shallow-rooted annuals or perennials. Apply water to the entire root zone, which in some plants can extend well beyond the leaves and branches.

Topography. Water may pond on flat ground and run off on slopes. Newly planted slopes should be mulched to slow runoff, and water should be applied in intervals with enough time in between applications for water to soak into the soil. Hot, south-facing sites will need more water more often than shady, north-facing sites. Mulch to keep the soil cool and water regularly until plants are well established.

Weather. In hot, dry weather, plants lose more water through their leaves and water evaporates more quickly from the soil than in cool, damp weather. Wind increases these effects. The combination of evaporation and transpiration (called evapotranspiration or ET) determines how much water is lost from the landscape. In winter, when temperatures are low and humidity is high, you probably won't need to water at all.

Fertilizing

Applying chemical fertilizers can cause adverse effects such as salt buildup in the soil, growth of weedy species, and inhibition or death of soil organisms. Even light fertilizing can result in root dieback and leaf burn in natives and dry-adapted plants. If your soil has been undisturbed for many years, and the plants you are growing are drought-adapted, it's probably safe to assume that you won't need to fertilize.

If you suspect that your soil is deficient—for example, if it is a highly disturbed "urban" soil—you can get a soil test to determine which nutrients are deficient. Use organic and slow-release amendments whenever possible. Keep in mind that soil pH, or the acidity or alkalinity of the soil, is an important determinant of levels of available nutrients and the health and activity of soil organisms. Acid soils register below 7.0, and alkaline soils are above that level. Consult your county cooperative extension office for advice on testing and amending soil.

Also consider the specific needs of the plants you intend to grow. For plants adapted to low-nutrient soils, adding nutrients may speed their growth but shorten their lives or simply encourage the growth of weeds.

RESEARCH ON RECYCLED WATER IN ORNAMENTAL LANDSCAPES

Use of recycled water is already the norm in some parts of the world with limited water supplies, and it is becoming increasingly common in California. As wastewater treatment plants expand their capacity to deliver recycled water to customers, landscape irrigation is expected to become the second largest use for recycled water after groundwater recharge.

Recycled water is wastewater treated to a quality high enough to be safe and effective for many purposes, including landscape irrigation. This water is clear, odorless, and free of harmful bacteria, but it does contain more salts and nutrients than are found in drinking water. Some of these, such as nitrogen, calcium, and magnesium, can enrich the soil and promote plant growth. Others, such as sodium and chloride, can cause leaf burn, dieback, stunted growth, and even death of salt-sensitive plants if the landscape is not carefully managed.

Most of the problems experienced with recycled water also occur with potable water if the site is poorly drained or the landscape is watered incorrectly. It just takes longer for plant symptoms to become serious enough to notice or a trained eye to see the early signs. Learning to use recycled water may help us become better gardeners by requiring that we pay close attention to soils, plants, and watering schedules.

A river cleans itself by depositing silt along its banks. Bacteria convert organic matter into more stable compounds that settle out. Water is disinfected by the sun's ultraviolet rays. As water percolates through rock and soil, impurities are left behind. We mimic these natural processes when we treat wastewater so it can be used again.

Research by the University of California at Davis and several northern California water utilities suggests that many of the plants most commonly used in California landscapes will thrive with recycled water. Field and greenhouse studies over a ten-year period tested the responses of a wide range of plants with varying cultural needs and growth habits. These studies have demonstrated that site management, particularly water management, is the key to successful use of recycled water in ornamental landscapes. Among the study findings are:

- Plants that show sensitivity to recycled water applied with overhead sprinklers often show no symptoms with drip irrigation.

- Sprinkler irrigation often has no negative effects if water is applied deeply and infrequently, allowing time for leaves to dry and salts to leach below the root zone.

- Salt buildup in soils is insignificant where annual rainfall is at least moderate and drainage is reasonably good.

- Even salt-sensitive plants in poorly draining soils may show no symptoms of distress if the right amount of water is applied at the right time.

Following are some of the plants that have proved tolerant or moderately tolerant of irrigation water containing 300ppm chloride and 200ppm sodium, levels comparable to or higher than most recycled waters.

SOME SALT-TOLERANT PLANTS

Trees

Albizia julibrissin (silk tree)
Cedrus deodara (deodar cedar)
Fraxinus augustifolia 'Raywood' (Raywood ash)
Koelreuteria paniculata (goldenrain tree)
Pinus cembroides (Mexican piñon pine)
Platanus x acerifolia 'Bloodgood' (London plane)
Quercus agrifolia (coast live oak)
Quercus lobata (valley oak)
Sequoia sempervirens 'Los Altos' (redwood)
Washingtonia filifera (California fan palm)

Shrubs

Acacia redolens (prostrate acacia)
Arbutus unedo (strawberry tree)
Arctostaphylos uva-ursi 'Point Reyes' (bearberry manzanita)
Baccharis pilularis 'Twin Peaks #2' (coyote brush)
Ceanothus 'Concha' (California lilac)
Ceanothus griseus var. horizontalis 'Yankee Point' (Carmel creeper)
Ceanothus thyrsiflorus (California lilac)
Cotoneaster dammeri 'Coral Beauty' (bearberry cotoneaster)
Cotoneaster microphyllus (rockspray cotoneaster)
Escallonia rubra (red escallonia)
Heteromeles arbutifolia (toyon)
Juniperis horizontalis 'Wiltonii' (juniper)
Lantana camara (lantana)
Mahonia pinnata (California holly grape)
Myrtus communis (myrtle)
Nandina domestica (heavenly bamboo)
Nerium oleander (oleander)
Olea europaea 'Montra' (dwarf olive)
Photinia x fraseri (photinia)
Pittosporum tobira (tobira)
Prunus caroliniana (Carolina laurel)
Rhaphiolepis indica (Indian hawthorn)

Rosmarinus officinalis 'Prostrata' (rosemary)
Sambucus nigra (elderberry)
Xylosma congestum (xylosma)

Ceanothus 'Concha'

Grasses

Bromus carinatus (California brome)
Deschampsia cespitosa (tufted hairgrass)
Deschampsia elongata (slender hairgrass)
Elymus glaucus (blue wild rye)
Festuca californica (California fescue)
Melica californica (California melic)
Muhlenbergia rigens (deergrass)
Sporobolus airoides (alkali sacaton)

Vine

Jasminum polyanthum (pink jasmine)

—Roger Waters, president
National Urban Agriculture Council
Woodacre, California

Mulching

Mulch is the natural gardener's most valuable ally. A layer of loose material spread over the soil surface, mulch reduces water loss from the soil, moderates soil temperature, reduces soil compaction from foot traffic or driving rain, inhibits germination of weed seeds, makes weeds easier to pull, and slows runoff and erosion. Organic mulch, consisting of partially or fully decomposed plant and animal matter, also enriches and aerates the soil and promotes the growth of beneficial soil organisms.

Conventional landscape practices—the grooming and clearing and offsite disposal routinely undertaken in so many landscapes—remove from the nutrient cycle much of the plant and animal matter on which healthy soil depends. Given enough time, regular application of organic matter can help restore even lifeless, compacted, "urban" soils to a more self-sustaining condition. Depending on the condition of your soil, renewal may take many years, but early signs of returning life—earthworms, beneficial insects, healthy plants—may begin to appear in a surprisingly short time.

The best place to obtain materials for mulch is in your own landscape. Recycling organic materials on site gives the gardener control over the quality and content of the mulch. You can use some materials directly, for example, leaves and grass clippings can be applied where needed or left where they fall. You can speed up the natural process of decomposition by composting a mixture of organic materials and using the finished product as mulch. Making your own compost, and applying it regularly to the surface of the soil, not only benefits your own small ecosystem but also helps to reduce the environmental costs of landfill disposal of this natural resource.

THE LANDSCAPE OVER TIME

If you have designed your landscape to take advantage of the site, selected plants that thrive in your microclimates, placed plants where they can grow to their full size and natural shape, and grouped plants according to their needs and tolerances, your landscape should require relatively little attention over time.

The main long-term tasks will be weeding and the care and feeding of your soil, which may be required for a decade—or a lifetime. Short-lived plants eventually will need replacing. Occasional pruning may be undertaken for corrective or aesthetic reasons. Once a year, grasses may be cut back and dead branches removed for fire safety. Plants in containers will need periodic repotting. Leaves may be swept from patios and decks and composted. A light tidying up in spring will satisfy most gardeners' needs for order.

The sustainable landscape takes time to develop, but most of the natural gardener's time will be spent watching the show. The time it takes for a landscape to reach maturity depends a great deal on how fast your plants grow. In the first year, most trees, shrubs, and woody groundcovers may show little change, but perennials and annuals can be counted on for an impressive display. By the third year, most woody plants will have put down roots and be starting to fill out. After five or six years, you will be able to envision the garden's ultimate shape. Some perennials will need division or replacement by this time. After ten years, most plants other than large trees will be approaching or have achieved their mature size. After fifteen or twenty years, you will be grateful for photographs to remind you of your newly planted landscape.

The best advice is don't rush it. There is no truly satisfactory way to speed up the process. You can choose fast-growing trees and shrubs, but these often are short-lived or rampant growers, requiring hard pruning to keep them in line. Some gardeners plant closely at the outset to achieve immediate effects, but up to half of these overcrowded plants may need removal or hard pruning over time. Mature trees and shrubs can be installed from large containers, but these often perform no better in the long run than smaller specimens, which tend to be more adaptable and less root-bound. Chemical fertilizers can be applied to speed growth, but excess growth may be susceptible to disease and certainly will require pruning and disposal. It's probably wise to embrace the long-term nature of gardening and to fill in the gaps temporarily with annuals, perennials, and shorter-lived shrubs.

If you must do something, work on the soil. Compost, mulch, and mulch again. Resist the urge to dig or tread on waterlogged winter soils. Stay on the paths and wait for those few glorious days in spring when soils are just right for easy weeding. In summer don't water until plants look like they'll suffer without your help. You may be surprised at how long they can wait, as most plants adapted to summer-dry climates will do better with less supplemental water. Gardening with regionally appropriate plants is one of few instances when less activity is required to attain better results. Sit back and enjoy it.

> *"We cannot decide who gets to stay aboard the ark: if we spray the caterpillars, we lose the butterflies."*
>
> —Sara Stein, *Noah's Garden*

RESOURCES

Brady, Nyle C. and Ray R. Weil, *Elements of the Nature and Properties of Soils*, 2nd ed., New York, Prentice-Hall, 2003.

Campbell, Stu, *Let It Rot: the gardener's guide to composting*, North Adams, MA, Storey Books, 1998.

Druse, Ken, *The Natural Habitat Garden*, New York, Clarkson N. Potter, 1994.

Harper, Peter, *The Natural Garden Book*, New York, Simon & Schuster, 1994.

Lowry, Judith Larner, *Gardening with a Wild Heart: restoring California's native landscapes at home*, Berkeley, University of California Press, 1999.

Ogden, Scott, *Gardening with Difficult Soils*, Eureka, CA, Taylor Publishing, 1992.

Olkowski, William, Sheila Daar, and Helga Olkowski, *Common Sense Pest Control: least toxic solutions for your home*, Newtown, CT, Taunton Press, 1991.

Osler, Mirabel, *A Gentle Plea for Chaos: the enchantment of gardening*, New York, Simon & Schuster, 1989.

Smillie, Joe and Grace Gershuny, *The Soul of Soil*, White River Junction, VT, Chelsea Green, 1999.

Smith & Hawken, *Composting*, by Liz Ball, New York, Workman Publishing, 1998.

Stein, Sara, *Noah's Garden*, Boston, Houghton-Mifflin, 1993.

Stell, Elizabeth P., *Secrets to Great Soil: a grower's guide to composting, mulching, and creating healthy, fertile soil*, North Adams, MA, Storey Books, 1998.

RESOURCES

Selected Readings

Place

Bakker, Elna, *An Island Called California: an ecological introduction to its natural communities*, Berkeley, University of California Press, 1971.

Barbour, M., B. Pavlik, F. Drysdale, and S. Lindstrom, *California's Changing Landscapes: diversity and conservation of California vegetation*, Sacramento, California Native Plant Society, 1993.

Barbour, M.G. and J. Major, eds., *Terrestrial Vegetation of California*, Sacramento, California Native Plant Society, 1988.

Blackburn, T.C. and K. Anderson, eds., *Before the Wilderness: environmental management by native Californians*, Menlo Park, CA, Ballena Press, 1993.

California Department of Fish and Game, *California's Wild Gardens*, Sacramento, California Native Plant Society, 1997.

Dallman, P.R., *Plant Life in the World's Mediterranean Climates*, Berkeley, University of California Press, 1998.

Francis, Mark, and Andreas Reimann, *The California Landscape Garden: ecology, culture, and design*, Berkeley, University of California Press, 1999.

Gutierrez, Ramon A. and Richard J. Orsi, *Contested Eden: California before the Gold Rush*, Berkeley, University of California Press, 1998.

Holland, V.L. and David Keil, *California Vegetation*, Dubuque, IA, 1996.

Jensen, D.B., M.S. Tom, and J. Harte, *In Our Own Hands: a strategy for conserving California's biological diversity*, Berkeley, University of California Press, 1993.

Keator, Glenn, *In Full View: three ways of seeing california plants*, Berkeley, CA, Heyday Books, 2001.

Keator, Glenn, *The Life of an Oak*, Berkeley, CA, Heyday Books, 1998.

Ornduff, Robert, Phyllis Faber, and Todd Keeler-Wolf, *Introduction to California Plant Life*, Berkeley, University of California Press, 2002.

Sawyer, John O. and Todd Keeler-Wolf, *A Manual of California Vegetation*, Sacramento, California Native Plant Society, 1995.

Schoenherr, Allan A., *A Natural History of California*, Berkeley, University of California Press, 1995.

Sullivan, Chip, *Garden and Climate*, New York, McGraw-Hill, 2002.

Waters, George, and Nora Harlow, eds., *The Pacific Horticulture Book of Western Gardening*, Boston, MA, David R. Godine, 1990.

Plants

American Horticultural Society, *Water-wise Gardening*, by Peter Robinson, New York, DK Publishing, 1999.

Aquatic Outreach Institute, *The Gardener's Guide to Native Plants of the East Bay: a home companion to growing native plants in Alameda and Contra Costa Counties*, Richmond, CA, 2001.

Beidleman, Linda and Eugene Kozloff, *Plants of the San Francisco Bay Region: Mendocino to Monterey*, Berkeley, University of California Press, 2003.

Boisset, Caroline, *Gardening in Time: planning future growth and flowering*, New York, Prentice-Hall, 1990.

Brooklyn Botanic Garden, *The Natural Lawn and Alternatives*, Brooklyn, N.Y., 1993.

Brickell, Christopher and Judith Zuk, *The American Horticultural Society A-Z Encyclopedia of Garden Plants*, New York, DK Publishing, 1996.

Clebsch, Betsy, *A Book of Salvias*, Portland, OR, Timber Press, 1997.

Courtright, Gordon, *Trees and Shrubs for Temperate Climates*, Portland, OR, Timber Press, 1979.

Crampton, Beecher, *Grasses in California*, Berkeley, University of California Press, 1974.

Darke, Rick, *The Color Encyclopedia of Ornamental Grasses*, Portland OR, Timber Press, 1999.

Denver Water Works Association, *Xeriscape Plant Guide*, by Rob Proctor, Golden, CO, Fulcrum Publishing, 1998.

Duffield, Mary Rose and Warren D. Jones, *Plants for Dry Climates: how to select, grow, and enjoy*, Cambridge, MA, Perseus Books, 2001.

Endicott, Katherine Grace, *Northern California Gardening*, San Francisco, Chronicle Books, 1996.

Ertter, Barbara and Mary L. Bowerman, *Flowering Plants and Ferns of Mt. Diablo, California*, Sacramento, California Native Plant Society, 2002.

Ferguson, Nicola, *Right Plant, Right Place*, New York, Simon & Schuster, 1992.

Grounds, Roger, *The Plantfinder's Guide to Ornamental Grasses*, Portland, OR, Timber Press, 1998.

Harlow, Nora and Kristin Jakob, eds., *Wild Lilies, Irises, and Grasses: gardening with California monocots*, Berkeley, University of California Press, 2004.

Hickman, James C., ed., *The Jepson Manual: higher plants of California*, Berkeley, University of California Press, 1993.

Johnson, Eric A. and Scott Millard, *The Low-Water Flower Gardener*, Tucson, AZ, Millard Publishing, 1993.

Keator, Glenn, *Complete Garden Guide to the Native Perennials of California*, San Francisco, Chronicle Books, 1990.

Keator, Glenn, *Introduction to Trees of the San Francisco Bay Region*, Berkeley, University of California Press, 2002.

King, Michael and Piet Oudolf, *Gardening with Grasses*, Portland, OR, Timber Press, 1996.

Lacey, Louise, *The Basics of Growing California Native Plants*, Berkeley, CA, Growing Native Research Institute, 1990.

Lancaster, Roy, *Mediterranean Plants and Gardens*, Sidney, B.C., CN, John Markham & Assocs., 1990.

Lancaster, Roy, *What Plant Where*, London, DK Publishing, 1995.

Lanner, Ronald M., *Conifers of California*, Los Olivos, CA, Cachuma Press, 1999.

Lenz, Lee W. and John Dourley, *California Native Trees and Shrubs*, Claremont, CA, Rancho Santa Ana Botanic Garden, 1981.

Muick, Pamela, Sharon Johnson, and Bruce M. Pavlik, *Oaks of California*, Los Olivos, CA, Cachuma Press, 1993.

Ondra, Nancy J., *Grasses: versatile partners for uncommon garden design*, North Adams, MA, Storey Books, 2002.

Ottesen, Carole, *Ornamental Grasses: the amber wave*, New York, McGraw-Hill, 1989.

Perry, Bob, *Trees and Shrubs for Dry California Landscapes: plants for water conservation*, San Dimas, CA, Land Design Publishing, 1989.

Perry, Bob, *Landscape Plants for Western Regions: an illustrated guide to plants for water conservation*, San Dimas, CA, Land Design Publishing, 1994.

Proctor, Rob, *Xeriscape Plant Guide*, Golden, CO, Fulcrum Press, 1998.

Schmidt, Marjorie, *Growing California Native Plants*, Berkeley, University of California Press, 1980.

Shuler, Carol, *Low Water Use Plants for California and the Southwest*, Tucson, AZ, Fisher Books, 1993.

Stuart, John David, John O. Sawyer, and Andrea Pickart, *Trees and Shrubs of California*, Berkeley, University of California Press, 2001.

Sunset Western Garden Book, Menlo Park, CA, Sunset Publishing, 2001.

Taylor, Jane, *Plants for Dry Gardens*, London, Frances Lincoln, 1993.

Turner, Richard and Ernie Wasson, *Botanica*, New York, Barnes & Noble, 1997.

Yronwode, Catherine, *The California Gardener's Book of Lists*, Eureka, CA, Taylor Publishing, 1998.

Landscape Design and Inspiration

Bauer, Nancy, *The Habitat Garden Book: wildlife landscaping for the San Francisco Bay Region*, Sebastopol, CA, Coyote Ridge Press, 2001.

Brookes, John, *The Book of Garden Design*, New York, Macmillan, 1991.

Chatto, Beth, *Beth Chatto's Gravel Garden: drought-resistant gardening throughout the year*, London, Frances Lincoln, 2003.

Conran, Terence, and Dan Pearson, *The Essential Garden Book: getting back to basics*, New York, Three Rivers Press, 1998.

Druse, Ken, *The Natural Garden*, New York, Clarkson N. Potter, 1989.

Druse, Ken, *The Natural Habitat Garden*, New York, Clarkson N. Potter, 1994.

Gildemeister, Heidi, *Mediterranean Gardening: a waterwise approach*, Berkeley, University of California Press, 2002.

Harper, Peter, *The Natural Garden Book*, New York, Simon & Schuster, 1994.

Latymer, Hugo, *The Mediterranean Gardener*, London, Frances Lincoln, 2001.

Lowry, Judith Larner, *Gardening with a Wild Heart: restoring California's native landscapes at home*, Berkeley, University of California Press, 1999.

Nottle, Trevor, *Gardens of the Sun*, Portland, OR, Timber Press, 1996.

Oudolf, Piet and Noel Kingsbury, *Designing with Plants*, Portland, OR, Timber Press, 1999.

Pollan, Michael, *Second Nature*, New York, Dell Publishing, 1993.

Roth, Sally, *Natural Landscaping*, Emmaus, PA, Rodale Press, 2002.

Smithen, Jan, *Sun-Drenched Gardens: the Mediterranean style*, New York, Harry N. Abrams, 2002.

Springer, Lauren, and Rob Proctor, *Passionate Gardening: good advice for challenging climates*, Golden, CO, Fulcrum Publishing, 2000.

Stein, Sara, *Noah's Garden: restoring the ecology of our own backyards*, Boston, Houghton-Mifflin, 1993.

Stevens, David, *The Garden Design Sourcebook: the essential guide to garden materials and structures*, London, Conran Octopus, 1995.

Stevens, David, Lucy Huntington, and Richard Key, *The Complete Book of Garden Construction, Design, and Planting*, London, Cassell Academic, 2002.

Wasowski, Andy, *The Landscaping Revolution*, Lincolnwood, IL, Contemporary Books, 2000.

Weinstein, Gayle, *The Xeriscape Handbook: a how-to guide to natural, resource-wise gardening*, Golden, CO, Fulcrum Publishing, 2003.

Technical and How-To

Bossard, Carla C., John M. Randall, and Marc C. Hoshovsky, eds., *Invasive Plants of California's Wildlands*, Berkeley, University of California Press, 2000.

Capon, Brian, *Botany for Gardeners*, Portland, OR, Timber Press, 1990.

Campbell, Craig S. and Michael Ogden, *Constructed Wetlands in the Sustainable Landscape*, New York, John Wiley, 1999.

Craul, Phillip J., *Urban Soil in Landscape Design*, New York, John Wiley, 1992.

Gershuny, Grace and Deborah L. Martin, eds., *The Rodale Book of Composting*, Emmaus, PA, Rodale Press, 1992.

Gilliam, Harold, *Weather of the San Francisco Bay Region*, Berkeley, University of California Press, 2002.

Hendrix, Howard and Stuart Straw, *Reliable Rain: a practical guide to landscape irrigation*, Newtown CT, Taunton Press, 1998.

Kourik, Robert and Heidi Schmidt, *Drip Irrigation for Every Landscape and All Climates*, Santa Rosa, CA, Metamorphic Press, 1993.

Mollison, Bill, *Introduction to Permaculture*, Tyalgum, Australia, Tagari Publications, 1991.

Norris, R.M. and R.W. Webb, *Geology of California*, 2nd ed., New York, Wiley, 1990.

Ogden, Scott, *Gardening with Difficult Soils*, Eureka, CA, Taylor Publishing, 1992.

Olkowski, William, Sheila Daar, and Helga Olkowski, *Common Sense Pest Control: least toxic solutions for your home*, Newtown, CT, Taunton Press, 1991.

Smillie, Joe and Grace Gershuny, *The Soul of Soil*, White River Junction, VT, Chelsea Green Publishing, 1999.

Smith & Hawken, *Composting*, by Liz Ball, New York, Workman Publishing, 1998.

Sunset Publishing, *Garden Watering Systems*, Menlo Park, CA, 1999.

Taylor, Jane, *Weather in the Garden*, London, John Murray Publishers, 1996.

Thompson, J. William and Kim Sorvig, *Sustainable Landscape Construction: a guide to green building outdoors*, Washington, D.C., Island Press, 2000.

Wasowski, Andy, *Building Inside Nature's Envelope: how new construction and land preservation can work together*, London, Oxford University Press, 2000.

Periodicals

Fine Gardening
Taunton Press
P.O. Box 5506
Newtown CT 06470

www.taunton.com

Fremontia
California Native Plant Society
2707 K Street, Suite 1
Sacramento, CA 95816

www.cnps.org

Garden Design
460 North Orlando Avenue, #200
Winter Park, FL 32789

www.gardendesignmag.com

Horticulture
98 North Washington Street
Boston, MA 02114

www.hortmag.com

The Mediterranean Garden
The Mediterranean Garden Society
P.O. Box 14
GR-190 02 Peania, Greece

www.mediterraneangardensociety.org

Organic Gardening
Rodale Press
33 East Minor Street
Emmaus, PA 18098

www.organicgardening.com

Pacific Horticulture
P.O. Box 485
Berkeley CA 94701

www.pacifichorticulture.org

Sunset Magazine
80 Willow Road
Menlo Park, CA 94025

www.sunsetmag.com

RESOURCES

Display Gardens

Elizabeth Gamble Garden
1431 Waverly Street
Palo Alto, CA 94301
(650) 329-1356
www.gamblegarden.org

The Gardens at Heather Farm
1450 Marchbanks Drive
Walnut Creek, CA 94598
(925) 947-1678
www.gardenshf.org

Gateway Emergency Preparedness Exhibit Center
 and Gardens
Tunnel Road and Caldecott Lane
Oakland, CA
www.ERGateway.org

Lester Rowntree Native Plant Garden
25800 Hatton Road
Carmel, CA 93923
(408) 624-3543

Markham Regional Arboretum
1202 La Vista Avenue
Concord, CA 94521
(925) 681-2968
www.markhamarboretum.org

Mendocino Coast Botanical Gardens
18220 North Highway One
Fort Bragg, CA 95437
www.gardenbythesea.org

Regional Parks Botanic Garden, Tilden Park
Wildcat Canyon Road and South Park Drive
Berkeley, CA 94708
(510) 841-8732
www.ebparks.org

Ruth Bancroft Garden
1500 Bancroft Road
PO Box 30845
Walnut Creek, CA 94598
(925) 210-9663
www.ruthbancroftgarden.org

Sierra Azul Nursery and Gardens
2660 East Lake Avenue
Watsonville, CA 95076
(831) 763-0939
www.sierraazul.com

Strybing Arboretum and Botanical Gardens
Ninth Avenue and Lincoln Way, Golden Gate Park
San Francisco, CA 94122
(415) 661-1316
www.strybing.org

University of California Botanical Garden
Centennial Drive
Berkeley, CA 94720
(510) 642-3343
www.mip.berkeley.edu/garden

University of California, Davis, Arboretum
La Rue Road
Davis, CA 95616
(530) 752-4880
www.arboretum.ucdavis.edu

INDEX

NOTE: In Chapter 3, plants are listed alphabetically by genus and species names. This index lists and cross-references alternative scientific and common names. Species are indexed only if shown in photographs. Pages on which photographs appear are in bold.

'Rose Glow' **78**
Bergenia 79
  crassifolia **79**
berms 27, **27**
Beschorneria 80
  yuccoides **80**
biennials 42, 264-5
big bluestem, see *Andropogon gerardii*
bigleaf maple, see *Acer macrophyllum*
Bignonia
  australis, see *Pandorea pandorana*
  cherere, see *Distictis buccinatoria*
  radicans, see *Campsis radicans*
birchleaf mountain mahogany, see
  Cercocarpus betuloides
bird's eyes, see *Gilia tricolor*
bishop's hat, see *Epimedium*
  grandiflorum
black oak, California, see *Quercus*
  kelloggii
black-eyed Susan, see *Rudbeckia hirta*
blazing star, see *Liatris spicata*
blood-red trumpet vine, see *Distictis*
  buccinatoria
blue dicks, see *Dichelostemma*
  capitatum
blue elderberry, see *Sambucus*
  mexicana
blue grama, see *Bouteloua gracilis*
blue hibiscus, see *Alyogne huegelii*
blue mist, see *Caryopteris* x
  clandonensis
blue oak, see *Quercus douglasii*
blue oat grass, see *Helictotrichon*
  sempervirens
blue palm, Mexican, see *Brahea edulis*
blue pimpernel, see *Anagallis monelli*
blue wild rye, see *Elymus glaucus*
bluebeard, see *Caryopteris incana*
bluebells, California desert, see
  Phacelia campanularia
blueblossom, see *Ceanothus*
  thyrsiflorus
blue-eyed grass, see *Sisyrinchium*
  bellum
blue-eyed Mary, see *Omphalodes verna*
Boston ivy, see *Parthenocissus*
  tricuspidata
bottle tree, see *Brachychiton populneus*
bottlebrush, see *Callistemon*
Bougainvillea 80, **80**, **304**
Bouteloua gracilis 81, **81**
Brachychiton populneus 81, **81**
Brachyscome 82
  multifida **82**
Brahea 82
  edulis **83**
bramble, see *Rubus*

breath of heaven, see *Coleonema*
Brisbane box, see *Lophostemon*
  confertus
brittlebush, see *Encelia farinosa*
Brodiaea 83
  laxa, see *Triteleia laxa*
  minor **83**
  uniflora, see *Ipheion uniflorum*
brome, see *Bromus*
Bromus 8
  hordeaceus 9
Brunsvigia rosea, see *Amaryllis*
  belladonna
buckeye, California, see *Aesculus*
  californica
buckthorn, Italian, see *Rhamnus*
  alaternus
buckwheat, wild, see *Eriogonum*
Buddleja 84
  alternifolia **42**
  davidii **84**
  'Lochinch' **84**
bugloss, see *Anchusa*
Bulbinella
  floribunda 84, **84**
  robusta, see *B. floribunda*
  setosa, see *B. floribunda*
bulbs 16
bull grass, see *Muhlenbergia emersleyi*
bush anemone, see *Carpenteria*
  californica
bush mallow, see *Malacothamnus*
bush marigold, Mexican, see *Tagetes*
  lemmonii
bush poppy, see *Dendromecon*
buttercup, see *Ranunculus*
butterfly bush, see *Buddleja*
butterfly weed, see *Asclepias*

C

cajeput tree, see *Melaleuca*
  quinquenervia
Calamagrostis 11, 85
  x *acutiflora* 'Karl Foerster' **ii-iii**, **85**
  foliosa **18**
calamint, see *Calamintha*
Calamintha 86
  nepeta **86**
  nepetoides, see *C. nepeta*
California aster, see *Aster chilensis*
California aster, see *Lessingia*
  filaginifolia
California black oak, see *Quercus*
  kelloggii
California buckeye, see *Aesculus*
  californica
California desert bluebells, see

Phacelia campanularia
California fan palm, see *Washingtonia*
  filifera
California fuchsia, see *Epilobium*
  canum
California holly, see *Heteromeles*
  arbutifolia
California holly grape, see *Mahonia*
  pinnata
California lilac, see *Ceanothus*
California native plant, see plants,
  native
California nutmeg, see *Torreya*
  californica
California pepper tree, see *Schinus*
  molle
California polypody fern, see
  Polypodium californicum
California poppy, see *Eschscholzia*
  californica
California sagebrush, see *Artemisia*
  californica
California wild grape, see *Vitis*
  californica
California wood fern, see *Dryopteris*
  arguta
Callirhoe involucrata 86-7, **86**
Callistemon 87
  viminalis **87**
    'Little John' **286**
Calocedrus decurrens 88, **88**
Calocephalus brownii 89, **89**, 119
Calochortus 89
  superbus **89**
  'Violet Queen' **89**
Calothamnus villosus 90, **90**
Calylophus 90
  hartwegii **90**
Campsis radicans 91, **91**
Canary Island date palm, see *Phoenix*
  canariensis
candlestick plant, see *Senna alata*
canyon live oak, see *Quercus*
  chrysolepis
Cape forget-me-not, see *Anchusa*
  capensis
Cape honeysuckle, see *Tecomaria*
  capensis
Cape mallow, see *Anisodontea* x
  hypomandarum
Cape marigold, see *Dimorphotheca*
Cape rush, see *Chondropetalum*
  tectorum
Carex **25**, 91-2
  morrowii 'Aurea-variegata' **35**
  secta **37**
    'Western Hills' **21**
  tumulicola **45**, **91**